THE NEW DEAL

THE NEW DEAL

Analysis and Interpretation

Edited by

ALONZO L. HAMBY

Ohio University

Weybright and Talley

New York

First Printing, February, 1969
Second Printing, February, 1970
Third Printing, February, 1971

© 1969 Weybright and Talley, Inc.
All rights reserved, including the right
to reproduce this book or portions
thereof in any form.
Published in the United States by
WEYBRIGHT AND TALLEY
750 Third Avenue
New York, New York 10017
Library of Congress Catalog Card No. 73-77161
PRINTED IN THE UNITED STATES OF AMERICA

PREFACE

THE PURPOSE of this volume is simply to provide a convenient collection of some of the best writings available on the New Deal. The selections do not, of course, cover all the topics or problems which have engaged historians of this complex reform movement; hopefully, they will serve as an introduction to the more important questions and stimulate further inquiry. The editor's interpretive introduction attempts to define some major issues; its judgments are purely personal and are in no way meant to represent any historical consensus.

This book would not have been possible without the help and guidance of others. Richard S. Kirkendall and William E. Leuchtenburg taught me most of what I know about the New Deal, and John A. Garraty has given me invaluable friendship and encouragement. Richard M. Dalfiume, John Lankford, Franklin D. Mitchell, and Harold D. Woodman all read my own contributions and made valuable suggestions for improving them. Miss Linda Webb xeroxed most of the selections and helped compile the bibliography. Mr. John T. Hawes of Weybright and Talley provided the advice and assistance which a young editor needs. My wife, Joyce, greatly facilitated the project, not just by tolerating it but by actively participating in it; her many suggestions have improved the book immeasurably. For the errors which remain I alone of course, am responsible.

A. L. H.

Athens, Ohio
September, 1968

CONTENTS

INTRODUCTION

THE NEW DEAL was the greatest epoch in the history of American reform. In the six years that it existed as an effective political force, 1933–1938, it produced (or perhaps was produced by) one of the most important political leaders in American history and instituted dramatic changes in American social and political patterns. Not surprisingly, it has brought forth some of the best and most significant historical writing of the generation which followed it.

To a remarkable extent, the analyses and interpretations in this book share common values. The American historical profession—as well as the American intellectual community in general—is dominated by men of a liberal social persuasion. It is true that some leading historical figures of the Right have found defenders among prominent historians; usually, however, these scholars have argued that their subjects were misunderstood carriers of progress. It is, to say the least, difficult to apply this defense to the opponents of the New Deal, and no significant historian has made the effort. There has been one important historical study written from a frankly conservative frame of reference, Edgar Eugene Robinson's *The Roosevelt Leadership* (1955). Robinson's work, however, has drawn much criticism, and its impact upon historical thought has been slight. The major dialogue in New Deal historiography is between those who accept and praise the reforms of the 1930's and those who feel that the New Deal was too moderate.

A historian seeking to understand the New Deal must attempt to discover its intellectual foundations. One method of doing so is to examine its relationship to early twentieth-century reform. To many, this relationship is direct and immediate: the Great Depression simply returned to power a progressive movement which had been disrupted by World War I and the decade of conservatism which had followed. According to this view, the New Deal drew the support of and was staffed by many old progressives, including President Roosevelt himself. Its use of national power to raise farm income was an idea which went at least as far back as the Populists, received some initial implementation from the farm credit acts of the Wilson administration, and was further advanced during the twenties by the fight for the McNary-Haugen bill. The debate which developed between economic planners and anti-trusters during the 1930's was reminiscent of the old argument between the New Nationalism and the New Freedom. The Social Security Act grew out of welfare legislation passed by the states, Wisconsin especially, during the progressive era, and FDR's conservation programs were simply a continuation of Theodore Roosevelt's efforts. The increasingly militant attacks on big business and privilege were part of the traditional rhetoric of American reform.

Some historians, however, among them Carl Degler and Richard Hofstadter, have presented an increasingly influential argument: the idea that the New Deal broke significantly with the old progressive tradition. To these authors, early twentieth-century progressivism was a middle-class reaction against both big business and organized labor. If the progressives sponsored some rudimentary welfare legislation, they did so out of a paternal, Victorian humanitarianism. They saw themselves as opponents of special privilege and sought to establish a government which would be subservient to neither the plutocratic power of the very wealthy nor the equally menacing threat of an organized proletariat; they wanted a state which would act as an impartial arbiter among competing groups, and in Theodore Roosevelt's apt phrase, give everyone, including the unorganized middle class, a Square Deal. The progressives thus saw only a limited role for government; Degler even seems to describe them as virtual believers in *laissez-faire*. The New Deal was different on all these counts. It completely abandoned the *laissez-faire* tradition; the depression was its first concern, and unlike progressivism it frankly attempted to manage the business cycle. The New Deal's strongest and most durable support came from labor and the lower classes, and it made the state a frank partisan of these classes. Its labor and welfare legislation, Richard Hofstadter argues, was the product of a "social democratic" outlook, not Victorian paternalism. Its appeal to class feeling, its flexibility, its downright opportunism shocked and alienated many old progressives.

The argument between these two schools of thought cannot really be resolved. Neither the progressives nor the New Dealers were as homogeneous as many of their interpreters seem to assume. There appears to have been an important progressive tradition upon which the New Deal drew; but not all of those reformers whom historians have called "progressives" subscribed to it. It is very difficult to determine if the advanced progressivism which paved the way for the New Deal represented the mainstream of early twentieth-century reform. It is certain that with a little selectivity one can find many examples to support either side of the argument. The debate over change and continuity in twentieth-century reform has been valuable and thought-provoking; it should continue but with more precise categories and better definitions of key terms.

An equally important, but separate, problem is to determine the extent of change that the New Deal actually made in American life, and it is unfortunate that those who discuss the change-and-continuity question have tended to blur the distinction. When one moves from the question of intellectual outlook and objectives to the fact of real accomplishment, it seems undeniable that the New Deal effected an important transformation in American society.

If previous reformers had worked for government action to raise farm prices and bring agricultural purchasing power toward parity, only the New Deal achieved their objective. It did so, moreover, with new methods—crop destruction and acreage allotments—which old agrarian reformers accepted with reluctance. Its programs brought a large degree of organization and prosperity to an agricultural community which, caught in the chaos of perfect competition, had been in a state of depression for almost a decade and a half.

The New Deal brought even greater changes to many American workers. It prohibited child labor, established national wage and hours legislation, and, most important of all, guaranteed the right of collective bargaining. Efforts to unionize unskilled workers generally had been unsuccessful since the days of the Knights of Labor. Since the end of World War I, even the trade unions had experienced difficulty, and the stolid, conservative American Federation of Labor had found its membership steadily decreasing. After an abortive beginning during the NRA period (1933–1935), the New Deal promoted the greatest and most successful organizing campaign in the history of American labor. The AFL recovered and began a period of growth. A new labor federation, the Congress of Industrial Organizations, established unions in the mass-production industries and openly entered politics to become an important element in the New Deal coalition. By the time the New Deal ended, organized labor occupied a more important and powerful position in American society than ever before, a development consolidated and institutionalized by World War II.

On the other hand, the New Deal brought few lasting changes to the business community. For two years, the National Recovery Administration attempted to bring a high degree of centralized economic coordination to American industry, but in practice it gave sanction to a loose cartelism. After the Supreme Court ruled the NRA unconstitutional, New Deal policy moved in general to a rhetorically militant antitrust program, which in the end accomplished little. The New Deal seemed, as Ellis Hawley brilliantly argues, to be caught in a dilemma which has plagued modern American reform. It accepted and for a time attempted to promote the benefits of organization and centralization; yet it also yearned for the opportunity and openness of the competitive, atomistic society. Consequently, it did little to alter the structure of American business, though it did impose some much-needed regulation upon the financial community.

Yet by enhancing the positions of agriculture and, especially, labor, the New Deal did manage to reduce in relative terms the prestige and authority of big business. It had created a system of "countervailing powers." And if it could not bring the nation out of the depression, it did succeed in putting a large variety of economic stabilizers into the economy. These stabilizers—ranging from deposit insurance and stock market regulation to minimum wages, agricultural price supports, and social security—have been instrumental in preventing a new depression.

The New Deal did more than bring these important changes to American society; it brought hope to a free world which had nearly lost faith in itself. Fascism was a steadily expanding force throughout the 1930's, and it seemed for a time that only Communism had the strength to oppose it. One of the most important accomplishments of the New Deal, as Arthur Schlesinger, Jr., has written, was its success in convincing so many Americans and Europeans that democratic reform represented a viable alternative to totalitarianism.

Despite all these achievements, the New Deal experienced important failures. Foremost among them was the failure to 'ift the nation entirely out of the depression; by mid-1939 unemployment was still at the intolerable level of ten million. It is true that the New Deal offered more to the unemployed than did its opponents on the Right; in fact, much of its political support was based on the benefits that its employment and mortgage relief programs distributed. Ultimately, however, the New Deal's faiiure to solve the problem of unemployment contributed heavily to its political defeat. If it ended the crisis of 1932–1933, its lack of success in dealing with the recession of 1937–1938 emboldened its opponents and greatly facilitated the formation of a conservative coalition in Congress. Its halfway measures, even if they lifted the nation above the low point of the depression, were an important factor in its undoing. Prosperity and full employment would come only with World War II.

Moreover, the benefits of countervailing power did not extend to all deprived Americans. When one considers that the New Deal could not end mass unemployment, it is hardly surprising that it also was unable to come to grips with the problem of hard-core poverty. Few of its programs were designed specifically for those who had been jobless or impoverished during the prosperous twenties. A notable exception was the Farm Security Administration, which attempted in a variety of ways to assist sharecroppers, tenant farmers, and migrant laborers. The FSA's objectives were noble, and the agency brought the problem of rural poverty to national attention. But the FSA existed on the fringes of the New Deal; its funds were limited, and its life was short and difficult. The New Deal gave great assistance to those who had lived on the margins of poverty; it lifted many blue-collar workers and small commercial farmers into the middle class. But it offered much less to those who lived in a state of deep and permanent poverty. Perhaps it would have been impossible to direct an attack upon hard-core poverty so long as the depression and mass unemployment continued; certainly, the New Deal was unable to do so. It gave the least to those who needed the most.

The New Deal perceived the problems of the American Negro only dimly. As with the unemployed and the poor, it could offer more than the conservatives. Such New Dealers as Harold Ickes and Eleanor Roosevelt displayed genuine sympathy for Negro aspirations, and the establishment of an informal "Black Cabinet" along with a few key appointments constituted token recognition. But there was never a New Deal civil rights program; Roosevelt's priorities lay elsewhere, and he was unwilling to give support to even such elementary measures as anti-lynching bills. With the threat of impending war and massive black demonstrations, the President established a Fair Employment Practices Commission, but he refused to end discrimination in the armed forces. Of course, the failure to understand the plight of the Negro was a national failure, and, given the overwhelming economic problems of the 1930's, it is difficult to question Roosevelt's sense of priorities. Nevertheless, on this problem, so crucial to present-day America, the New Deal was largely another period of postponement.

To some historians, many of them identified with the new political radicalism of the 1960's, these failures have overshadowed even the accomplishments of the New Deal; certainly, they raise the question of why the New Deal could not have accomplished more. One answer may lie in the leadership of Franklin D. Roosevelt and the intellectual style of the New Deal.

Arthur Schlesinger, Jr., has eloquently depicted Roosevelt's receptivity to new ideas and the New Deal's eagerness to experiment as a triumph of the pragmatic mood. Its rejection of dogma, he believes, was the central element in its success. But others, most notably James MacGregor Burns, argue that flexibility and opportunism should not be confused with pragmatism. Following the contemporary criticism of the great American pragmatist, John Dewey, these historians assert that the half-planned, compromised, and inconsistent improvisations of the New Deal were indicative simply of a lack of coherence and direction; their prime example, of course, is Roosevelt's failure to grasp Keynesian economic theory and make the wholehearted commitment which it required. In addition, they believe that Roosevelt failed as a party leader. Lacking the imagination to effect the political realignment which the nation required, he was unable to rebuild the Democratic party and make it a genuinely liberal force. As these critics see it, FDR failed to give America the truly great leadership which the times demanded and may actually have done long-range harm to the cause of reform.

Yet it is impossible to place sole responsibility for the unfinished nature of the New Deal upon Roosevelt. After 1938, reform was blocked in Congress by a conservative coalition whose pivotal element was composed of Democrats. Some flaws in Roosevelt's leadership may have encouraged the formation of this informal but powerful coalition; however, its existence was possible only because of the loosely structured and undisciplined character of the American party system, and because of the rigid separation of powers in the American constitution. An American president acting as party leader has little disciplinary power; his party members in Congress are not constitutionally responsible to him, and the patronage at his disposal is limited. He may appeal to public opinion, but in order to bring results, his appeals must bring a response from the specific constituencies of unfriendly congressmen. The formation of the conservative coalition became possible only when a large number of Democratic congressmen, unfavorably disposed toward the New Deal, realized that their constituencies differed sufficiently from President Roosevelt's national constituency to tolerate an anti-administration voting record. Unable to control the constituencies of these congressmen, Roosevelt could not wield effective power as a party leader. He could and did continue to dominate the Democratic "presidential party," the coalition which controlled the Democratic nominating conventions and provided the margin of victory in presidential elections. However, he could not control the Democratic "congressional party"; after 1938, he could hope to achieve legislation only through the weak and largely ineffective method of persuasion.

Many liberals, then and since, felt that the conservative coalition was an undemocratic and illegitimate conspiracy. Actually, it was a natural development of the American political system; one need only read James Madison's contributions to *The Federalist* to understand that the Constitution was designed to protect different interests by giving each a veto on important legislation. On the whole, the Founding Fathers sought to contain government, not promote change. It was remarkable that the New Deal was able to break through these carefully devised constitutional barriers for so long.

By 1939, however, Congress was so hopelessly deadlocked that it was balking at even the inadequate relief appropriations which Roosevelt was requesting. The massive spending suggested by John Maynard Keynes and his followers was now impossible; so long as peacetime conditions continued, the nation could look forward only to a permanent depression and mass unemployment. Had not World War II intervened with its huge defense expenditures and resultant prosperity, the New Deal might well have been considered a failure. In fact, the war may have saved more than the New Deal; it is hard to see how American representative government could have endured had the depression persisted indefinitely. The continuance of prosperity after the war ended mass unemployment. But prosperity did not solve the problems of the Negro and the poor; instead it made these problems more difficult to handle. By the 1960's these issues had assumed the dimensions of a national crisis. Whatever the failures in FDR's leadership, no future reform-minded president surpassed or even approached Roosevelt's dual ability to appeal to both Congress and the public. It seemed more certain than ever that reform was being blocked by those flaws in the American political system which had ended the New Deal. And it was evident that this time war could not provide a solution.

THE NEW DEAL: AN OVERVIEW

Frank Freidel

THE NEW DEAL IN HISTORICAL PERSPECTIVE

FRANK FREIDEL, Professor of History at Harvard University, is one of the major biographers of Franklin D. Roosevelt; in the three volumes which he has published thus far, he has carried the story of Roosevelt's life through his election to the Presidency. The essay below is Freidel's major statement on the nature of the New Deal. It provides a convenient, if necessarily sketchy, overview of its subject, and its interpretations represent the mature opinion of one of the most eminent students of the Roosevelt era.

Stressing what he believes to be the essential moderation of Roosevelt and the New Deal, Freidel attempts to show that both the man and the movement had strong connections with the Progressive Era. He also argues that despite important continuities in Roosevelt's attitude, there was, beginning in 1935, a definite shift in the style and policies of the New Deal, a change so significant that one may speak of a "first New Deal" characterized by relatively conservative consensus politics and a "second New Deal" based on class politics. The reader should attempt to find the evidence for each interpretation; he should remember also that both are controversial and by no means have won unanimous acceptance among historians.

From *The New Deal in Historical Perspective* by Frank Freidel, 2d ed. (Washington, D.C.: American Historical Association Service Center for Teachers of History, 1965), pp. 1–20. Copyright © 1959 by the American Historical Association. Reprinted by permission of the publisher and the author.

In less than a generation, the New Deal has passed into both popular legend and serious history. The exigencies of American politics long demanded that its partisans and opponents paint a picture of it either in the most glamorous whites or sinister blacks. Long after the New Deal was over, politicians of both major parties tried at each election to reap a harvest of votes from its issues.

Gradually a new generation of voters has risen which does not remember the New Deal and takes for granted the changes that it wrought. Gradually too, politicians have had to recognize that the nation faces new, quite different problems since the second World War, and that campaigning on the New Deal has become as outmoded as did the "bloody shirt" issue as decades passed after the Civil War. At the same time, most of the important manuscript collections relating to the New Deal have been opened to scholars so rapidly that careful historical research has been possible decades sooner that was true for earlier periods of United States history. (The Franklin D. Roosevelt papers and the Abraham Lincoln papers became available for research at about the same time, just after the second World War.)

It has been the task of the historians not only to analyze heretofore hidden aspects of the New Deal on the basis of the manuscripts, but also to remind readers of what was once commonplace and is now widely forgotten. A new generation has no firsthand experience of the depths of despair into which the depression had thrust the nation, and the excitement and eagerness with which people greeted the new program. Critics not only have denied that anything constructive could have come from the New Deal but they have even succeeded in creating the impression in the prosperous years since 1945 that the depression really did not amount to much. How bad it was is worth remembering, since this is a means of gauging the enormous pressure for change.

Estimates of the number of unemployed ranged up to thirteen million out of a labor force of fifty-two million, which would mean that one wage-earner out of four was without means of support for himself or his family. Yet of these thirteen million unemployed, only about a quarter were receiving any kind of assistance. States and municipalities were running out of relief funds; private agencies were long since at the end of their resources. And those who were receiving aid often obtained only a pittance. The Toledo commissary could allow for relief only 2.14 cents per person per meal, and the Red Cross in southern Illinois in 1931 was able to provide families with only seventy-five cents a week for food. It was in this crisis that one of the most flamboyant members of the Hoover administration suggested a means of providing sustenance for the unemployed: restaurants should dump left-overs and plate scrapings into special sanitary cans to be given to worthy unemployed people willing to work for the food. It was a superfluous suggestion, for in 1932 an observer in Chicago reported:

> Around the truck which was unloading garbage and other refuse were about thirty-five men, women, and children. As soon as the truck pulled away from the pile, all of them started digging with sticks, some with their hands, grabbing bits of food and vegetables.

The employed in some instances were not a great deal better off. In December 1932 wages in a wide range of industries from textiles to iron and steel, averaged from a low of 20 cents to a high of only 30 cents an hour. A quarter of the women working in Chicago were receiving less than 10 cents an hour. In farming areas, conditions were equally grim. In bitter weather on the Great Plains, travelers occasionally encountered a light blue haze that smelled like roasting coffee. The "old corn" held over from the crop of a year earlier would sell for only $1.40 per ton, while coal cost $4 per ton, so many farmers burned corn to keep warm. When Aubrey Williams went into farm cellars in the Dakotas in the early spring of 1933 farm wives showed him shelves and shelves of jars for fruits and vegetables—but they were all empty. Even farmers who could avoid hunger had trouble meeting payments on their mortgages. As a result a fourth of all farmers in the United States lost their farms during these years.

Despairing people in these pre-New Deal years feared President Herbert Hoover had forgotten them or did not recognize the seriousness of their plight. As a matter of fact he had, more than any other depression president in American history, taken steps to try to bring recovery. But he had functioned largely through giving aid at the top to prevent the further collapse of banks and industries, and the concentric rings of further collapses and unemployment which would then ensue. Also he had continued to pin his faith upon voluntary action. He felt that too great federal intervention would undermine the self-reliance, destroy the "rugged individualism" of the American people, and that it would create federal centralization, thus paving the way for socialism.

President Hoover was consistent in his thinking, and he was humane. But it would have been hard to explain to people like those grubbing on the Chicago garbage heap, why, when the Reconstruction Finance Corporation was loaning $90,000,000 to a single Chicago bank, the President would veto a bill to provide federal relief for the unemployed, asserting, "never before has so dangerous a suggestion been seriously made in this country." It was not until June 1932 that he approved a measure permitting the RFC to loan $300,000,000 for relief purposes.

It seems shocking in retrospect that such conditions should have existed in this country, and that any president of either major party should so long have refused to approve federal funds to alleviate them. It adds to the shock when one notes that many public figures of the period were well to the right of the President—for instance, Secretary of the Treasury Andrew Mellon—and that almost no one who was likely to be in a position to act, including Governor Roosevelt of New York, was ready at that time to go very far to the left of Hoover.

Roosevelt, who was perhaps the most advanced of the forty-eight governors in developing a program to meet the depression, had shown little faith in public works spending. When he he had established the first state relief agency in the United States in the fall of 1931, he had tried to finance it through higher taxes, and only later, reluctantly, abandoned the pay-as-you-go basis. He was, and he always remained, a staunch believer in a balanced budget. He was never more sincere than when, during the campaign of 1932, he accused the Hoover administration of having run up a deficit of three and three-quarters billions of dollars in the previous two years. This, he charged, was "the most reckless and extravagant past that I have been able to discover in the statistical record of any peacetime Government anywhere, any time."

Governor Roosevelt's own cautious record did not exempt him from attack. In April 1932, seeking the presidential nomination, he proclaimed himself the champion of the "forgotten man," and talked vaguely about raising the purchasing power of the masses, in part through directing Reconstruction Finance Corporation loans their way. This little was sufficient to lead many political leaders and publicists, including his Democratic rival, Al Smith, to accuse Roosevelt of being a demagogue, ready to set class against class.

Smith and most other public figures, including Roosevelt, favored public works programs. A few men like Senators Robert F. Wagner of New York and Robert M. La Follette of Wisconsin visualized really large-scale spending on public construction, but most leaders also wanted to accompany the spending with very high taxes which would have been deflationary and thus have defeated the program. None of the important political leaders, and none of the economists who had access to them, seemed as yet to visualize the decisive intervention of the government into the economy of the sort that is considered commonplace today. The term "built-in stabilizers" had yet to be coined.

The fact was that Roosevelt and most of his contemporaries, who like him were products of the Progressive Era, were basically conservative men who unquestioningly believed in the American free enterprise system. On the whole, they were suspicious of strong government, and would indulge in it only as a last resort to try to save the system. This was their limitation in trying to bring about economic recovery. On the other hand, part of their Progressive legacy was also a humanitarian belief in social justice. This belief would lead them to espouse reforms to improve the lot of the common man, even though those reforms might also take them in the direction of additional government regulation. Roosevelt as governor had repeatedly demonstrated this inconsistency in his public statements and recommendations. He had ardently endorsed states rights and small government in a truly Jeffersonian way. Then in quite contrary fashion (but still in keeping with Jeffersonian spirit applied to twentieth century society) he had pointed out one or another area, such as old age security, in which he believed the government must intervene to protect the individual.

At this time, what distinguished Governor Roosevelt from his fellows were two remarkable characteristics. The first was his brilliant political skill, which won to him an overwhelming proportion of the Democratic politicians and the general public. The second was his willingness to experiment, to try one or another improvisation to stop the slow economic drift downward toward ruin. During the campaign of 1932, many a man who had observed Roosevelt felt as did Harry Hopkins that he would make a better president than Hoover, "chiefly because he is not afraid of a new idea."

Roosevelt's sublime self-confidence and his willingness to try new expedients stood him in good stead when he took over the presidency. On that grim March day in 1933 when he took his oath of office, the American economic system was half-paralyzed. Many of the banks were closed; the remainder he quickly shut down through presidential proclamation. Industrial production was down to 56 per cent of the 1923–25 level. Yet somehow, Roosevelt's self-confidence was infectious. People were ready to believe, to follow, when he said in words that were not particularly new, "The only thing we have to fear is fear itself." He offered "leadership of frankness and vigor," and almost the whole of the American public and press—even papers like the Chicago *Tribune* which soon became bitter critics—for the moment accepted that leadership with enthusiasm.

For a short period of time, about one hundred days, Roosevelt had behind him such overwhelming public support that he was able to push through Congress a wide array of legislation which in total established the New Deal. It came in helter-skelter fashion and seemed to go in all directions, even at times directions that conflicted with each other. There was mildly corrective legislation to get the banks open again, a slashing of government costs to balance the budget, legalization of 3.2 beer, establishment of the Civilian Conservation Corps, of the Tennessee Valley Authority, and of a wide variety of other agencies in the areas of relief, reform, and, above all in those first months, of recovery.

What pattern emerged in all of this legislation? How sharply did it break with earlier American political traditions? The answer was that it represented Roosevelt's efforts to be president to all the American people, to present something to every group in need. And it was based squarely on American objectives and experience in the Progressive Era and during the first World War. It went beyond the Hoover program in that while the word "voluntary" remained in many of the laws, they now had behind them the force of the government or at least strong economic incentives.

It has been forgotten how basically conservative Roosevelt's attitudes remained during the early period of the New Deal. He had closed the banks, but reopened them with relatively little change. Indeed, the emergency banking measure had been drafted by Hoover's Treasury officials. What banking reform there was came later. His slashing of the regular government costs was something he had promised during his campaign, and in which he sincerely believed and continued to believe. He kept the regular budget of the government low until the late thirties. While he spent billions through the parallel emergency budget, he did that reluctantly, and only because he felt it was necessary to keep people from starving. He was proud that he was keeping the credit of the government good, and never ceased to look forward to the day when he could balance the budget. For the first several years of the New Deal he consulted frequently with Wall Streeters and other economic conservatives. His first Director of the Budget, Lewis Douglas, parted ways with him, but late in 1934 was exhorting: "I hope, and hope most fervently, that you will evidence a real determination to bring the budget into actual balance, for upon this, I think, hangs not only your place in history but conceivably the immediate fate of western civilization." (Douglas to FDR, November 28, 1934)

Remarks like this struck home with Roosevelt. Douglas's successors as Director of the Budget held much the same views, and Henry Morgenthau, Jr., who became Secretary of the Treasury at the beginning of 1934, never failed to prod Roosevelt to slash governmental expenditures.

We should add parenthetically that Roosevelt always keenly resented the untrue newspaper stories that his parents had been unwilling to entrust him with money. As a matter of fact he was personally so thrifty when he was in the White House that he used to send away for bargain mail-order shirts, and when he wished summer suits, switched from an expensive New York tailor to a cheaper one in Washington. This he did despite the warning of the New York tailor that he might thus lose his standing as one of the nation's best-dressed men.

Financial caution in governmental affairs rather typifies Roosevelt's economic thinking throughout the entire New Deal. He was ready to go much further than Hoover in construction of public works, but he preferred the kind which would pay for themselves, and did not think there were many possibilities for them in the country. His estimate before he became president was only one billion dollars worth. In 1934, he once proposed that the government buy the buildings of foundered banks throughout the nation and use them for post-offices rather than to construct new buildings. This is how far he was from visualizing huge public works expenditures as a means of boosting the country out of the depression. His course in this area was the middle road. He wished to bring about recovery without upsetting the budget any further than absolutely necessary. He did not launch the nation on a program of deliberate deficit financing.

When Roosevelt explained his program in a fireside chat at the end of July 1933, he declared:

"It may seem inconsistent for a government to cut down its regular expenses and at the same time to borrow and to spend billions for an emergency. But it is not inconsistent because a large portion of the emergency money has been paid out in the form of sound loans . . . ; and to cover the rest . . . we have imposed taxes. . . .

"So you will see that we have kept our credit good. We have built a granite foundation in a period of confusion."

It followed from this that aside from limited public works expenditures, Roosevelt wanted a recovery program which would not be a drain on governmental finances. Neither the Agricultural Adjustment Administration nor the National Recovery Administration were. He had promised in the major farm speech of his 1932 campaign that his plan for agricultural relief would be self-financing; this was achieved through the processing tax on certain farm products. The NRA involved no governmental expenditures except for administration.

Both of these programs reflected not the progressivism of the first years of the century, but the means through which

Progressives had regulated production during the first World War. This had meant regulation which would as far as possible protect both producers and consumers, both employers and employees. Here the parallel was direct. The rest of Roosevelt's program did not parallel the Progressives' wartime experience, for during the war, in terms of production regulation had meant output of what was needed to win the war. Now the problem in the thirties was one of reducing output in most areas rather than raising it, and of getting prices back up rather than trying to hold them down.

Certainly the nation badly needed this sort of a program in 1933. The products of the fields and mines and of highly competitive consumers' goods industries like textiles were being sold so cheaply that producers and their employees alike were close to starvation. The overproduction was also wasteful of natural resources. In an oilfield near Houston, one grocer advertised when 3.2 beer first became legal that he would exchange one bottle of beer for one barrel of oil. They were worth about the same. In other heavy industries like automobiles or farm machinery, production had been cut drastically while prices remained high. One need was to bring prices throughout industry and agriculture into a more equitable relationship with each other, and with the debt structure.

The NRA scheme in theory would help do this. Its antecedents were in the regulatory War Industries Board of the first World War, and indeed it was run by some of the same men. The War Industries Board had functioned through industrial committees; in the twenties these committees had evolved into self-regulatory trade associations. Unfortunately, as Roosevelt had found when he headed the association created to discipline one of the largest and most chaotic of industries, the American Construction Council, self-regulation without the force of law behind it, had a tendency to break down. When the depression had hit, some businessmen themselves had advocated the NRA scheme, but Hoover would have none of it. Roosevelt was receptive.

The theory was that committees in a few major fields like steel, textiles, bituminous coal and the like, would draw up codes of fair practice for the industry. These would not only stabilize the price structure, but also protect the wages and working conditions of labor. Even consumers would benefit, presumably through receiving more wages or profits, and thus enjoying larger purchasing power with which to buy goods at somewhat higher prices.

In practice, the NRA program went awry. Too many committees drew up too many codes embodying many sorts of unenforceable provisions. There was a code even for the mopstick industry. What was more important, some manufacturers rushed to turn out quantities of goods at the old wage and raw material level before the code went into effect, hoping then to sell these goods at the new higher prices. Consequently during the summer of 1933 there was a short NRA boom when industrial production jumped to 101 per cent of the 1923–25 level, and wholesale prices rose from an index figure of 60.2 in March to 71.2 by October. The crop reduction program of the AAA led to a corresponding rise in agricultural prices.

Had consumers at the same time enjoyed a correspondingly higher purchasing power, the recovery scheme might well have worked. Some of its designers had visualized pouring the additional dollars into consumers' pockets through a heavy public works spending program. Indeed the bill which created the NRA also set up a Public Works Administration with $3,300,000,000 to spend. This money could have been poured here and there into the economy where it was most needed to "prime the pump." But Roosevelt and his most influential advisers did not want to give such an enormous spending power to the administrator of the NRA, nor had they really accepted the deficit spending school of thought. Hence while some of the money being spent by the New Deal went for immediate relief of one form or another, it went to people so close to starvation that they were forced to spend what they received on bare necessities. This was of little aid in priming the pump. The public works fund, which could have served that purpose, went to that sturdy old Progressive, "Honest Harold" Ickes. He slowly went about the process of allocating it in such a way that the government and the public would get a return of one hundred cents (or preferably more) on every dollar spent. Raymond Moley has suggested that if only the cautious Ickes had headed the NRA and the impetuous [Hugh] Johnson the Public Works Administration the scheme might have worked.

Without a huge transfusion of dollars into the economy, the industrial and agricultural recovery programs sagged in the fall of 1933. Roosevelt turned to currency manipulation to try to get prices up. He explained to a critical Congressman, "I have always favored sound money, and do now, but it is 'too darn sound' when it takes so much of farm products to buy a dollar." Roosevelt also accepted a makeshift work relief program, the Civil Works Administration, to carry the destitute through the winter.

Already the New Deal honeymoon was over, and in 1934 and 1935 a sharp political struggle between Roosevelt and the right began to form. To conservatives, Roosevelt was shattering the constitution with his economic legislation. Al Smith was attacking the devaluated currency as "baloney dollars," and was writing articles with such titles as "Is the Constitution Still There?" and "Does the Star-Spangled Banner Still Wave?" Former President Hoover published his powerful jeremiad, *The Challenge to Liberty.*

Many businessmen complained against the NRA restrictions, the favoritism allegedly being shown to organized labor, and the higher taxes. Although some of them had advocated the NRA, the significant fact was that the thinking of most businessmen seems to have remained about what it had been in the 1920's. They were eager for aid from the government, as long as it involved no obligations on their part or restrictions against them. They wanted a government which could protect their domestic markets with a high tariff wall, and at the same time seek out foreign markets for them, a court system which could discipline organized labor with injunctions, and a tax structure which (as under Secretary of the Treasury Mellon) would take no enormous bite of large profits, and yet retain disciplinary levies on the lower-middle income groups. All these policies they could understand and condone. The New Deal, which would confer other benefits upon them, but require corresponding obligations, they could not.

This hostile thinking which began to develop among the business community was sincere. Businessmen genuinely believed that under the New Deal program too large a share of their income had to go to organized labor, and to much to the government. They freely predicted federal bankruptcy as the deficit began to mount. If they had capital to commit, they refused to expend it on new plants and facilities (except for some introduction of labor-saving machinery). They were too unsure of the future, they complained, because they could not tell what that man in the White House might propose next. Business needed a "breathing spell," Roy Howard wrote Roosevelt, and the President promised one. Nevertheless, the legislative requests continued unabated.

All this, important though it is in delineating the ideology of businessmen, is not the whole story. The fact is that during the long bleak years after October 1929 they had slipped into a depression way of thinking. They regarded American industry as being over-built; they looked upon the American market as being permanently contracted. By 1937 when industrial production and stock dividends were up to within ten percent of the 1929 peak, capital expenditures continued to drag along the depression floor. Industrialists did not engage in the large-scale spending for expansion which has been a significant factor in the boom since 1945. As late as 1940 to 1941, many of them were loathe to take the large defense orders which required construction of new plants. Unquestionably the pessimism of businessmen during the thirties, whether or not linked to their hatred of Roosevelt and fear of the New Deal, was as significant a factor in perpetuating the depression, as their optimism since the war has been in perpetuating the boom.

The paradox is that some of the New Deal measures against which the businessmen fought helped introduce into the economy some of the stabilizers which today help give businessmen confidence in the continuation of prosperity. These came despite, not because of, the businessmen. Roosevelt long continued to try to co-operate with the leaders of industry and banking. Their anger toward him, and frequently-expressed statements that he had betrayed his class, at times bewildered and even upset him. For the most part he laughed them off. He hung in his bedroom a favorite cartoon. It showed a little girl at the door of a fine suburban home, apparently tattling to her mother. "Johnny wrote a dirty word on the sidewalk." And the word, of course, was "Roosevelt."

To some of his old friends who complained to him, he would reply with patience and humor. Forever he was trying to point out to them the human side of the problem of the depression. Perhaps the best illustration is a witty interchange with a famous doctor for whom he had deep affection. The doctor wired him in March 1935:

"Pediatricians have long been perplexed by difficulty of weaning infant from breast or bottle to teaspoon or cup. The shift often establishes permanent neurosis in subsequent adult. According to report in evening paper twenty-two million citizen infants now hang on federal breasts. Can you wean them doctor and prevent national neurosis?"

Roosevelt promptly replied:

"As a young interne you doubtless realize that the interesting transitional process, which you describe in your telegram, presupposes that the bottle, teaspoon, or cup is not empty. Such vehicles of feeding, if empty produce flatulence and the patient dies from a lack of nutrition.

"The next question on your examination paper is, therefore, the following:

"Assuming that the transitional period has arrived, where is the Doctor to get the food from to put in the new container?"

As time went on, and the attacks became virulent from some quarters, at times even passing the bounds of decency, Roosevelt struck back vigorously. During his campaign in 1936 he excoriated the "economic royalists." When he wound up the campaign in Madison Square Garden, he declared:

"We had to struggle with the old enemies of peace—business and financial monopoly, speculation, reckless banking, class antagonism, sectionalism, war profiteering. They had begun to consider the Government of the United States as a mere appendage to their own affairs. And we know now that Government by organized money is just as dangerous as Government by organized mob.

"Never before in all our history have these forces been so united against one candidate as they stand today. They are unanimous in their hate for me—and I welcome their hatred."

To these sharp words Roosevelt had come from his position early in the New Deal as the impartial arbiter of American economic forces. He had come to them less because of what he considered as betrayal from the right than through pressure from the left. How had this pressure applied between 1934 and the campaign of 1936?

Back in 1934, while the economic temperature chart of the near frozen depression victim had fluctuated up and down, still dangerously below normal, the dispossessed millions began to look at the New Deal with despair or even disillusion. Those workers going on strike to obtain the twenty-five or thirty-five cents an hour minimum wage or the collective bargaining privileges promised by the NRA began to wisecrack that NRA stood for the National Run-Around. Some of them and of the unemployed millions in northern cities still dependent upon meager relief handouts, began to listen to the stirring radio addresses of Father Charles Coughlin. Old people began to pay five cents a week dues to Dr. Francis Townsend's clubs, which promised them fantastically large benefits. Throughout the South (and even in parts of the North) the dispossessed small farmers listened with enthusiasm to the exhortations of the Louisiana Kingfish, Huey Long, that he would share the wealth to make every man a king.

Many Democratic politicians were surprisingly oblivious to these rumblings and mutterings. Much of the private conversation of men like Vice President John Nance Garner sounded like the public demands of the Liberty Leaguers: cut relief and balance the budget. Garner, who spent the 1934 campaign hunting and fishing in Texas, predicted the usual mid-term loss of a few congressional seats back to the Republicans. Instead the Democrats picked up a startling number of new seats in both houses of Congress. The dispossessed had continued to vote with the Democratic party—but perhaps because there was no alternative but the Republicans who offered only retrenchment. Charles Beard commented that the 1934 election was "thunder on the left."

President Roosevelt, who was brilliantly sensitive to political forces, sensed fully the threat from the left. At the beginning of that crisis year 1935 he proposed in his annual message to Congress the enactment of a program to reinforce "the security of the men, women, and children of the nation" in their livelihood, to protect them against the major hazards and vicissitudes of life, and to enable them to obtain decent homes. In this increased emphasis upon security and reform, Professor Basil Rauch sees the beginnings of a second New Deal.

Certainly the pattern as it emerged in the next year was a brilliant one. Roosevelt neutralized Huey Long with the "soak the rich" tax, the "holding company death sentence," and with various measures directly of benefit to the poorer farmers of the South. Before an assassin's bullet felled Long, his political strength was already undercut. Similarly Roosevelt undermined the Townsend movement by pressing passage of the Social Security Act, which provided at least small benefits for the aged, at the same time that a congressional investigation disclosed how men around Townsend were fattening themselves on the nickels of millions of the aged. As for Father Coughlin, the Treasury announced that money from his coffers had gone into silver speculation at a time he had been loudly advocating that the government buy more silver at higher prices. More important, Coughlin had less appeal to employed workers after the new National Labor Relations Act raised a benign federal umbrella over collective bargaining. For the unemployed, a huge and substantial work relief program, the Works Progress Administration, came into existence.

Partly all this involved incisive political counterthrusts; partly it was a program Roosevelt had favored anyway. In any event, combined with Roosevelt's direct and effective appeal in radio fireside chats, it caused the dispossessed to look to him rather than to demagogues as their champion. Millions of them or their relations received some direct aid from the New Deal, whether a small crop payment or a WPA check. Millions more received wage boosts for which they were more grateful to Roosevelt than to their employers. Others through New Deal mortgage legislation had held onto their farms or homes. All these people, benefitting directly or indirectly, looked to Roosevelt as the source of their improved economic condition, and they were ready to vote accordingly. Roosevelt, who had been nominated in 1932 as the candidate of the South and the West, the champion of the farmer and the middle-class "forgotten man," after 1936 became increasingly the leader of the urban masses and the beneficiary of the growing power of organized labor.

What happened seems sharper and clearer in retrospect than it did at the time. Secretary Ickes, recording repeatedly in his diary during the early months of 1935 that the President was losing his grip, was echoing what many New Dealers and part of the public felt. They did not see a sharp shift into a second New Deal, and that is understandable. Roosevelt ever since he had become president had been talking about reform and from time to time recommending reform measures to Congress. He seems to have thought at the outset in two categories, about immediate or short-range emergency recovery measures to bring about a quick economic upswing, and also in terms of long-range reform legislation to make a recurrence of the depression less likely. Some of these reform measures like TVA had been ready for immediate enactment; others, like a revision of banking legislation and the social security legislation, he had planned from the beginning but were several years in the making. Frances Perkins has vividly described in her memoirs the lengthly task she and her associates undertook of drafting and selling to Congress and the public what became the Social Security Act of 1935.

Then Roosevelt had to face the additional factor that the emergency legislation had not succeeded in bringing rapid recovery. He had to think in terms of more permanent legislation with which to aim toward the same objectives. That meant he ceased trying to save money with a temporary program of cheaper direct relief, and switched instead to work relief (in which he had always believed) to try to stop some of the moral and physical erosion of those unfortunates who had been without employment for years.

In part the Supreme Court forced the recasting of some of his legislation. It gave a mercy killing in effect to the rickety, unwieldy NRA code structure when it handed down the Schechter or "sick chicken" decision of May 1935. On the whole the NRA had been unworkable, but it had achieved some outstanding results—in abolishing child labor, in bringing some order in the chaotic bituminous coal industry, and the like. Roosevelt was furious with the court, since the decision threatened to undermine all New Deal economic regulation. He charged that the justices were taking a horse and buggy view of the economic powers of the government. There followed six months later the court invalidation of the Triple-A processing tax, which for the moment threw out of gear the agricultural program.

The answer to these and similar Supreme Court decisions was Roosevelt's bold onslaught against the court after he had been reelected in the great landslide of 1936. He had carried every state but Maine and Vermont; he considered himself as having a great mandate from the people to continue his program. Nor had he any reason to doubt his ability to push a court reform program through Congress, since the already bulging New Deal majorities had become still bigger. He was wrong; he failed. His failure came as much as anything through a great tactical error. He disguised his program as one to bring about a speedier handling of cases, when he should have presented it frankly as a means of ending the court obstruction of the New Deal. This obstruction was real. Many corporations openly flaunted the National Labor Relations Act, for example, they were so confident that the Supreme Court would invalidate it.

However laudable the end, to many a well-educated member of the middle class who had supported Roosevelt even through the campaign of 1936, Roosevelt's resort to subterfuge smacked of the devious ways of dictators. In 1937, Americans were all too aware of the way in which Hitler and Mussolini had gained power. It was not that any thinking man expected Roosevelt to follow their example, but rather that many objected to any threat, real or potential, to the constitutional system including the separation of powers. After Roosevelt, they argued, the potential dictator might appear. It may be too that times had improved sufficiently since March 1933 so that constitutional considerations could again overweigh economic exigencies. In any event, Roosevelt lost his battle—and won his war.

While the struggle was rocking the nation, the justices began exercising the judicial self-restraint which one of their number, Harlan F. Stone, had urged upon them the previous year. They surprised the nation by upholding the constitutionality of the National Labor Relations Act and the Social Security Act. In large part this eliminated the necessity for the New Dealers to make any change in the personnel of the court, and thus helped contribute to Roosevelt's defeat in Congress. Further, the fight had helped bring into existence a conservative coalition in Congress which from this time on gave Roosevelt a rough ride. Many old-line Democratic congressmen now dared proclaim in public what they had previously whispered in private. All this added up to a spectacular setback for Roosevelt—so spectacular that it is easy to overlook the enormous and permanent changes that had come about.

In the next few years the Supreme Court in effect rewrote a

large part of constitutional law. The federal and state governments were now able to engage in extensive economic regulation with little or no court restraint upon them. The limits upon regulation must be set for the most part by the legislative branch of the government, not the judiciary. Not only were the National Labor Relations Act and Social Security constitutional, but a bulging portfolio of other legislation.

These laws were not as spectacular as the measures of the Hundred Days, but in the bulk they were far more significant, for they brought about lasting changes in the economic role of the federal government. There was the continued subsidy to agriculture in order to maintain crop control—based upon soil conservation rather than a processing tax. There were all the agricultural relief measures which came to be centralized in the Farm Security Administration. Although that agency has disappeared, most of its functions have continued in one way or another. There was a beginning of slum clearance and public housing, and a continuation of TVA, held constitutional even before the court fight. There was a stiffening of securities regulation. There was a continuation of much that Roosevelt had considered beneficial in the NRA through a group of new laws usually referred to as the "little NRA." These perpetuated the coal and liquor codes, helped regulate oil production, tried to prevent wholesale price discriminations and legalized the establishment of "fair trade" prices by manufacturers. Most important of all, the Fair Labor Standards Act of [1938] set a national minimum of wages and maximum of hours of work, and prohibited the shipping in interstate commerce of goods made by child labor. These are lasting contributions of the New Deal, either substantial laws in themselves or the seeds for later legislation.

What then, is to be said of the recession and the anti-monopoly program? A Keynesian point of view is that public works spending, the other New Deal spending programs, and the payment of the bonus to veterans of the first World War (over Roosevelt's veto, incidentally), all these together had poured so much money into the economy that they brought about a substantial degree of recovery, except in employment, by the spring of 1937. At this point Roosevelt tried to balance the budget, especially by cutting public works and work relief expenditures. The result was a sharp recession. Roosevelt was forced to resort to renewed pump-priming, and in a few months the recession was over.

Even this recession experience did not convert Roosevelt to Keynesianism. Keynes once called upon Roosevelt at the White House and apparently tried to dazzle him with complex mathematical talk. Each was disappointed in the other. In 1939, after the recession when a protégé of Mrs. Roosevelt's proposed additional welfare spending, Roosevelt replied by listing worthwhile projects in which the government could usefully spend an additional five billions a year. Then he pointed out that the deficit was already three billions, which could not go on forever. How, he inquired, could an eight billion dollar deficit be financed.

As for economists, many of them saw the answer in the enormous spending power which would be unleashed if the government poured out billions in time of depression. To most of them the lesson from the recession was that the only way to right the economy in time of upset was through spending.

As for businessmen, they could see in the recession only the logical outcome of Roosevelt's iniquitous tinkering with the economy. They had been especially angered by the protection the Wagner act had given to protective bargaining with the resulting militant expansion of organized labor. Roosevelt reciprocated the businessmen's feelings and blamed the recession upon their failure to co-operate. To a considerable degree he went along with a powerful handful of Progressive Republicans and Western Democrats in the Senate, like William E. Borah of Idaho and Joseph O'Mahoney of Wyoming, in attacking corporate monopoly as the villain. There are some indications, however, that the anti-monopoly program that he launched in the Department of Justice through the urbane Thurman Arnold was intended less to bust the trusts than to forestall too drastic legislation in the Congress. Roosevelt gave his strong backing to Arnold's anti-trust division only for the first year or two, and Arnold functioned for the most part through consent decrees. These in many instances allowed industries to function much as they had in the NRA days. The new program was in some respects more like a negative NRA than the antithesis of the NRA.

Thus from the beginning of the New Deal to the end, Roosevelt functioned with a fair degree of consistency. He heartily favored humanitarian welfare legislation and government policing of the economy, so long as these did not dangerously unbalance the budget. He preferred government co-operation with business to warfare with it.

Many of the New Dealers went far beyond Roosevelt in their views, and sometimes saw in his reluctance to support them, betrayal rather than a greater degree of conservatism. They had valid grievances some of the time when Roosevelt stuck to a middle course and seemed to them to be compromising away everything for which they thought he stood, in order to hold his motley political coalitions together. It is a serious moral question whether he compromised more than necessary, and whether at times he compromised his principles. It has been charged that his second four years in the White House represented a failure in political leadership.

In terms of gaining immediate political objectives, like the fiasco of the court fight, and the abortive "purge" in the 1938 primaries, this is undoubtedly true. In terms of the long-range New Deal program, I think the reverse is the case. These were years of piece-meal unspectacular consolidation of the earlier spectacular changes. It was many years before historians could say with certainty that these changes were permanent. By 1948 various public opinion samplings indicated that an overwhelming majority of those queried, even though Republican in voting habits, favored such things as social security and the TVA. The election of a Republican president in 1952 did not signify a popular repudiation of these programs. In the years after 1952 they were accepted, and in some instances even expanded, by the Republican administration. The only serious debate over them concerned degree, in which the Republicans were more cautious than the Democrats. The New Deal changes have even come for the most part to be accepted by the business community, although the United States Chamber of Commerce now issues manifestoes against federal aid to education with all the fervor it once directed against Roosevelt's proposals. The fact is that the business community in part bases its plans for the future upon some things that began as New Deal reforms. It takes for granted such factors as the "built-in stabilizers" in the social security system—something, incidentally, that Roosevelt pointed out at the time the legislation went into effect.

In January 1939 Roosevelt, concerned about the threat of

world war, called a halt to his domestic reform program. What he said then, concerning the world crisis of 1939, is remarkably applicable to the United States more than two decades later:

"We have now passed the period of internal conflict in the launching of our program of social reform. Our full energies may now be released to invigorate the processes of recovery in order to preserve our reforms, and to give every man and woman who wants to work a real job at a living wage.

"But time is of paramount importance. The deadline of danger from within and from without is not within our control. The hour-glass may be in the hands of other nations. Our own hour-glass tells us that we are off on a race to make democracy work, so that we may be efficient in peace and therefore secure in national defense."

THE POLITICAL ECONOMY OF THE NEW DEAL

Christiana McFadyen Campbell

THE NEW DEAL AND THE AGRICULTURAL ESTABLISHMENT

IN A SENSE, New Deal agricultural policy was remarkably successful from the beginning. The new Agricultural Adjustment Administration quickly brought basic commodity prices back up to tolerable levels. To this extent, the First New Deal undeniably effected a substantial degree of recovery for agriculture. In addition, its mortgage relief programs saved many farms from foreclosure, and a vigorous soil conservation program worked to preserve America's land.

These early programs, however, despite such apparently radical innovations as acreage allotments and at times even crop destruction, were fundamentally moderate in purpose and accomplishment. They were designed essentially to restore a decent living to the rural middle class. The First New Deal offered little or nothing to those farmers, sharecroppers, and agricultural workers who had lived in poverty before the depression. Sharecroppers seldom received a fair share of allotment payments, and acreage reduction even made it profitable to evict many from the land they had worked. In 1935, a group of reform-minded intellectuals within the AAA attempted to change its regulations in order to protect sharecroppers; they were "purged" from the agency. This was the

From *The Farm Bureau and the New Deal* by Christiana McFadyen Campbell, pp. 57–59, 156–157, 159–162, 165–178, 186. Copyright © 1962 by the University of Illinois Press. Reprinted by permission of the University of Illinois Press.

clearest indication that the dominating force in the First New Deal's agricultural policy was a coalition which represented the interests of the larger commercial farmer. The major components of this "agricultural establishment" were the land-grant colleges, the United States Extension Service, and the American Farm Bureau Federation.

Christiana Campbell, Lecturer in American history at the University of Sydney in Australia, explores the relationship between the agricultural establishment and the New Deal in this selection from her book, *The Farm Bureau and the New Deal,* winner of the Agricultural History Society award in 1961. Mrs. Campbell's focus on the AFBF is appropriate. Fundamentally a coalition of Southern and Midwestern farmers, it was the largest and most influential agrarian pressure group. Much of its power stemmed from its close connection with the Extension Service and the land-grant colleges, and these in turn could not have asked for a more vigilant defender. The colleges and the Extension Service were limited in their political activity by their public character; the AFBF served as their political representative.

As Mrs. Campbell demonstrates in her initial discussion of AFBF President Ed O'Neal, there was a close relationship between the First New Deal and the establishment. By the end of 1936, however, this official friendship was beginning to cool; in succeeding years, the AFBF became increasingly alienated from the Roosevelt administration. Two factors stand out in her analysis of this important development: (1) struggles for power between both rival pressure groups and competing government agencies, (2) a general change in the substance and ideology of the New Deal. The Farm Bureau began to discover that it could not easily influence the recently-created New Deal agencies, which were overshadowing the AFBF's old allies. Moreover, a rival and more liberal farm group, the National Farmers Union, was establishing an increasingly closer relationship with the administration. At the same time, the New Deal's concerns and objectives in agriculture were becoming broader; especially important were the attempts of Rexford Tugwell's Resettlement Administration (1935–1937) and its successor, the Farm Security Administration (1937–1946), to deal with problems of rural poverty. A Second New Deal had materialized, one which was moving away from the moderation of the establishment and attempting to assert its independence. The power of the establishment seemed, at least in relative terms, to be diminishing, and the AFBF began a fight to retain its old authority. The consensus which had characterized the agricultural politics of the First New Deal was irreparably shattered.

Mrs. Campbell's interpretation provides important evidence for those who argue that the New Deal may be divided into two distinct phases. It also seems to give support to those who stress the changes the New Deal made, or at least attempted to make, in American life and politics. Certainly, it shows that the agrarian side of the New Deal, as is the case with most political programs, was the product of a series of conflicts between the ambitions and aspirations of diverse groups.

ED O'NEAL AND THE NEW DEAL FOR AGRICULTURE

The A.F.B.F.'s role in the making of the New Deal for agriculture was . . . a crucial one, for two reasons. First, it served as a unifying agency within agriculture, both in bringing about sectional agreement between the Southern and the Midwestern farmers within its own organization, and (under the leadership of President O'Neal) in working earnestly in 1932 to bring about agreement among the major farm organizations. Second, as Henry A. Wallace himself has stated, the Farm Bureau gave the Department of Arigculture its strongest political support. Wallace did not elaborate this statement, but a study of the activities and statements of Farm Bureau leaders indicates that such support consisted both in winning farmer support at the local level and in pressing Congress on the national level. By virtue of its federal structure, the Farm Bureau was superbly equipped to do both.

The history of both the A.F.B.F. and of the New Deal would have been different if any other man than Ed O'Neal had been president of the A.F.B.F. during that critical period. The role of personalities was a significant one particularly in the early New Deal period.

The best assessment of O'Neal is that of M. L. Wilson.

"O'Neal was a mediator," says Wilson. "He brought together the South and the Midwest. And Wallace thought so too."

In addition to being a mediator, O'Neal was a Democrat. He was a friend of education. And he was a hard-drinking Presbyterian. O'Neal did not mind saying he was a Democrat. He always had been. Besides, he liked President Roosevelt. He liked Henry Wallace. And he even liked Rex Tugwell, though sometimes he disagreed with his ideas. He understood these people. . . .

O'Neal was a Southern aristocrat of the old school—the type whom William Faulkner describes as being progressively displaced in the South by the Snopes family. Owner of a plantation which he had inherited in the Tennessee Valley region of northern Alabama, O'Neal was no dirt farmer, but he had the affection for farming and the interest in intelligent methods of agriculture of an eighteenth-centuury English gentleman. It was while he was on a tour of Europe (he made the "grand tour" of a young Southern gentleman after his graduation from Washington and Lee College) that he said he got the idea of better farming. When he came back home, he went to the land-grant colleges at Auburn, Alabama, and at Urbana, Illinois, where he acquired solid basis for his inspiration for intelligent methods. He became a staunch supporter of agricultural education as carried out by the Alabama Extension Service, and an early supporter of the Farm Bureau work sponsored by the Extension Service in Alabama. He attempted to make a model of his own farm to show that under progressive methods of cultivation "that old red land" of the former cotton kingdom could be made as productive and rich as any in the world.

O'Neal had no desire to change the social order of his region. But he had a paternalistic interest in improving conditions for all, both high and low. It was M. L. Wilson's impression that O'Neal was something like Senator Bankhead, who, going around little farms in Alabama and talking with even the lowest Negro farmers, said: "We must do something to give opportunities to these people." Bankhead may have been more willing to alter the system. O'Neal wished to give them greater opportunities within the existing social order. In this matter O'Neal was representative of his section, for welfare policies generally had far greater support within the A.F.B.F. from the

Southern section than from the Midwestern, where Farm Bureau members simply saw no need for them.

At first Midwestern farmers, as staunchly Protestant as they were Republican, were bewildered by the fact that O'Neal openly both cursed and drank, in the manner of a gentleman, but not according to their conception of a Presbyterian. Their initial wariness soon dissolved. According to the testimony of Midwestern leaders who knew him well, the Midwestern farmers came to love him and to forgive in him the "vices" which they would not have tolerated in anyone else.

Besides agricultural reform, O'Neal's other great enthusiasm was for his own region—that of northern Alabama and Nashville, Tennessee, the heart of the Tennessee Valley. His attitude toward it was more that of a Westerner of 1812 than of a Southerner. It was Andrew Jackson's old region, and O'Neal's great-grandfather, Alex Coffee, had been a close friend and partner of Jackson in land speculation. O'Neal treasured family correspondence between his ancestors and Jackson.

In Franklin D. Roosevelt, O'Neal felt that he had found a kindred spirit who shared his enthusiasm for Andrew Jackson and for Jacksonian principles. Letters from Roosevelt to O'Neal reveal that at one time or another O'Neal sent him a picture pertaining to the Coffee family's connection with Andrew Jackson, a newspaper clipping about Jackson, and some of Jackson's correspondence which was in O'Neal's possession. Roosevelt always seems to have expressed his appreciation, a typical Roosevelt reply being: "Those letters from good old Andrew Jackson are magnificent. It is absolutely true that his opponents represented the same social outlook and the same element in the population that ours do."

THE BEGINNING OF THE BREAK WITH THE NEW DEAL

After the Presidential election of 1936, there began a titanic struggle between the U.S. Department of Agriculture and the A.F.B.F. To say "began" is not precisely correct, for it is impossible to determine exactly when it started. By coeval processes, the Department of Agriculture consulted less freely about farm policy with the Farm Bureau, and the leaders of the Farm Bureau became more insistent in their demands that it was their right to be consulted. The role of the Extension Service was a central issue in this conflict. The Department of Agriculture sought to lessen its early dependence on the Extension Service for the local administration of the New Deal farm programs and to establish straight-line administration through agencies of the Department. At the same time, the A.F.B.F. attempted to place the administration of practically everything under the Extension Service.

Previous to the New Deal, federal aid to agriculture had been chiefly through grants-in-aid for agricultural education rather than through direct action. And agricultural education was (and is) carried out chiefly through the Extension Service administered by the land-grant colleges. The key figure in this system is the county agent, who carries the expert technical advice of the colleges to the local farmers. Federal control over the county agents has been negligible under the decentralized system by which the Extension Service has traditionally operated. While the procedure by which a county agent is appointed varies somewhat from state to state, the appointing procedure most frequently followed is for the state Extension Service to recommend qualified candidates, from among whom the local sponsoring body appoints the agent. Final approval must be given by the director of the Federal Extension Service, who is an officer of the U.S. Department of Agriculture, but this has usually been a formal matter only. Until the Farm Bureau was separated from the Extension Service in 1954, the local sponsoring body was in some cases the county farm bureau. However, legal ties were not always as binding as informal reciprocal undestandings between the Farm Bureau and the Extension Service.

The new agricultural programs undertaken by the federal government during the period of the New Deal were chiefly "action" programs designed to give economic aid to farmers, as distinguished from the traditional educational programs. "Action" agencies were accordingly set up in order to carry these programs out. In the beginning, the most important of these, the A.A.A., worked through the county agents of the Extension Service.

However, the mushroom growth of agencies of the new type eventually brought about basic changes in the structure of the federal Department of Agriculture, and in the relationships of the Extension Service to the new programs. Some of the new action agencies, such as the Rural Resettlement Administration, the Farm Credit Administration, and the Rural Electrification Administration, were originally outside the Department of Agriculture. But after 1936 these outside agencies were gradually brought within the Department, and moreover responsibilities for the local administration of the A.A.A. were withdrawn from the county agents of the Extension Service. Thus the administration of "action" programs, as distinct from educational programs, was increasingly centralized in the federal Department of Agriculture, which reached farmers directly through its "action" agencies. The A.A.A., for instance, had its own county offices, and its own local farmer committeemen. While the Farm Bureau was in some cases able to dominate the farmer committeemen of the A.A.A., the influence of the Farm Bureau with a centralized agency was not likely to be as strong as with a decentralized agency like the Extension Service, since the organization and development of the Farm Bureau virtually paralleled that of the Extension Service.

In 1936 the A.F.B.F. detected signs that its own influence with the federal Department of Agriculture was beginning to wane, and that simultaneously other agencies of the Department were gaining in importance relative to the Extension Service.

In contrast to the situation early in 1936, when the Farm Bureau was profoundly satisfied with its relationship with the Department of Agriculture and in particular with Secretary Wallace, between 1936 and 1940 O'Neal frequently expressed resentment over the fact that the Department did "policy things" without talking with the Farm Bureau leaders about them. O'Neal felt that the Farm Bureau's advice should be asked, though the Secretary of Agriculture would not have to follow that advice unless he wanted to. Thus Farm Bureau leaders believed that the Department of Agriculture was denying them what was perhaps the most vital right which a national farm organization could posses—the right to be consulted in the making of agricultural policy.

The first Administration to grant such a right in any significant degree to the leaders of farm organizations had been that of Franklin D. Roosevelt, whose Secretary of Agcriulture had called in farm leaders to assist in formulating the Agricultural Adjustment Act of 1933 and the Soil Conservation Act of 1936, and who had consulted less formally with the Farm Bureau leaders on other occasions. The recognition thus accorded the Farm Bureau had been a most significant factor in promoting the prestige and influence of the organization. Now it appeared that this recognition was being progressively withdrawn by the same Administration and even under the same Secretary of Agriculture who had originally granted it.

This struggle between the Department of Agriculture and the Farm Bureau remained chiefly underground, only occasionally coming to the surface in isolated incidents or specific conflicts, such as those over the Farm Credit Administration and the Farm Security Administration. Most of the time the relations between the Department of Agriculture and the Farm Bureau remained superficially much as usual, except for a perceptible waning of the old mutual confidence. Much of the time they continued to work together on those policies which both supported. It was not until 1940 that the lid really came off.

Involved in the major struggle for power were many sorts of conflicts, the threads of which are exceedingly tangled. Among the major sources of conflict were: (1) differences in concepts of the proper role of the Department of Agriculture; (2) the issue of centralization versus decentralization of power in the administration of the federal farm programs; (3) increasing divergence over the substance of the farm program; (4) rivalry between government agencies ("empire-building"); (5) rivalry between farm organizations; (6) partisan politics; (7) the influence of personalities; and (8) fundamental differences over how farm policy should be made in a democracy.

The A.F.B.F.'s concept of the Department of Agriculture was based upon a premise which was becoming more and more unacceptable to the Administration. This premise, which applied to all agricultural agencies whether federal or state, was explicitly stated by O'Neal soon after he became president of the A.F.B.F. in 1931. He said then: "Thinking farmers have a jealous regard for these institutions, feeling that they in very deed belong to them and that these institutions were created for the purpose of serving the farmers alone. In no case do we farmers question the right of the Department of Commerce to aggressively serve business nor of the Department of Labor to vigorously promote the welfare of the group it represents. In turn, we must demand that those serving agriculture be anxiously concerned only in the welfare of the group they represent." This obviously was a "clientele" concept of the departments of government.

The more politically sophisticated members of the Administration, however, looked upon themselves as representative of the chief executive, who in turn was the one official elected by the vote of all the people and presumably therefore the representative of the interests of all. Even apart from the fact that at least some of the officers of the Department of Agriculture conceived its role broadly as that of serving the general public, rather than narrowly that of promoting the interests of farmers alone, there were two interest groups other than farmers which felt they had special claims for consideration by the Department of Agriculture. These were: (1) consumers and (2) processors of agricultural products. While during the early New Deal the Farm Bureau considered that processors were the worst enemy of the farm program, there was never any suspicion on the Farm Bureau's part that the Department of Agriculture was unduly protecting the interests of this group. During the latter days of the New Deal, however, there were many expressions of alarm over what was called in Farm Bureau circles "consumer dominance" in the Department of Agriculture.

The second major source of conflict, the issue of centralization as against decentralization, is basic in explaining the "divorce" of the A.A.A. from the Extension Service in 1936. . . . [T]he state and local A.A.A. committees had to be divorced from informal domination by the Farm Bureau as well, and this was a long, drawn-out process. Trouble centered in the state of Iowa, which seems to have been made a test case by the Department of Agriculture in its attempt to wrench the A.A.A. (and other action programs) out from under Extension Service-Farm Bureau domination and place the administration of them instead under the more direct control of the federal Department of Agriculture. As early as 1935, when Dr. A. G. Black was administrator of the corn-hog section of the A.A.A., this struggle had come intermittently into the open. For instance, the *Cedar Rapids Gazette* declared: "The Farm Bureau was ignored when the state corn and hog committee was named by Dr. A. G. Black and it again was 'slapped in the face,' so organization leaders say, when district fieldmen carefully were selected last fall from men who are not active Farm Bureau boosters, and when Farm Bureau leaders such as Allan B. Kline of Vinton, Paul P. Stewart of Maynard, and others were summarily dismissed by Dr. Black, without explanation."

The issue of centralization as against decentralization of power was a genuine one in this struggle. The Department of Agriculture held, logically, that it had been charged with the responsibility for carrying out certain programs, and that it could not discharge its responsibilities through an agency like the Extension Service, over which the federal Department had only nominal authority and over which the states had the real authority. The Department of Agriculture had turned to the Extension Service for assistance in administering the Agricultural Adjustment Act in 1933 only as an emergency measure. Conversely, the Farm Bureau, while convinced of the necessity of a national program for agriculture, sought to maintain the traditional agrarian opposition to the centralization of power in government by insisting that the *administration* of federal programs should be decentralized. To Farm Bureau leaders the Extension Service seemed the ideal agency for such purposes. The cynical explanation that the Extension Service was often allied with the Farm Bureau, though true, ignores the deep-rooted value which farm people placed upon the cherished Jeffersonian concept of decentralization of power.

While the developing conflict between the Department of Agriculture and the Farm Bureau appears chiefly as a struggle for power, there might have been no power conflict had not a widening divergence of views developed over the substance of the programs. Once the extreme need for emergency programs in the early New Deal period was past, agreement on more permanent programs was much more difficult to obtain. The early A.A.A. and other similar programs had been based on the spirit if not the letter of McNary-Haugenism, in which Farm Bureau members had been educated for years, and which they thoroughly understood. If it is assumed that the New Deal program for agriculture had three facets—relief, recovery, and reform—the Farm Bureau went enthusiastically along on the first two of them, and balked on the third. Farm Bureau people were the repository of the old American values of the homestead era. They were innately resistant to reforms which went counter to these values, particularly when they were proposed not by one of their own farm people, like Henry A. Wallace, but by an urban liberal like Rex Tugwell. When the Rural Resettlement Administration (and its successor, the Farm Security Administration) confined its activities primarily to rural relief, the Farm Bureau let it fairly much alone. But when the F.S.A. embarked on an aggressive program of reform, the Farm Bureau went on the warpath.

A basic assumption of Farm Bureau people, which was challenged by the F.S.A., was that the best possible system of land tenure was that of private, individual ownership. This principle was taken so much for granted that it was not even mentioned in the A.F.B.F. resolutions of 1934, which summarized the land utilization policies of the Farm Bureau. In fact it was not until President Roosevelt's Committee on Farm Tenancy made its report in 1937 that the A.F.B.F. felt called upon to defend this principle. The report of the President's committee began with an expression of alarm over the increasing incidence of tenancy, then stated categorically: "The land policy adopted by this country, under which title to practically all of the agricultural land of the Nation passed to private owners in fee simple absolute, has proved defective as a means of keeping the land in the ownership of those who work it." The report recommended that the federal government purchase land and sell it under long-term contracts to operating farmers, who would not, however, be allowed to repay all the principal and obtain title to the land until after 20 years. Thus it was hoped that speculation, ownership by non-farmers, and uneconomic subdivisions might be prevented. While the report in general favored family-size farms, it suggested that co-operative groups might in some cases be aided to acquire land by purchase or long lease for subleasing to group members.

The Farm Bureau's insistence upon the fee simple ownership of farm land followed the tradition of those who fought for the homestead policy and other measures by which the public domain had passed into private ownership.

O'Neal, who was a member of the committee, stated that he

could not be a signer of the report unless his objections to the proposed restrictions on the alienation of land were called to the attention of the reader. O'Neal's view was that more individuals should be aided to become landowners, as quickly as they had proved themselves to be good farmers.

This conflict of views reappeared later in the fight between the Farm Bureau and the F.S.A., when the latter was alleged to be following the same policy regarding land ownership as that recommended by the President's committee. That is, the F.S.A. was charged with refusing to allow its clients to pay off the principal of the mortgage indebtedness on their farms as soon as they were able, and thus refusing to allow them to gain title to their farms. A Southern Farm Bureau leader expressed the hostility of Farm Bureau leaders in his region to this sort of practice: "We thought the Farm Security Administration was to help tenants to become farm owners; we did not know it was to reform us." O'Neal himself had a genuine patriarchal interest in providing greater opportunities for the more poverty-stricken farmers of the South, but he wished these opportunities to be provided within the traditional social order. Farm Security officers thought it could not be done without changing the social order. The payment of poll taxes for Farm Security clients falls into the category of controversies of this nature.

Rivalry among governmental agencies contributed to such conflicts as that over the F.S.A. In the case of both the Soil Conservation Service and the Rural Resettlement Administration it is fairly clear that at least part of the initiative for the A.F.B.F.'s policies toward these agencies came from some state Extension Services. . . .

O'Neal was also alarmed about the Soil Conservation Service, for he felt, rightly, that Hugh Bennett, who was head of it, "was driving right along" to keep it separate and increase its power and influence. "As you know," wrote O'Neal to a college president, "I am against all these things, running away from the proper foundation—the Land Grant College." . . .

It was not only the Southern state colleges which feared that they were being bypassed by the regional offices of the Soil Conservation Service and the Resettlement Administration. The Extension directors of eight North-Central states protested, in 1937: "At the present time there is a strong tendency on the part of certain bureaus and agencies in the U.S. Department of Agriculture to go direct to the individual farmer, thus overlooking the possibilities of making larger use of state and local agencies. . . ." These Extension directors found the regional offices of the Soil Conservation Service and the Resettlement Administration the most threatening aspect of the agencies in question, for it was by means of the regional offices that a centralized system of administration, straight from Washington to the farmer, could be maintained. . . .

It appears very much as if various land-grant college and Extension officials prodded O'Neal and the Farm Bureau into a battle with other agencies, and then when the battle became rough and the Farm Bureau wished to carry it further than the gentlemen of the colleges and the Extension Service wished, the politicians of academe began to run for cover. When the director of the Alabama Extension Service, P. O. Davis, whom O'Neal called his "best buddy," informed O'Neal that the Southern directors of Extension had passed a resolution asking only that all educational work of the Department of Agriculture be done through the land-grant colleges, O'Neal was indignant: "We are leading this battle for you, but you are leaving us. I want to tell your Southerners you are leaving me out on a limb. . . ."

Rivalry between farm organizations was at least as important as interagency rivalry in explaining many of the issues of the late New Deal period. As the star of the Farm Bureau waned with the Department of Agriculture and the Roosevelt administration, that of another farm organization waxed. From being almost a voluntary outcast at the beginning of the New Deal period, the National Farmers Union seems rapidly to have achieved prosperity and prestige (in Democratic circles) in the late New Deal period.

The Farm Bureau suspected the Administration of deliberately building up the Farmers' Union in order to have a strong lobby for the type of reform programs in agriculture which both the Administration and the Farmers' Union favored. (The fact that the Farm Bureau had developed out of just this sort of relationship with the Extension Service was overlooked. Anyway, that process probably had not been deliberate.) The

Farmers' Union was the only national farm organization which would lobby for appropriations for the F.S.A. On the other hand, federal funds were channeled through the F.S.A. into the Farmers' Union Grain Terminal Association, which became under M. W. Thatcher the strongest and most prosperous part of the Farmers' Union.

What the Farm Bureau officials considered as evidence that the resources of the F.S.A. were being used to build up the Farmers' Union was found in the loans made by the F.S.A. to its clients to enable them to purchase stock in co-operatives affiliated with the Farmers' Union. F.S.A. officials readily admitted that they did make such loans, but pointed out that the F.S.A. of course did not lay down any requirements that these co-operatives should be affiliated with any organization. Its interest was merely in the organization and development of farm co-operatives. In reply to a request from the Farm Bureau for information, the director of information for the F.S.A. stated that in the northern Great Plains area, the F.S.A. had made 9,696 loans to individual farmers to enable them to purchase stock in 99 local grain elevator associations, all of which were affiliated with the Farmers' Union Grain Terminal Association. Moreover, 9,216 loans had been made by the F.S.A. to enable individual rehabilitation borrowers to purchase preferred stock in the Farmers' Union Grain Terminal Association.

This looked more like a plot than a coincidence to the Farm Bureau. Moreover, M. W. Thatcher, chairman of the Legislative Committee of the Farmers' Union, who was also general manager of the Farmers' Union Grain Terminal Association, had pointed with pride in his report to the fact that the F.S.A. had made such loans: "The Farm Security Administration has made loans to low-income farmers to enable them to participate in the purchase of preferred stock in our association."

In allying itself with the National Farmers' Union, the F.S.A. entered the wars of agricultural politics, and invited political annihilation. The Farm Bureau accepted the invitation.

In explaining the closer relations between the Department of Agriculture and the National Farmers' Union, former officials of the Administration stressed the point that the Farmers' Union was helping the Department to carry out programs which it wished to promote, such as co-operative marketing. Furthermore, from the standpoint of the power complex, the

Department of Agriculture preferred to have three or four farm organizations to deal with rather than only one (the Farm Bureau).

The alignment of the Farmers' Union with organized labor, at a time when the harmonious relationship between the Farm Bureau and urban labor was breaking up, increased the rivalry between the two farm organizations. That there was a special link between the Farmers' Union and organized labor was, of course, a fact not denied but rather proclaimed by both. A public statement of a sympathetic understanding between the Farmers' Union and the Congress of Industrial Organizations was made on November 18, 1941, in a broadcast on a two-way radio hookup with James G. Patton, President of the Farmers' Union, speaking from the Farmers' Union convention at Topeka, Kansas, and James B. Carey, Secretary of the C.I.O., speaking from the C.I.O. convention in Detroit. As the Farm Bureau moved away from close relationships with both the Administration and with urban labor, the Farmers' Union appeared to be more than willing to fill the vacuum.

An instance of the vital role of personalities in explaining the origin of some conflicts is to be found in the reorganization of the Farm Credit Administration in 1939. "The Farm Credit fight," as it was generally called in the Farm Bureau papers, brought on the open break between the Midwestern Farm Bureau leaders and the Roosevelt administration. In the first place, the principle of centralization of power was followed when President Roosevelt, in the spring of 1939, ordered the transfer of the Farm Credit Administration to the Department of Agriculture. It had previously been an independent agency. The Farm Bureau was in general opposed to centralization of power, but withheld opposition in this instance in the hope that Wallace would bring in "an outstanding man" (i.e., a sympathetic administrator), as governor. Certain farm bureaus were hopeful too that, under the new setup, credit facilities might be broadened. In particular there were complaints from the New England and California farm bureaus that many of their farmer members were too poor to obtain credit from the Farm Credit Administration, and too prosperous to obtain it from the F.S.A. O'Neal himself seemed not so much interested at that time in what Wallace might do with the Farm Credit Administration as in the possibility that the credit facilities of the F.S.A. might be extended to help the middle group of farmers not then being satisfactorily served by either of the major credit agencies.

It was not until Wallace told O'Neal, confidentially, who the new governor was going to be that the fireworks began. Undoubtedly the man whom Wallace named to O'Neal was Dr. A. G. Black. O'Neal then warned Wallace of what Wallace must have known already—that the Midwestern farm bureaus would be very hostile to his choice.

Dr. A. G. Black had been *persona non grata* to the Midwestern farm bureaus ever since the days when, as administrator of the corn-hog section of the A.A.A., he had been thought to be deliberately ignoring the Farm Bureau people in the naming of A.A.A. committeemen. The appointment of Black therefore appeared to be confirmation of what Farm Bureau leaders had suspected for several years, namely, that the Department of Agriculture was determined to ignore them in the making of agricultural policy. If the Farm Bureau was to function as a policy-making organization for agriculture, it had to able not only to get the laws passed, but it had to be able also to influence the administrators. Midwestern farm bureaus had reasons for believing that they would not be able to influence Black.

When Wallace not only recommended the appointment of Black as governor of the Farm Credit Administration, but subsequently supported a bill to increase the powers of the governor over farm credit, the Farm Bureau became aroused on the issue of decentralization of power as well.

The fact that Wallace went out to a National Farmers' Union meeting at St. Paul, Minnesota, on April 27, 1940, to explain and defend his views on the farm credit situation did nothing to reassure the Farm Bureau. Henceforth, interfarm organization rivalries became an important element in the controversy over farm credit. Numerous confidential letters from Midwestern Farm Bureau leaders to O'Neal expressed the belief that the agencies of the Department of Agriculture in the Midwest, particularly the A.A.A., were being used to promote attendance at the Farmers' Union meeting in St. Paul.

Another case, apart from that of the Farm Credit Administration, in which the personality of the administrator was important in precipitating conflict, was that of the F.S.A. The intense hostility of the Farm Bureau to the F.S.A. was not aroused until C. B. Baldwin became administrator. His predecessor, Dr. Will Alexander, had preferred to compromise on the best program he could get rather than to bring conflict into the open. O'Neal could work with him. But he could not work with Baldwin, who seemed to prefer an open fight to a compromise.

The archetype of the administrator whom farmers of the Farm Bureau sort could neither understand nor like was Rex Tugwell. Tugwell was an urban liberal, which was quite a different species from an agrarian liberal. As another agricultural statesman has said, he had a lovely free spirit, but farmers were alternately bewildered, amused, and enraged by some of the frills that his agencies sponsored—frills such as the "special skills" program, encouragement of folk-singing, and the like. Besides, Tugwell apparently took a positive delight in insulting people of the Farm Bureau-Extension Service sort. This personality clash was just an added irritant to the basic clash over the nature of the farm program.

For his part, Tugwell viewed the Farm Bureau as "the most sinister influence in America." . . .

The influence of personalities in farm organization politics was also significant. When John Simpson, who had been president of the Farmers' Union at the opening of the New Deal period, was replaced by James G. Patton as president, with M. W. Thatcher as the power behind the throne, the Roosevelt administration found the new Farmers' Union leadership much more congenial to work with. This was particularly true of Thatcher.

The part played by partisan political considerations in explaining conflicts among agricultural forces is everywhere suggested and nowhere easy to grasp. Farm Bureau officials believed that an important reason for the attempts of the Department of Agriculture to centralize control over the administration of action programs, thus reducing the authority and influence of the land-grant colleges and Extension Services, was a political one. This arose from the fact that Extension officials in some Northeastern and Midwestern states were likely to be Republican or to be controlled by state administrations which were Republican. They were presumed therefore to be nuclei of Republican influence, which the Administration naturally had no wish to strengthen. Since farm policy was a bipartisan product according to the Farm Bureau creed, it did not matter whether Extension officials administering the New Deal farm program were Republican or not.

The heart of the conflict between the Farm Bureau and the Department of Agriculture was reached in the contest over the county land-use planning committees. The basic issue was: How should farm policy be made, and by whom? Of course it was granted that Congress had the final voice and the final decision-making power in agricultural legislation, along with the President. But farm policy-making had not normally originated with Congress, at least not in recent times.

Through the county land-use planning system, the Department of Agriculture sought to solve many of the problems of relationships between agencies with which it was plagued; and at the same time to take democratic planning of programs down to the "grass roots." Actually there was far more to the system than the county committees, but these were considered the heart of it, and it was usually designated as county land-use planning. . . .

A basic assumption of those who originated the land-use planning program was that "the trend toward strong central governments . . . is universal and inevitable." The problem, as they saw it, was how to keep both policy-making and administration democratic. The answer, they believed, lay in farmer participation in the democratic process.

The essential framework for the land-use planning program consisted of a state committee in each state, a county committee in each agricultural county, and some community committees as well. The state committee consisted of a representative of each of the action agencies in the Department of Agriculture (such as the A.A.A. and the F.S.A.), the state director of Extension (as chairman), the director of the state experiment station, representatives of any other state agencies having responsibility for land-use programs, and a number of representative farm men and women.

The county committees were considered more important from the standpoint of democratic planning in agriculture. The county agent of the Extension Service was the secretary of the county committee, which consisted of 10 to 20 farm men and women (democratically elected), as well as the county representatives of the agricultural action agencies. The farmer membership on the county committee was supposed always to be in the majority. The community committees, consisting of farm men and women, were expected to help the county committees.

The purely administrative work involved in the various action programs was carried out by the agencies of the Department, though the state committee was expected to assist in such matters as adjudication of conflicts. The Department's really great expectations of the county land-use planning program lay in the realm of policy formulation. The Department hoped, through the land-use planning committees, to reach directly down to the grass roots, and tap great reservoirs of ideas among the farmers themselves at the local level. M. L. Wilson, who more than anyone else was probably the philosophical father of the plan, spoke of the need, in a world threatened by totalitarianism, "to battle for a renaissance of democracy and for new democratic patterns in farm life and the rural community." Echoing John Dewey, he maintained, "The best way to save democracy is to use it."

It soon became clear to the Department of Agriculture "that the Department itself was in need of a central planning agency through which local people could make themselves heard." To meet this need, the Bureau of Agricultural Economics was reorganized and given the responsibility for the general planning work of the Department.

No more unfortunate term or concept could have been employed than that of "a central planning agency." To Farm Bureau leaders this sounded more like bureaucracy than democracy. Additionally, they believed that the whole system of state and county committees was designed to reduce the Extension Service to a minor role and to bypass the Farm Bureau altogether. Instead of being chief among agricultural agencies on the state and local level, the Extension Service would be only *primus inter pares*, and perhaps not even *primus*, if the other agencies chose to combine against it.

It was part of the Farm Bureau creed that national policy for agriculture should be formulated by independent national farm organizations (i.e., the A.F.B.F.). It was frequently reiterated in Farm Bureau circles that farmers should speak through their own independent organizations, rather than through government organizations, even if these were designated "co-operative."

In Departmental thinking, however, the Farm Bureau was not an independent organization on account of its special relationship with the Extension Service. And further, it was alleged that farm policy as produced by the A.F.B.F. was more a product of its resolutions committee, over which Earl Smith presided, than it was of farmers at the grass roots.

In any case, a nationwide system of farmer committees always contained potentialities, in the eyes of the leaders of the A.F.B.F., that it might develop into a powerful rival farm organization. . . .

The county land-use planning program was buried in the early 1940's, and there is no doubt that the A.F.B.F. was the chief undertaker. By 1940 the Farm Bureau had already demonstrated two parts of its strategy. One was to make sure that Farm Bureau members were elected to the county land-use planning committees. This was easy in the states in which the Farm Bureau was the most powerful farm organization. The other was to come out with a sweeping plan of its own for the co-ordination of the administration of government programs. The third and most effective part of the strategy was held in reserve until 1941, when the A.F.B.F. began to use its influence in Congress to reduce appropriations for the offending agencies. The A.F.B.F. was not wholly responsible for the burial of county land-use planning, for there were inherent weaknesses in the system, as Gross has pointed out. One was that instead of the spontaneous democracy that was assumed to exist among farmers at the local level, there was apathy against which special efforts should have been made to arouse a desire for self-help. The other was that the system *was* far too heavily weighted on the side of bureaucracy, with one in every four members of committees a government employee. There was the further fact that involvement in World War II turned major attention to other matters.

The Farm Bureau's master plan to counter the Department's efforts at co-ordination and county planning was contained in a "Resolution for the Co-ordination of Agricultural Agencies" adopted at the annual meeting of the A.F.B.F. in December, 1940. . . .

Two main areas of change were proposed. (1) On the national level a five-man, nonpartisan board should be set up within the Department of Agriculture to administer the A.A.A., the Soil Conservation Service, and other similar agencies, as well as the planning activities of the Bureau of Agricultural Economics. "This board should be representative of the nation's agriculture." Furthermore, "it should be independent in its position with respect to other bureaus and agencies of government." (2) In the field of state and local administration, the gist of the recommendation was that most of the programs should be turned over to the Extension Service. For some of those regulatory and other functions which the Extension Service was known to be very wary of accepting, other arrangements were to be made, but even in such cases the Extension director would nominate the persons to compose the state committee, after consultation with statewide farm organizations.

If this appears to be a plan to place all of the national programs for agriculture under the Extension Service, it was only superficially so. The fundamental aim was to take control of agricultural programs away from the Department of Agriculture, which was believed to be no longer the farmers' advocate, and give it to the farmers themselves (i.e., the organized farmers). . . .

The A.F.B.F.'s resolution on co-ordination was never adopted by the government.

In the later part of the New Deal period, a shifting alignment of forces helps to explain much of the conflict that occurred. New relationships among interest groups, and between them and the Administration, were forming. The new alignment placed organized labor with the Administration on the one side, and most of organized agriculture along with business on the other. In time of depression, the A.F.B.F. had found its best ally in urban labor. As prosperity returned, and as farmers no longer found themselves so dependent on the support of the representatives of urban labor to gain Congressional appropriations, the Farm Bureau leaders tended to align themselves more with the forces of organized business.

During the early New Deal period, the common enemy in Congress of both labor and agriculture had been the "economy bloc." As late as 1937 O'Neal characterized both the senators from Virginia as reactionary. But by the early 1940's the A.F.B.F. had become one of the strongest supporters of Senator Byrd of Virginia, spearhead of the drive for economy, in his activities as chairman of the Joint Committee on the Reduction of Non-Essential Federal Expenditures. In this case the chief target of both Senator Byrd's committee and of the A.F.B.F. was the F.S.A. O'Neal's frank recognition of the shifting relationships among labor, agriculture, and business is stated in a letter from him to the editor of *Fortune:* "Frankly, you know also that labor has, in the last few years come along in a fine fashion with our farm organization group to a greater degree than have the industrialists. A number of the industrialists, however, are now having a much broader vision of the farm problem."

David Brody

THE NEW DEAL AND THE EMERGENCE OF MASS-PRODUCTION UNIONISM

IN THE FOLLOWING selection, David Brody, Professor of History at the University of California (Davis) and one of the foremost American labor historians, demonstrates the New Deal's revolutionary impact upon the American worker. He argues persuasively that the Wagner Act and the general pro-labor political climate of the New Deal era made it possible to organize the skilled and semiskilled labor of the mass-production industries. By guaranteeing the right of collective bargaining, providing protection for union members and organizers, and establishing procedures for determining bargaining agents, the Wagner Act brought unprecedented change to American labor-management relations. The pro-labor attitude of New Deal politicians insured full and benevolent enforcement of labor's rights; as a result, many of the problems which had destroyed young unions in the past were eliminated.

Yet even the legislation of the New Deal could not compel genuine collective bargaining; nor could it assure that stubborn corporations would grant anything more than union recognition. Unionism in the mass-production industries received its initial impetus from the New Deal, but was made secure only by World

From "The Emergence of Mass-Production Unionism," by David Brody in *Change and Continuity in Twentieth-Century America*, edited by John Braeman, Robert H. Bremner, and Everett Walters, pp. 243–262. Copyright © 1964 by the Ohio State University Press. All rights reserved. Reprinted by permission of the Ohio State University Press.

War II. Full employment and a friendly federal intervention in the collective bargaining process established the new industrial unionism beyond recall. The war had consolidated and institutionalized labor's New Deal.

In the 1930's, a new legal framework for industrial relations emerged. In the past, the right to organize had fallen outside the law; unionization, like collective bargaining, had been a private affair. Within normal legal limits, employers had freely fought the organization of their employees. Now that liberty was being withdrawn. World War I had first raised the point. The National War Labor Board had protected workers from discrimination for joining unions and thus contributed substantially to the temporary union expansion of the war period. The lesson was inescapable. Unionization in the mass-production industries depended on public protection of the right to organize. The drift of opinion in this direction was discernible in the Railway Labor Act of 1926 and the Norris-LaGuardia Act of 1932. But the real opportunity came with the advent of the New Deal. Then key union spokesmen, notably [William] Green and [John L.] Lewis, pressed for the insertion of the famous section 7a in the National Industrial Recovery Act. After an exhilarating start, section 7a foundered; loopholes developed and enforcement broke down long before the invalidation of the NRA. But the intent of section 7a was clear, and it soon received effective implementation.

"If the Wagner bill is enacted," John L. Lewis told the AF of L Executive Council in May, 1935, "there is going to be increasing organization. . . ." The measure, enacted on July 5, 1935, heavily influenced Lewis' decision to take the initiative that led to the CIO. For the Wagner Act did adequately protect the right to organize through a National Labor Relations Board clothed with powers of investigation and enforcement. Employer opposition was at long last neutralized.

The Act made it an unfair labor practice for an employer "to interfere with, restrain, or coerce employees in the exercise" of "the right of self-organization." This protection unquestionably freed workers from fear of employer discrimination. Stipulation cases required the posting of such notices as the following at a Sioux City plant:

> The Cudahy Packing Company wants it definitely understood that . . . no one will be discharged, demoted, transferred, put on less desirable jobs, or laid off because he joins Local No. 70 or any other labor organization. . . . If the company, its officers, or supervisors have in the past made any statements or taken any action to indicate that its employees were not free to join Local No. 70 or any other labor organization, these statements are now repudiated.

Even more persuasive was the reinstatement with back pay of men discharged for union activities. The United Auto Workers' cause at Ford was immensely bolstered in 1941 by the rehiring of twenty-two discharged men as the result of an NLRB decision which the company had fought up to the Supreme Court. By June 30, 1941, nearly twenty-four thousand charges of unfair labor practices—the majority involving discrimination—had been lodged with the NLRB. More important in the long run, vigorous enforcement encouraged obedience of the law among employers. Assured of their safety, workers flocked into the unions.

The law also resolved the knotty problems of determining union representation. During the NRA period, company unions had been widely utilized to combat the efforts of outside organizations. The Wagner Act now prohibited employers from dominating or supporting a labor union. Legal counsel at first held that "inside" unions could be made to conform with the law by changing their structure, that is, by eliminating management participation from the joint representation plans. The NLRB, however, required the complete absence of company interference or assistance. Few company unions could meet this high standard, and large numbers were disestablished by NLRB order or by stipulation. In meat-packing, for instance, the Big Four companies had to withdraw recognition for over fifteen company unions. Only in the case of some Swift plants did such bodies prevail over outside unions in representation elections and become legal bargaining agents. Besides eliminating employer-dominated unions, the law put the selection of bargaining representatives on the basis of majority rule. By mid-1941, the NLRB had held nearly six thousand elections and cross-checks, involving nearly two million workers. Given a free choice, they overwhelmingly preferred a union to no union (the latter choice resulting in only 6 per cent of elections in 1937 and, on the average, in less than 20 per cent up to the passage of the Taft-Hartley Act). Having proved its majority in an "appropriate" unit, a union became the certified bargaining agent for all employees in the unit.

An unexpected dividend for union organization flowed from the Wagner Act. In the past, the crisis of mass-production unions had occurred in their first stage. Rank-and-file pressure normally built up for quick action. Union leaders faced the choice of bowing to this sentiment and leading their organizations into suicidal strikes—as happened on the railroads in 1894, in the stockyards in 1904, and in steel in 1919—or of resisting the pressure and seeing the membership melt away or break up in factional conflict—as occurred in meat-packing after World War I. The Wagner Act, while it did not eliminate rank-and-file pressures, eased the problem. A union received NLRB certification on proving its majority in a plant. Certification gave it legal status and rights which could be withdrawn only by formal evidence that it lacked majority support. Defeat in a strike did not in any way affect the status of a bargaining agent. Restraint, on the other hand, became a feasible policy. The CIO unions as a whole were remarkably successful in resisting workers' demands for national strikes in the early years, although not in preventing local trouble. The resulting dissidence could be absorbed. The Packinghouse Workers Organizing Committee, for instance, was in continual turmoil from 1939 to 1941 because of the conservative course of Chairman Van A. Bittner; but internal strife did not lead to organizational collapse there or elsewhere. NLRB certification permitted labor leaders to steer between the twin dangers—external and internal—that earlier had smashed vigorous mass-production unionism.

Years later, the efficacy of the Wagner Act was acknowledged by an officer of the most hostile of the major packing firms: ". . . The unions would not have organized Wilson [& Company] if it had not been for the Act." That judgment was certainly general in open-shop circles.

Yet the Wagner Act was not the whole story. For nearly two years while its constitutionality was uncertain, the law was virtually ignored by anti-union employers. And after the Jones and Laughlin decision in April, 1937, the effect was part of a larger favoring situation. John L. Lewis was not reacting to a single piece of legislation. He saw developing in the mid-1930's a general shift toward unionization.

The change was partly in the workers themselves. Their accommodation to the industrial system had broken down under the long stretch of depression. The resulting resentment was evident in the sitdown strikes of 1936–37, which involved almost half a million men. These acts were generally not a calculated tactic of the union leadership; in fact President Sherman Dalrymple of the Rubber Workers at first opposed the sitdowns. Spontaneous sitdowns within the plants accounted for the initial victories in auto and rubber. Much of Lewis' sense of urgency in 1935 sprang from his awareness of the pressure mounting in the industrial ranks. A local auto-union leader told Lewis in May, 1935, of talk about craft unions' taking skilled men from the federal unions. "We say like h—— they will and if it is ever ordered and enforced there will be one more independent union." Threats of this kind, Lewis knew, would surely become actions under existing AF of L policy, and, as he warned the Executive Council, then "we are facing the merging of these independent unions in some form of national organization." That prophecy, Lewis was determined, should come to pass under his control. The CIO succeeded in large measure because it became the vehicle for channeling the militancy released by the Great Depression.

The second factor that favored union organization was the impact of the depression on the major employers. They had operated on a policy of welfare capitalism: company paternalism and industrial-relations methods were expected to render employees impervious to the blandishments of trade unionism. The depression forced the abandonment of much of this expense and, beyond that, destroyed the workers' faith in the company's omnipotence on which their loyalty rested. Among themselves, as an official of Swift and Company said, industrialists had to admit that grounds existed for "the instances of open dissatisfaction which we see about us, and perhaps with us. . . ."

The depression also tended to undermine the will to fight unionization. Anti-union measures were costly, the La Follette investigation revealed. The resulting labor troubles, in addition, cut deeply into income. The Little Steel companies, Republic in particular, operated significantly less profitably in 1937 than did competitors who were free of strikes. Economic considerations seemed most compelling, not when business was bad, but when it was getting better. Employers then became very reluctant to jeopardize the anticipated return of profitable operations. This apparently influenced the unexpected decision of U. S. Steel to recognize the Steel Workers Organizing Committee. In 1937 the Steel Corporation was earning substantial profits for the first time during the depression; net income before taxes that year ultimately ran to 130 million dollars. And the first British purchases for defense were just then in the offing. During the upswing, moreover, the competitive factor assumed increasing importance. Union firms had the advantage of avoiding the disruptions incident to conflict over unionization. Certainly a decline of 15 per cent in its share of the automobile market from 1939 to 1940 contributed to the Ford Company's retreat of the following year.

Finally, the political situation—the Wagner Act aside—was heavily weighted on the side of labor. Management could no longer assume governmental neutrality or, under stress, assistance in the labor arena. The benefits accruing to organized labor took a variety of forms. The Norris-LaGuardia Act limited the use of injunctions that had in the past hindered union tactics. A federal law prohibited the transportation of strikebreakers across state lines. The *Thornhill* decision (1940) declared that antipicketing laws curbed the constitutional right of free speech. Detrimental governmental action, standard in earlier times of labor trouble, was largely precluded now by the emergence of sympathetic officeholders on all levels, from the municipal to the national. Indeed, the inclination was in the opposite direction. The response to the sitdown strike illustrated the change. "Well, it is illegal," Roosevelt commented. "But shooting it out and killing a lot of people because they have violated the law of tresspass . . . [is not] the answer. . . . There must be another way. Why can't those fellows in General Motors meet with the committee of workers?" This tolerance of unlawful labor acts, as sitdowns were generally acknowledged to be, could not have happened at any earlier period of American history. These were negative means of forwarding the labor cause.

But political power was also applied in positive ways. The La Follette investigation * undermined antiunion tactics by exposure and, among other ways, by feeding information on spies to the unions. At critical junctures, there was intercession by public officials ranging from President Roosevelt and Labor Secretary Perkins down to Mayor Kelly of Chicago. Governor Frank Murphy's role in the General Motors controversy is only the best known of a number of such mediating contributions to the union cause. At the start of the CIO steel drive Pennsylvania's Lieutenant-Governor Thomas Kennedy, a Mine Workers' officer, announced that organizers were free to move into steel towns and that state relief funds would be available in the event of a steel strike. The re-election of Roosevelt in 1936 no doubt cast out lingering hopes; many employers bowed to the inevitable after F.D.R.'s smashing victory with labor support.

These broader circumstances—rank-and-file enthusiasm, economic pressures on management, and the political condition—substantially augmented the specific benefits flowing from the Wagner Act. In fact, the great breakthroughs at U.S. Steel and General Motors in early 1937 did not result from the law. The question of constitutionality was resolved only some weeks later. And the agreements themselves did not accord with the provisions of the Wagner Act. The unions dared not utilize procedures for achieving certification as bargaining agents in the auto and steel plants. Lee Pressman, counsel for the SWOC, later admitted that recognition could not then have been won "without Lewis' brilliant move" in his secret talks with U.S. Steel's Myron C. Taylor.

> There is no question that [the SWOC] could not have filed a petition through the National Labor Relations Board . . . for an election. We could not have won an election for collective bargaining on the basis of our own membership or the results of the organizing campaign to date. This certainly applied not only to Little Steel but also to Big Steel.

Similarly, the *New York Times* reported on April 4, 1937:

* In the late 1930's, a Senate committee headed by Robert La Follette, Jr., extensively investigated anti-labor activities in the United States.—Ed.

"Since the General Motors settlement, the union has been spreading its organization rapidly in General Motors plants, which were weakly organized at the time of the strike." The NLRB could not require either U. S. Steel or General Motors to make agreements with unions under those circumstances. Nor did the companies grant the form of recognition contemplated in the Wagner Act, that is, as *exclusive* bargaining agents. (This would have been illegal under the circumstances.) Only employees who were union members were covered by the two agreements. These initial CIO victories, opening the path as they did for the general advance of mass-production unionism, stemmed primarily from the wider pressures favorable to organized labor.

The Wagner Act proved indecisive for one whole stage of unionization. More than the enrollment of workers and the attainment of certification as bargaining agent was needed in unionization. The process was completed only when employers and unions entered bona fide collective bargaining. But this could not be enforced by law. Meaningful bargaining was achievable ultimately only through the interplay of non-legislative forces.

The tactics of major employers had shifted significantly by the 1920's. Their open-shop doctrine had as its declared purpose the protection of workingmen's liberties. "We do not believe it to be the wish of the people of this country," a U. S. Steel official had said, "that a man's right to work shall be made dependent upon his membership in any organization." Since the closed shop was assumed to follow inevitably from collective bargaining, the refusal to recognize unions was the fixed corollary of the open shop. The argument, of course, cut both ways. Open-shop employers insisted that their employees were free to join unions (whether or not this was so). The important fact, however, was that the resistance to unionism was drawn tight at the line of recognition and collective bargaining. That position had frustrated the attempt of the President's Industrial Conference of October, 1919, to formulate principles for "genuine and lasting cooperation between capital and labor." The union spokesmen had withdrawn in protest against the insistence of the employer group that the obligation to engage in collective bargaining referred only to shop committees, not to trade unions. In effect, the strategy was to fight organized labor by withholding its primary function.

Federal regulation of labor relations gradually came to grips with the question of recognition and collective bargaining. During World War I, the NWLB only required employers to deal with shop committees. Going further, the NRA granted employees the right to "bargain collectively through representatives of their own choosing. . . ." This was interpreted to imply an obligation of employers to deal with such representatives. The major failing of section 7a was that the NRA did not implement the interpretation. In practice, determined employers were able, as earlier, to escape meaningful negotiation with trade unions. It seems significant that the permanent union gains of the NRA period came in those areas—the coal and garment industries—where collective bargaining did not constitute a line of employer resistance. Profiting by the NRA experience, the Wagner Act established the procedure for determining bargaining agents and the policy of exclusive representation and, by the device of certification, withdrew recognition from the option of an employer.

But recognition did not mean collective bargaining. Section 8 (5) did require employers to bargain with unions chosen in accordance with the law. Compliance, however, was another matter. In the first years, hostile employers attempted to withhold the normal attributes of collective bargaining. When a strike ended at the Goodyear Akron plant in November, 1937, for example, the company insisted that the agreement take the form of a "memorandum" signed by the mediating NLRB regional director, not by company and union, and added that "in no event could the company predict or discuss the situation beyond the first of the year." (Although the Rubber Workers' local had already received certification, it would not secure a contract for another four years.) Westinghouse took the position that collective bargaining "was simply an opportunity for representatives of the employees to bring up and discuss problems affecting the working force, with the final decision reserved to the company. It rejected the notion of a signed agreement because business conditions were too uncertain. . . ." Some companies—for instance, Armour in April, 1941—unilaterally raised wages while in union negotiations. The contractual forms were resisted: agreements had to be verbal, or take the form of a "statement of policy," or, if in contractual terms, certainly with no signatures. These blatant evasions of the intent of section 8 (5) were gradually eliminated: a series of NLRB and court rulings prohibited the refusal to negotiate or make counteroffers, the unilateral alteration of the terms of employment, and opposition to incorporating agreements into written and signed contracts.

The substance proved more elusive than the externals of collective bargaining. "We have no trouble negotiating with Goodyear," a local union president observed, "but we can never bargain. The company stands firmly against anything which does not give them the absolute final decision on any question." The law, as it was interpreted, required employers to bargain "in good faith." How was lack of good faith to be proved? The NLRB tried to consider the specific circumstances and acts, rather than the words, of the employer in each case. That cumbersome procedure was almost useless from the union standpoint. Delay was easy during the case, and further evasion possible afterward. Barring contempt proceedings after a final court order, moreover, the employer suffered no penalties for his obstruction; there was no counterpart here for the back-pay provisions in dismissal cases. The union weakness was illustrated at Wilson & Co. The Cedar Rapids packing plant had been well organized since the NRA period, but no agreement was forthcoming from the hostile management. In 1938 the union filed charges with the NLRB. Its decision came in January, 1940, and another year was consumed by the company's unsuccessful appeal to the Circuit Court. The negotiations that followed (interrupted by a strike which the union lost) led nowhere because, a union official reported, Wilson "as always . . . tried to force the Union to accept the Company's agreement or none at all." The contract which was finally consummated in 1943 resulted neither from an NLRB ruling nor from the free collective bargaining that was the aim of the Wagner Act. Clearly, "good faith" was not to be extracted from recalcitrant employers by government fiat.

The collective-bargaining problem had a deeper dimension. The bitter-enders themselves constituted a minority group in American industry. For every Westinghouse, Goodyear, Ford, and Republic Steel there were several major competitors prepared to abide by the intent of the law and enter "sincere negotiations with the representatives of employees." But, from the union standpoint, collective bargaining was important for the results it could yield. Here the Wagner Act stopped. As the Supreme Court noted in the Sands case, "from the duty of the employer to bargain collectively . . . there does not flow any duty . . . to accede to the demands of the employees." No legal force sustained the objectives of unions either in improving wages, hours, and conditions or in strengthening their position through the union shop, master contracts, and arbitration of grievances.

The small utility of the law in collective bargaining was quickly perceived by labor leaders. The CIO packinghouse union, for instance, did not invoke the Wagner Act at all in its three-year struggle with Armour. The company, in fact, objected to the intercession of Secretary of Labor Perkins in 1939 on the ground that the union had not exhausted, or even utilized, the remedies available through the NLRB. The dispute actually did involve issues which fell within the scope of the Wagner Act. But the union clearly was seeking more effective ways—federal pressure in this case—of countering Armour's reluctance to negotiate and sign contracts. For the prime union objective was a master contract covering all the plants of the company organized by the union, a concession which could only be granted voluntarily by the company. Collective bargaining, both the process itself and the fruits, depended on the working of the other advantages open to the unions in the New Deal era.

Where negotiation was undertaken in "good faith," there were modest initial gains. The year 1937, marking the general beginning of collective bargaining in mass production, saw substantial wage increases as the result of negotiations and/or union pressure. In steel, the advances of November, 1936, and March, 1937, moved the unskilled hourly rate from 47 cents to 62½ cents. In rubber, average hourly earnings rose from 69.8 cents to 76.8 cents; in automobiles, from 80 to 93 cents. Other gains tended to be slender. The U. S. Steel agreement, for instance, provided the two major benefits of time-and-a-half after eight hours and a grievance procedure with arbitration. The vacation provision, on the other hand, merely continued an existing arrangement, and silence prevailed on many other questions. The contracts were, in contrast to later ones, very thin documents. Still, the first fruits of collective bargaining were encouraging to labor.

Then the economy faltered again. In 1938 industrial unions had to fight to stave off wage cuts. They succeeded in most, but not all, cases. Rates were reduced 15 per cent at Philco after a four months' strike. Less visible concessions had to be granted in some cases. For example, the SWOC and UAW accepted changes which weakened the grievance procedure at U. S. Steel and General Motors. The mass-production unions were, in addition, hard hit by the recession. Employment fell sharply. The UAW estimated that at the end of January, 1938, 320,000 auto production workers were totally unemployed and most of the remainder of the normal complement of 517,000 were on short time. The union's membership was soon down to 90,000. It was the same story elsewhere. In the Chicago district of the SWOC, dues payments fell by two-thirds in the twelve months after July, 1937 (that is, after absorbing the setback in Little Steel). Declining membership and, in some cases, internal dissension rendered uncertain the organizational viability of the industrial unions. And their weakness in turn further undermined their effectiveness in collective bargaining. They faced a fearful choice. If they became quiescent, they would sacrifice the support of the membership. If they pressed for further concessions, they would unavoidably become involved in strikes. By so doing, they would expose their weakened ranks in the one area in which labor legislation permitted the full expression of employer hostility—and in this period few even of the law-abiding employers were fully reconciled to trade unionism.

Collective bargaining was proving a severe obstacle to the new mass-production unions. The Wagner Act had little value here; and the other favoring circumstances had declining effectiveness after mid-1937. Hostile employers were evading the requirement of negotiating in good faith. For the larger part, the industrial unions achieved the first approximation of collective bargaining. But from 1937 to 1940 very little more was forthcoming. The vital function of collective bargaining seemed stalled. The situation was, in sum, still precarious five years after the formation of the CIO.

John L. Lewis had made something of a miscalculation. The promise of the New Deal era left mass-production unionism short of permanent success. Ultimately, two fortuitous circumstances rescued the industrial unions.

The outbreak of World War II finally ended the American depression. By 1941, the economy was becoming fully engaged in defense production. Corporate profits before taxes leaped from 6½ billion dollars in 1939 to 17 billion in 1941. The number of unemployed fell from 8½ million in June, 1940, to under 4 million in December, 1941. It was this eighteen-month period that marked the turning point for the CIO. Industry's desire to capitalize on a business upswing, noted earlier, was particularly acute now; and rising job opportunities and prices created a new militancy in the laboring ranks. The open-shop strongholds began to crumble. Organization came to the four Little Steel companies, to Ford, and to their lesser counterparts. The resistance to collective bargaining, where it had been the line of conflict, was also breaking down. First contracts were finally being signed by such companies as Goodyear, Armour, Cudahy, Westinghouse, Union Switch and Signal. Above all, collective bargaining after a three-year gap began to produce positive results. On April 14, 1941, U. S. Steel set the pattern for its industry with an increase of ten cents an hour. For manufacturing generally, average hourly earnings from 1940 to 1941 increased over 10 per cent and weekly earnings 17 per cent; living costs rose only 5 per cent. More than wages was involved. Generally, initial contracts were thoroughly renegotiated for the first time, and this produced a wide range of improvements in vacation, holiday, and seniority provisions and in grievance procedure. Mass-production workers could now see the tangible benefits flowing from their union membership. These results of the defense prosperity were reflected in union growth: CIO membership jumped from 1,350,000 in 1940 to 2,850,000 in 1941.

The industrial unions were arriving at a solid basis. That achievement was insured by the second fortuitous change. American entry in the war necessitated a major expansion of the federal role in labor-management relations. To prevent strikes and inflation, the federal government had to enter the hitherto private sphere of collective bargaining. The National War Labor Board largely determined the wartime terms of employment in American industry. This emergency circumstance, temporary although it was, had permanent consequences for mass-production unionism. The wartime experience disposed of the last barriers to viable collective bargaining.

For one thing, the remaining vestiges of anti-unionism were largely eliminated. The hard core of resistance could now be handled summarily. In meat-packing, for instance, Wilson & Co. had not followed Armour, Swift, and Cudahy in accepting collective bargaining. In 1942 the NWLB ordered the recalcitrant firm to negotiate a master contract (Wilson was holding to the earlier Big Four resistance to company-wide bargaining). Years later in 1955, a company official was still insisting that Wilson would not have accepted "a master agreement if it had not been for the war. Such an agreement is an unsatisfactory arrangement; today or yesterday." Subsequent negotiations having yielded no results, a Board panel itself actually wrote the first Wilson contract.

Beyond such flagrant cases, the NWLB set to rest an issue deeply troubling to the labor-management relationship in mass production. With few exceptions, the open shop remained dogma even after the acceptance of unionism. "John, it's just as wrong to make a man join a union," Benjamin Fairless of U. S. Steel insisted to Lewis, ". . . as it is to dictate what church he should belong to." The union shop had been granted in auto by Ford only; in rubber, by the employers of a tenth of the men under contract; in steel, by none of the major producers (although they had succumbed under pressure in the "captive mines"). The issue was profoundly important to the new unions. The union shop meant membership stability and, equally significant, the full acceptance of trade unionism by employers. The NWLB compromised the charged issue on the basis of a precedent set by the prewar National Defense Mediation Board. Maintenance-of-membership prevented members from withdrawing from a union during the life of a contract. Adding an escape period and often the dues checkoff, the NWLB had granted this form of union security in 271 of 291 cases by February, 1944. The CIO regarded maintenance-of-membership as a substantial triumph. And, conversely, some employers took the measure, as Bethlehem and Republic Steel asserted, to be a "camouflaged closed shop." Among the expressions of resentment was the indication in contracts, following the example of Montgomery Ward, that maintenance-of-membership was being granted "over protest." This resistance, however, was losing its force by the end of the war. The union shop then generally grew from maintenance-of-membership.

The war experience also served a vital educational function. A measure of collective bargaining remained under wartime government regulation. Both before and after submission of cases to the NWLB, the parties involved were obliged to negotiate, and their representatives had to participate in the lengthy hearings. From this limited kind of confrontation, there grew the consensus and experience essential to the labor-management relationship. Wartime education had another aspect. The wage-stabilization policy, implemented through the Little Steel formula by the NWLB, tended to extend the issues open to negotiation. Abnormal restraint on wages convinced labor, as one CIO man said, that "full advantage must be taken of what leeway is afforded" to achieve "the greatest possible gains. . . ." As a result the unions began to include in their demands a variety of new kinds of issues (some merely disguised wage increases) such as premium pay, geographical differentials, wage-rate inequalities, piece-rate computation, and a host of "fringe" payments. Thus were guidelines as to what was negotiable fixed for use after the war and a precedent set that would help further to expand the scope of collective bargaining. The collapse of economic stabilization then also would encourage the successive wage increases of the postwar rounds of negotiation. However illusory these gains were in terms of real income, they endowed the industrial unions with a reputation for effectiveness.

Finally, the wartime restrictions permitted the groping advance toward stable relations to take place in safety. The danger of strikes that might have pushed the parties back to an earlier stage of hostilities was eliminated. Strikes there were in abundance in the postwar period, but these could then be held to the objective of the terms of employment, not the issue of unionism itself. Nothing revealed more of the new state of affairs than the first major defeat of an industrial union. The packing-house strike of 1948 was a thorough union disaster in an industry traditionally opposed to trade unionism. Yet the United Packinghouse Workers of America recovered and prospered. As one of its officials noted with relief, it was the first time in the history of the industry that a " 'lost' strike did not mean a lost union."

Unionization thus ran its full course in mass production. The way had been opened by the New Deal and the Great Depression. The legal right to organize was granted, and its utilization was favored by contemporary circumstances. John L. Lewis seized the unequalled opportunity. Breaking from the bounds of the labor establishment, he created in the CIO an optimum instrument for organizing the mass-production workers. These developments did not carry unionization to completion. There was, in particular, a failure in collective bargaining. In the end, the vital progress here sprang fortuitously from the defense prosperity and then the wartime impact on labor relations. From the half-decade of war, the industrial unions advanced to their central place in the American economy.

Ellis W. Hawley

THE NEW DEAL AND THE PROBLEM OF MONOPOLY

IN THIS SELECTION from his brilliant monograph, *The New Deal and the Problem of Monopoly,* Ellis W. Hawley, Professor of History at Ohio State University, argues that New Deal policy toward business was economically illogical, yet politically successful because it reflected the divided yearnings of the American people. Americans, he believes, had accepted the benefits and practical necessity of corporate bigness but longed for the simplicity and opportunity of an old competitive order. Roosevelt's approach to the question of monopoly was highly inconsistent but, "His mixed emotions so closely reflected the popular mind that they were a political asset rather than a liability." This inconsistency, this divided mind, Hawley argues, characterized the New Deal from beginning to end.

Hawley does feel that there was a rough shift in emphasis from a First New Deal built around the concept of central economic planning to a Second New Deal based on anti-trust sentiment. But the First New Deal failed to impose any real central planning on the economy; indeed the American tradition of competitive individualism made genuine central planning impossible. Acting through the NRA, the First New Deal instead gave government sanction to many disjointed and uncoordinated monopolistic agree-

From *The New Deal and the Problem of Monopoly* by Ellis W. Hawley, pp. 472–490. Copyright © 1966 by the Princeton University Press. Reprinted by permission of the Princeton University Press.

ments; it also maintained a rhetorical commitment to the competitive ethic.

On the other hand, when the New Deal emphasis moved to antimonopoly, the shift was sharply limited by practical considerations. However much Americans might idealize the past, they appreciated the progress which bigness had brought. In addition, a serious antitrust program might well have caused deflationary business disruptions and worsened the depression. Consequently, the effort which developed was ritualistic. Thurman Arnold's program "made no real effort to rearrange the underlying industrial structure itself, no real attempt to dislodge vested interests, disrupt controls that were actual checks against deflation, or break up going concerns." And the creation of the Temporary National Economic Committee in Congress was a method of avoiding decisions rather than arriving at definite programs.

In the end, the New Deal made little change in the structure of American business. It instead attempted to restore prosperity by organizing agriculture and labor as countervailing powers and by moving toward a policy of compensatory government spending. These were rather radical departures, but they allowed the nation to continue its evasion of an even more fundamental decision.

Two souls dwell in the bosom of this Administration," wrote Dorothy Thompson in 1938, "as indeed, they do in the bosom of the American people. The one loves the Abundant Life, as expressed in the cheap and plentiful products of large-scale mass production and distribution. . . . The other soul yearns for former simplicities, for decentralization, for the interests of the 'little man,' revolts against high-pressure salesmanship, denounces 'monopoly' and 'economic empires,' and seeks means of breaking them up." "Our Administration," she continued, "manages a remarkable . . . stunt of being . . . in favor of organizing and regulating the Economic Empires to greater and greater efficiency, and of breaking them up as a tribute to perennial American populist feeling."

Dorothy Thompson was a persistent critic of the Roosevelt Administration; yet her remarks did show considerable insight into the dilemma that confronted New Dealers, and indeed, the dilemma that confronted industrial America. The problem of reconciling liberty and order, individualism and collective organization, was admittedly an ancient one, but the creation of a highly integrated industrial system in a land that had long cherished its liberal, democratic, and individualistic traditions presented the problem in a peculiarly acute form. Both the American people and their political leaders tended to view modern industrialism with mingled feelings of pride and regret. On one hand, they tended to associate large business units and economic organization with abundance, progress, and a rising standard of living. On the other, they associated them with a wide variety of economic abuses, which, because of past ideals and past standards, they felt to be injurious to society. Also, deep in their hearts, they retained a soft spot for the "little fellow." In moments of introspection, they looked upon the immense concentrations of economic power that they had created and accused them of destroying the good life, of destroying the independent businessman and the satisfactions that came from owning one's own business and working for oneself, of reducing Americans to a race of clerks and machine tenders, of creating an impersonal, mechanized world that destroyed man as an individual.

The search in twentieth-century America, then, was for some solution that would reconcile the practical necessity with the individualistic ideal, some arrangement that would preserve the industrial order, necessarily based upon a high degree of collective organization, and yet would preserve America's democratic heritage at the same time. Americans wanted a stable, efficient industrial system, one that turned out a large quantity of material goods, insured full employment, and provided a relatively high degree of economic security. Yet at the same time they wanted a system as free as possible from centralized direction, one in which economic power was dispersed and economic opportunity was really open, one that preserved the dignity of the individual and adjusted itself automatically to market forces. And they were unwilling to renounce the hope of achieving both. In spite of periodic hurricanes of anti-big-business sentiment, they refused to follow the prophets that would destroy their industrial system and return to former simplicities. Nor did they pay much attention to those that would sacrifice democratic ideals and liberal traditions in order to create a more orderly and more rational system, one that promised greater security, greater stability, and possibly even greater material benefits.

There were times, of course, when this dilemma was virtually forgotten. During periods of economic prosperity, when Americans were imbued with a psychological sense of well-being and satiated with a steady outflow of material benefits, it was hard to convince them that their industrial organization was seriously out of step with their ideals. During such periods, the majority rallied to the support of the business system; so long as it continued to operate at a high level, they saw no need for any major reforms. So long as the competitive ideal was embodied in statutes and industrial and political leaders paid lip service to it, there was a general willingness to leave it at that. If there were troubled consciences left, these could be soothed by clothing collective organizations in the attributes of rugged individuals and by the assurances of economic experts that anything short of pure monopoly was "competition" and therefore assured the benefits that were supposed to flow from competition.

In a time of economic adversity, however, Americans became painfully aware of the gap between ideal and reality. Paradoxically, this awareness produced two conflicting and contradictory reactions. Some pointed to the gap, to the failure of business organizations to live by the competitive creed, and concluded that it was the cause of the economic debacle, that the breakdown of the industrial machine was the inevitable consequence of its failure to conform to competitive standards. Others pointed to the same gap and concluded that the ideal itself was at fault, that it had prevented the organization and conscious direction of a rational system that would provide stability and security. On one hand, the presence of depression conditions seemed to intensify anti-big-business sentiment and generate new demands for antitrust crusades. On the other, it inspired demands for planning, rationalization, and the creation of economic organizations that could weather deflationary forces. The first general effect grew directly out of the loss of confidence in business leadership, the conviction that industrial leaders had sinned against the economic creed, and the determination that they should be allowed to sin no more. The second grew out of the black fear of economic death, the urgent desire to stem the deflationary tide, and the mounting conviction that a policy of laissez-faire or real implementation of the competitive ideal would result in economic disaster.

During such a period, moreover, it would seem practically inevitable that the policy-making apparatus of a democracy should register both streams of sentiment. Regardless of their logical inconsistency, the two streams were so intermixed in the ideology of the average man that any administration, if it wished to retain political power, had to make concessions to both. It must move to check the deflationary spiral, to provide some sort of central direction, and to salvage economic groups through the erection of cartels and economic controls. Yet while it was doing this, it must make a proper show of maintaining competitive ideals. Its actions must be justified by an appeal to competitive traditions, by showing that they were designed to save the underdog, or if this was impossible, by an appeal to other arguments and other traditions that for the moment justified making an exception. Nor could antitrust action ever be much more than a matter of performing the proper rituals and manipulating the proper symbols. It might attack unusually privileged and widely hated groups, break up a few loose combinations, and set forth a general program that was presumably designed to make the competitive ideal a reality. But the limit of the program would, of necessity, be that point at which changes in business practice or business structures would cause serious economic dislocation. It could not risk the disruption of going concerns or a further shrinkage in employment and production, and it would not subject men to the logical working out of deflationary trends. To do so would amount to political suicide.

To condemn these policies for their inconsistency was to miss the point. From an economic standpoint, condemnation might very well be to the point. They were inconsistent. One line of action tended to cancel the other, with the result that little was accomplished. Yet from the political standpoint, this very inconsistency, so long as the dilemma persisted, was the safest method of retaining political power. President Roosevelt, it seems, never suffered politically from his reluctance to choose between planning and antitrust action. His mixed emotions so closely reflected the popular mind that they were a political asset rather than a liability.

II

That New Deal policy was inconsistent, then, should occasion little surprise. Such inconsistency, in fact, was readily apparent in the National Industrial Recovery Act, the first major effort to deal with the problems of industrial organization. When Roosevelt took office in 1933, the depression had reached its most acute stage. Almost every economic group was crying for salvation through political means, for some sort of rationalization and planning, although they might differ as to just who was to do the planning and the type and amount of it that would be required. Pro-business planners, drawing upon the trade association ideology of the nineteen twenties and the precedent of the War Industries Board, envisioned a semi-cartelized business commonwealth in which industrial leaders would plan and the state would enforce the decisions. Other men, convinced that there was already too much planning by businessmen, hoped to create an order in which other economic groups would participate in the policy-making process. Even under these circumstances, however, the resulting legislation had to be clothed in competitive symbols. Proponents of the NRA advanced the theory that it would help small businessmen and industrial laborers by protecting them from predatory practices and monopolistic abuses. The devices used to erect monopolistic controls became "codes of fair competition." And each such device contained the proper incantation against monopoly.

Consequently, the NRA was not a single program with a single objective, but rather a series of programs with a series of objectives, some of which were in direct conflict with each other. In effect, the National Industrial Recovery Act provided a phraseology that could be used to urge almost any approach to the problem of economic organization and an administrative machine that each of the conflicting economic and ideological groups might possibly use for their own ends. Under the circumstances, a bitter clash over basic policies was probably inevitable.

For a short period these inconsistencies were glossed over by the summer boomlet of 1933 and by a massive propaganda campaign appealing to wartime precedents and attempting to create a new set of cooperative symbols. As the propaganda wore off, however, and the economic indices turned downward again, the inconsistencies inherent in the program moved to the forefront of the picture. In the code-writing process, organized business had emerged as the dominant economic group, and once this became apparent, criticism of the NRA began to mount. Agrarians, convinced that rising industrial prices were canceling out any gains from the farm program, demanded that businessmen live up to the competitive faith. Labor spokesmen, bitterly disillusioned when the program failed to guarantee union recognition and collective bargaining, charged the Administration had sold out to management. Small businessmen, certain that the new code authorities were only devices to increase the power of their larger rivals, raised the ancient cry of monopolistic exploitation. Antitrusters, convinced that the talk about strengthening competition was sheer hypocrisy, demanded that this disastrous trust-building program come to a halt. Economic planners, alienated by a process in which the businessmen did the planning, charged that the government was only sanctioning private monopolistic arrangements. And the American public, disillusioned with rising prices and the failure of the program to bring economic recovery, listened to the criticisms and demanded that its competitive ideals be made good.

The rising tide of public resentment greatly strengthened the hand of those that viewed the NRA primarily as a device for raising the plane of competition and securing social justice for labor. Picking up support from discontented groups, from other governmental agencies, and from such investigations as that conducted by Clarence Darrow's National Recovery Review Board, this group within the NRA had soon launched a campaign to bring about a reorientation in policy. By June 1934 it had obtained a formal written policy embodying its views, one that committed the NRA to the competitive ideal, renounced the use of price and production controls and promised to subject the code authorities to strict public supervision.

By this time, however, most of the major codes had been written, and the market restorers were never able to apply their policy to codes already approved. The chief effect of their efforts to do so was to antagonize businessmen and to complicate the difficulties of enforcing code provisions that were out of line with announced policy.

The result was a deadlock that persisted for the remainder of the agency's life. Putting the announced policy into effect would have meant, in all probability, the complete alienation of business support and the collapse of the whole structure. Yet accepting and enforcing the codes for what they were would have resulted, again in all probability, in an outraged public and congressional opinion that would have swept away the whole edifice. Thus the NRA tended to reflect the whole dilemma confronting the New Deal. Admittedly, declared policy was inconsistent with practice. Admittedly, the NRA was accomplishing little. Yet from a political standpoint, if the agency were to continue at all, a deadlock of this sort seemed to be the only solution. If the Supreme Court had not taken a hand in the matter, the probable outcome would have been either the abolition of the agency or a continuation of the deadlock.

The practical effect of the NRA, then, was to allow the erection, extension, and fortification of private monopolistic arrangements, particularly for groups that already possessed a fairly high degree of integration and monopoly power. Once these arrangements had been approved and vested interests had developed, the Administration found it difficult to deal with them. It could not move against them without alienating powerful interest groups, producing new economic dislocations, and running the risk of setting off the whole process of deflation again. Yet, because of the competitive ideals, it could not lend much support to the arrangements or provide much in the way of public supervision. Only in areas where other arguments, other ideals, and political pressure justified making an exception, in such areas as agriculture, natural resources, transportation, and to a certain extent labor, could the government lend its open support and direction.

Moreover, the policy dilemma, coupled with the sheer complexity of the undertaking, made it impossible to provide much central direction. There was little planning of a broad, general nature, either by businessmen or by the state; there was merely the half-hearted acceptance of a series of legalized, but generally uncoordinated, monopolistic combinations. The result was not over-all direction, but a type of partial, piecemeal, pressure-group planning, a type of planning designed by specific economic groups to balance production with consumption regardless of the dislocations produced elsewhere in the economy.

III

There were, certainly, proposals for other types of planning. But under the circumstances, they were and remained politically unfeasible, both during the NRA period and after. The idea of a government-supported business commonwealth still persisted, and a few men still felt that if the NRA had really applied it, the depression would have been over. Yet in the political context of the time, the idea was thoroughly unrealistic. For one thing, there was the growing gap between businessmen and New Dealers, the conviction of one side that cooperation would lead to bureaucratic socialism, of the other that it would lead to fascism or economic oppression. Even if this quarrel had not existed, the Administration could not have secured a program that ran directly counter to the anti-big-business sentiment of the time. The monopolistic implications in such a program were too obvious, and there was little that could be done to disguise them. Most industrial leaders recognized the situation, and the majority of them came to the conclusion that a political program of this sort was no longer necessary. With the crisis past and the deflationary process checked, private controls and such governmental aids as tariffs, subsidies, and loans would be sufficient.

The idea of national economic planning also persisted. A number of New Dealers continued to advocate the transfer of monopoly power from businessmen to the state or to other organized economic groups. Each major economic group, they argued, should be organized and allowed to participate in the formulation of a central plan, one that would result in expanded production, increased employment, a more equitable distribution, and a better balance of prices. Yet this idea, too, was thoroughly impractical when judged in terms of existing political realities. It ran counter to competitive and individualistic traditions. It threatened important vested interests. It largely ignored the complexities of the planning process or the tendency of regulated interests to dominate their regulators. And it was regarded by the majority of Americans as being overly radical, socialistic, and un-American.

Consequently, the planning of the New Deal was essentially single-industry planning, partial, piecemeal, and opportunistic, planning that could circumvent the competitive ideal or could be based on other ideals that justified making an exception. After the NRA experience, organized business groups found it increasingly difficult to devise these justifications. Some business leaders, to be sure, continued to talk about a public agency with power to waive the antitrust laws and sanction private controls. Yet few of them were willing to accept government participation in the planning process, and few were willing to come before the public with proposals that were immediately vulnerable to charges of monopoly. It was preferable, they felt, to let the whole issue lie quiet, to rely upon unauthorized private controls, and to hope that these would be little disturbed by antitrust action. Only a few peculiarly depressed groups, like the cotton textile industry, continued to agitate for government-supported cartels, and most of these groups lacked the cohesion, power, and alternative symbols that would have been necessary to put their programs through.

In some areas, however, especially in areas where alternative symbols were present and where private controls had broken down or proven impractical, it was possible to secure a type of partial planning. Agriculture was able to avoid most of the agitation against monopoly, and while retaining to a large extent its individualistic operations, to find ways of using the state to fix prices, plan production, and regularize markets. Its ability to do so was attributable in part to the political power of the farmers, but it was also due to manipulation of certain symbols that effectively masked the monopolistic implications in the program. The ideal of the yeoman farmer—honest, independent, and morally upright—still had a strong appeal in America, and to many Americans it justified the salvation of farming as a "way of life," even at the cost of subsidies and the violation of competitive standards. Agriculture, moreover, was supposed to be the basic industry, the activity that supported all others. The country, so it was said, could not be prosperous unless its farmers were prosperous. Finally, there was the conservation argument, the great concern over conservation of the soil, which served to justify some degree of public planning and some type of production control.

Similar justifications were sometimes possible for other areas of the economy. Monopolistic arrangements in certain food-processing industries could be camouflaged as an essential part of the farm program. Departures from competitive standards in such natural resource industries as bituminous coal and crude oil production could be justified on the grounds of conservation. Public controls and economic cartelization in the fields of transportation and communication could be justified on the ground that these were "natural monopolies" in which the public had a vital interest. And in the distributive trades, it was possible to turn anti-big-business sentiment against the mass distributors, to brand them as "monopolies," and to obtain a series of essentially anti-competitive measures on the theory that they were designed to preserve competition by preserving small competitors.* The small merchant, however, was never able to dodge the agitation against monopoly to the same extent that the farmer did. The supports granted him were weak to begin with, and to obtain them he had to make concessions to the competitive ideal, concessions that robbed his measures of much of their intended effectiveness.

In some ways, too, the Roosevelt Administration helped to create monopoly power for labor. Under the New Deal program, the government proceeded to absorb surplus labor and prescribe minimum labor standards; more important, it encouraged labor organization to the extent that it maintained a friendly attitude, required employer recognition of unions, and restrained certain practices that had been used to break unions in the past. For a time, the appeals to social justice, humanitarianism, and anti-big-business sentiment overrode the appeal of business spokesmen and classical economists to the competi-

* The Robinson-Patman Act (1936) and the Miller-Tydings Act (1937) were designed to protect small business by prohibiting wholesalers from practicing price discrimination and by establishing "fair trade" price floors on numerous items. Neither bill received the active support of the Roosevelt administration.—Ed.

tive ideal and individualistic traditions. The doctrine that labor was not a commodity, that men who had worked and produced and kept their obligations to society were entitled to be taken care of, was widely accepted. Along with it went a growing belief that labor unions were necessary to maintain purchasing power and counterbalance big business. Consequently, even the New Dealers of an antitrust persuasion generally made a place in their program for social legislation and labor organization.

The general effect of this whole line of New Deal policy might be summed up in the word counterorganization, that is, the creation of monopoly power in areas previously unorganized. One can only conclude, however, that this did not happen according to any preconceived plan. Nor did it necessarily promote economic expansion or raise consumer purchasing power. Public support of monopolistic arrangements occurred in a piecemeal, haphazard fashion, in response to pressure from specific economic groups and as opportunities presented themselves. Since consumer organizations were weak and efforts to aid consumers made little progress, the benefits went primarily to producer groups interested in restricting production and raising prices. In the distributive trades, the efforts to help small merchants tended, insofar as they were successful, to impede technological changes, hamper mass distributors, and reduce consumer purchasing power. In the natural resource and transportation industries, most of the new legislation was designed to restrict production, reduce competition, and protect invested capital. And in the labor and agricultural fields, the strengthening of market controls was often at the expense of consumers and in conjunction with business groups. The whole tendency of interest-group planning, in fact, was toward the promotion of economic scarcity. Each group, it seemed, was trying to secure a larger piece from a pie that was steadily dwindling in size.

From an economic standpoint, then, the partial planning of the post-NRA type made little sense, and most economists, be they antitrusters, planners, or devotees of laissez-faire, felt that such an approach was doing more harm than good. It was understandable only in a political context, and as a political solution, it did possess obvious elements of strength. It retained the antitrust laws and avoided any direct attack upon the competitive ideal or competitive mythology. Yet by appealing to other goals and alternative ideals and by using these to justify special and presumably exceptional departures from competitive standards, it could make the necessary concessions to pressure groups interested in reducing competition and erecting government-sponsored cartels. Such a program might be logically inconsistent and economically harmful. Perhaps, as one critic suggested at the time, it combined the worst features of both worlds, "an impairment of the efficiency of the competitive system without the compensating benefits of rationalized collective action." But politically it was a going concern, and efforts to achieve theoretical consistency met with little success.

Perhaps the greatest defect in these limited planning measures was their tendency toward restriction, their failure to provide any incentive for expansion when an expanding economy was the crying need of the time. The easiest way to counteract this tendency, it seemed, was through government expenditures and deficit financing; in practice, this was essentially the path that the New Deal took. By 1938 Roosevelt seemed willing to accept the Keynesian arguments for a permanent spending program, and eventually, when war demands necessitated pump-priming on a gigantic scale, the spending solution worked. It overcame the restrictive tendencies in the economy, restored full employment, and brought rapid economic expansion. Drastic institutional reform, it seemed, was unnecessary. Limited, piecemeal, pressure-group planning could continue, and the spending weapon could be relied upon to stimulate expansion and maintain economic balance.

IV

One major stream of New Deal policy, then, ran toward partial planning. Yet this stream was shaped and altered, at least in a negative sense, by its encounters with the antitrust tradition and the competitive ideal. In a time when Americans distrusted business leadership and blamed big business for the prevailing economic misery, it was only natural that an antitrust approach should have wide political appeal. Concessions had to be made to it, and these concessions meant that planning had to be limited, piecemeal, and disguised. There could be no over-all program of centralized controls. There could be no government-sponsored business commonwealth. And there could be only a minimum of government participation in the planning process.

In and of itself, however, the antitrust approach did not offer a politically workable alternative. The antitrusters might set forth their own vision of the good society. They might blame the depression upon the departure from competitive standards and suggest measures to make industrial organization correspond more closely to the competitive model. But they could never ignore or explain away the deflationary and disruptive implications of their program. Nor could they enlist much support from the important political and economic pressure groups. Consequently, the antitrust approach, like that of planning, had to be applied on a limited basis. Action could be taken only in special or exceptional areas, against unusually privileged groups that were actively hated and particularly vulnerable, in fields where one business group was fighting another, in cases where no one would get hurt, or against practices that violated common standards of decency and fairness.

This was particularly true during the period prior to 1938. The power trust, for example, was a special demon in the progressive faith, one that was actively hated by large numbers of people and one that had not only violated competitive standards but had also outraged accepted canons of honesty and tampered with democratic political ideals. For such an institution, nothing was too bad, not even a little competition; and the resulting battle, limited though its gains might be, did provide a suitable outlet for popular antitrust feeling. Much the same was also true of the other antitrust activities. Financial reform provided another outlet for antitrust sentiment, although its practical results were little more than regulation for the promotion of honesty and facilitation of the governmental spending program. The attacks upon such practices as collusive bidding, basing-point pricing,* and block-booking†

* A practice followed by several major industries. The delivered price of a product was calculated by adding freight charges from an agreed-upon "basing point," rather than the actual point from which the shipment originated. The Federal Trade Commission began to move against this system in 1937.—Ed.

† A system by which the major motion picture companies forced independent theaters to accept their entire output of films. Thurman Arnold, head of the Antitrust Division in the Department of Justice, began a relatively mild campaign against the practice in 1938.—Ed.

benefited from a long history of past agitation. And the suits in the petroleum and auto-finance industries had the support of discontented business groups. The result of such activities, however, could hardly be more than marginal. When the antitrusters reached for real weapons, when they tried, for example, to use the taxing power or make drastic changes in corporate law, they found that any thorough-going program was simply not within the realm of political possibilities.

Under the circumstances, it appeared, neither planning nor antitrust action could be applied in a thorough-going fashion. Neither approach could completely eclipse the other. Yet the political climate and situation did change; and, as a result of these changes, policy vacillated between the two extremes. One period might see more emphasis on planning, the next on antitrust action, and considerable changes might also take place in the nature, content, and scope of each program.

Superficially, the crisis of 1937 was much like that of 1933. Again there were new demands for antitrust action, and again these demands were blended with new proposals for planning, rationalization, and monopolistic controls. In some respects, too, the results were similar. There was more partial planning in unorganized areas, and eventually, this was accompanied by a resumption of large-scale federal spending. The big difference was in the greater emphasis on an antitrust approach, which could be attributed primarily to the difference in political circumstances. The alienation of the business community, memories of NRA experiences, and the growing influence of antimonopolists in the Roosevelt Administration made it difficult to work out any new scheme of business-government cooperation. These same factors, coupled with the direct appeal of New Dealers to the competitive ideal, made it difficult for business groups to secure public sanction for monopolistic arrangements. The political repercussions of the recession, the fact that the new setback had occurred while the New Deal was in power, made it necessary to appeal directly to anti-big-business sentiment and to use the administered price thesis* to explain why the recession had occurred and why the New Deal

* Many leading figures within the Roosevelt administration, including apparently Roosevelt himself for a time, attributed the recession of 1937–1938 to artificially high prices "administered" by corporate monopoly. —Ed.

had failed to achieve sustained recovery. Under the circumstances, the initiative passed to the antitrusters, and larger concessions had to be made to their point of view.

One such concession was the creation of the Temporary National Economic Committee. Yet this was not so much a victory for the antitrusters as it was a way of avoiding the issue, a means of minimizing the policy conflict within the Administration and postponing any final decision. Essentially, the TNEC was a harmless device that could be used by each group to urge a specific line of action or no action at all. Antimonopolists hoped that it would generate the political sentiment necessary for a major breakthrough against concentrated economic power, but these hopes were never realized. In practice, the investigation became largely an ineffective duplicate of the frustrating debate that produced it, and by the time its report was filed, the circumstances had changed. Most of the steam had gone out of the monopoly issue, and antitrust sentiment was being replaced by war-induced patriotism.

The second major concession to antimonopoly sentiment was Thurman Arnold's revival of antitrust prosecutions, a program that presumably was designed to restore a competitive system, one in which prices were flexible and competition would provide the incentive for expansion. Actually, the underlying assumptions behind such a program were of doubtful validity. Price flexibility, even if attainable, might do more harm than good. The Arnold approach had definite limitations, even assuming that the underlying theories were sound. It could and did break up a number of loose combinations; it could and did disrupt monopolistic arrangements that were no necessary part of modern industrialism. It could and, in some cases, did succeed in convincing businessmen that they should adopt practices that corresponded a bit more closely to the competitive model. But it made no real effort to rearrange the underlying industrial structure itself, no real attempt to dislodge vested interests, disrupt controls that were actual checks against deflation, or break up going concerns. And since the practices and policies complained of would appear in many cases to be the outgrowth of this underlying structure, the Arnold program had little success in achieving its avowed goals.

Even within these limits, moreover, Arnold's antitrust campaign ran into all sorts of difficulties. Often the combinations that he sought to break up were the very ones that the earlier New Deal had fostered. Often, even though the arrangements involved bore little relation to actual production, their sponsors claimed that they did, that their disruption would set the process of deflation in motion again and impair industrial efficiency. Arnold claimed that his activities enjoyed great popular support, and as a symbol and generality they probably did. But when they moved against specific arrangements, it was a different story. There they succeeded in alienating one political pressure group after another. Then, with the coming of the war, opposition became stronger than ever. As antitrust sentiment was replaced by wartime patriotism, it seemed indeed that the disruption of private controls would reduce efficiency and impair the war effort. Consequently, the Arnold program gradually faded from the scene.

It is doubtful, then, that the innovations of 1938 should be regarded as a basic reversal in economic policy. What actually happened was not the substitution of one set of policies for another, but rather a shift in emphasis between two sets of policies that had existed side by side throughout the entire period. Policies that attacked monopoly and those that fostered it, policies that reflected the underlying dilemma of industrial America, had long been inextricably intertwined in American history, and this basic inconsistency persisted in an acute form during the nineteen thirties. Policy might and did vacillate between the two extremes; but because of the limitations of the American political structure and of American economic ideology, it was virtually impossible for one set of policies to displace the other. The New Deal reform movement was forced to adjust to this basic fact. The practical outcome was an economy characterized by private controls, partial planning, compensatory governmental spending, and occasional gestures toward the competitive ideal.

FDR AND THE NEW DEAL

Arthur M. Schlesinger, Jr.

FDR: PRAGMATIST-DEMOCRAT

FEW HISTORIANS have combined careers in scholarship and politics so remarkably as Arthur Schlesinger, Jr. The son of an eminent Harvard historian, Schlesinger won the Pulitzer Prize at the age of 28 for his brilliant and controversial book, *The Age of Jackson* (1945). After a brief career as a Washington journalist, he returned to Harvard as a faculty member and began a study of the era of Franklin D. Roosevelt, three volumes of which are now in print. He also maintained an active interest in public affairs and liberal politics as one of the founders of the Americans for Democratic Action, author of *The Vital Center* (1949), a major statement of non-Communist liberalism, and as an aide to Adlai Stevenson during the presidential campaigns of 1952 and 1956. Leaving his position at Harvard, he became a special assistant to President John F. Kennedy and subsequently wrote a best-selling account of the Kennedy administration, *A Thousand Days* (1965). As Albert Schweitzer Professor of Humanities at the City University of New York, he has returned to his work on the *Age of Roosevelt*, a study which when completed probably will rank as one of the most important enterprises in the whole history of American historical writing.

Schlesinger is a strong and articulate believer in the ability of

---

From The *Age of Roosevelt: The Politics of Upheaval* by Arthur M. Schlesinger, Jr., pp. 647–657. Copyright © 1960 by Arthur M. Schlesinger, Jr. Reprinted by permission of the publisher, Houghton Mifflin Company.

great men to influence history. He pictures Roosevelt as a towering individual who determined the basic character of the New Deal and probably preserved American democracy. FDR, he believes, was a pragmatist who rejected the absolute systems which attracted so many social thinkers of the 1930's. Roosevelt felt that Herbert Hoover's philosophy of absolute individualism had failed to meet the problems of the depression and at the same time saw himself and the New Deal as fighters against the absolute totalitarianisms of Fascism and Communism. He sought to lead America down a middle way, establish a non-systematic, mixed economy, preserve democracy, and provide security for all. In so doing, he established himself as the international leader of democracy, a "trustee for those in every country" who believed in freedom and democratic experimentation.

Schlesinger's critics, including James MacGregor Burns and Howard Zinn, question his designation of Roosevelt as a real pragmatist. They argue that FDR rejected not simply ideological systems but also systematic thinking. They feel that his vague affirmations of democracy, freedom, and security failed to provide a basis for the type of reform movement which would have ended the depression and rebuilt American society. The argument is, one should remember, between two types of liberals, those who prefer to stress Roosevelt's accomplishments and those who think he should have accomplished much more.

Was no middle way possible between freedom and tyranny—no mixed system which might give the state more power than Herbert Hoover would approve, enough power, indeed, to assure economic and social security; but still not enough to create a Hitler or a Stalin? This was the critical question.

To this question the Hoovers, no less than the Hitlers and Stalins, had long since returned categorical answers. They all—the prophets of individualism and the prophets of totalitarianism—agreed on this if on nothing else: no modified capitalism was possible, no mixed economy, no system of partial and limited government intervention. One could have one thing or the other, but one could never, never, never mix freedom and control. There was, in short, no middle way.

If this conclusion were true, it would have the most fateful consequences for the future of the world.

The assumption that there were two absolutely distinct economic orders, capitalism and socialism, expressed, of course, an unconscious Platonism—a conviction that reality inhered in theoretical essences of which any working economy, with its compromises and confusions, could only be an imperfect copy. If in the realm of essences capitalism and socialism were wholly separate phenomena based on wholly separate principles, then they must be rigorously kept apart on earth. Thus abstractions became more "real" than empirical reality: both doctrinaire capitalists and doctrinaire socialists fell victim to what Whitehead called the "fallacy of misplaced concreteness." Both ideological conservatism and ideological radicalism dwelt in the realm of either-or. Both preferred essence to existence.

The distinction of the New Deal lay precisely in its refusal to approach social problems in terms of ideology. Its strength lay in its preference of existence to essence. The great central source of its energy was the instinctive contempt of practical, energetic, and compassionate people for dogmatic absolutes. Refusing to be intimidated by abstractions or to be overawed by ideology, the New Dealers responded by doing things. Walt Whitman once wrote, "To work for Democracy is good, the exercise is good—strength it makes and lessons it teaches." The whole point of the New Deal lay in its faith in "the exercise of Democracy," its belief in gradualness, its rejection of catastrophism, its denial of either-or, its indifference to ideology, its conviction that a managed and modified capitalist order achieved by piecemeal experiment could best combine personal freedom and economic growth. "In a wórld in which revolutions just now are coming easily," said Adolf Berle, "the New Deal chose the more difficult course of moderation and rebuilding." "It looks forward toward a more stable social order," said Morgenthau, "but it is not doctrinaire, not a complete cut-and-dried program. It involves the courage to experiment." "The course that the new administration did take," wrote Ickes, "was the hardest course. It conformed to no theory, but it did fit into the American system—to meet concrete needs, a system of courageous recognition of change." Tugwell, rejecting laissez faire and Communism, spoke of the "third course." *Hold Fast the Middle Way* was the title of a book by John Dickinson.

Roosevelt hoped to steer between the extreme of chaos and tyranny by moving always, in his phrase, "slightly to the left of center." "Unrestrained individualism" had proved a failure; yet "any paternalistic system which tries to provide for security for everyone from above only calls for an impossible task and a regimentation utterly uncongenial to the spirit of our people." He deeply agreed with Macaulay's injunction to reform if you would preserve. Once, defending public housing to a press conference, he said, "If you had knowledge of what happened in Germany and England and Vienna, you would know that 'socialism' has probably done more to prevent Communism and rioting and revolution than anything else in the last four or five years."

Roosevelt had no illusions about revolution. Mussolini and Stalin seemed to him "not mere distant relatives" but "blood brothers." When Emil Ludwig asked him his "political motive," he replied, "My desire to obviate revolution. . . . I work in a contrary sense to Rome and Moscow." He said during the 1932 campaign:

> Say that civilization is a tree which, as it grows, continually produces rot and dead wood. The radical says: "Cut it down." The conservative says: "Don't touch it." The liberal compromises: "Let's prune, so that we lose neither the old trunk nor the new branches." This campaign is waged to teach the country to march upon its appointed course, the way of change, in an orderly march, avoiding alike the revolution of radicalism and the revolution of conservatism.

His "speech material" file contained a miscellany of material indexed according to the random categories of the President's mind. One folder bore the revealing label: "Liberalism vs. Communism and Conservatism."

As Roosevelt saw it, he was safeguarding the constitutional system by carrying through reforms long overdue. "The principal object of every Government all over the world," he once said, "seems to have been to impose the ideas of the last generation upon the present one. That's all wrong." As early as 1930 he had considered it time for America "to become fairly radical for at least one generation. History shows that where this occurs occasionally, nations are saved from revolution." In 1938 he remarked, "In five years I think we have caught up twenty years. If liberal government continues over another ten years we ought to be contemporary somewhere in the late nineteen forties."

For Roosevelt, the technique of liberal government was pragmatism. Tugwell talked about creating "a philosophy to fit the Roosevelt method"; but this was the aspiration of an intellectual. Nothing attracted Roosevelt less than rigid intellectual systems. "The fluidity of change in society has always been the despair of theorists," Tugwell once wrote. This fluidity was Roosevelt's delight, and he floated upon it with the confidence of an expert sailor, who could detect currents and breezes invisible to others, hear the slap of waves on distant rocks, smell squalls beyond the horizon and make infallible landfalls in the blackest of fogs. He respected clear ideas, accepted them, employed them, but was never really at ease with them and always ultimately skeptical about their relationship to reality.

His attitude toward economists was typical. Though he acknowledged their necessity, he stood in little awe of them. "I brought down several books by English economists and leading American economists," he once told a press conference. ". . . I suppose I must have read different articles by fifteen different experts. Two things stand out: The first is that no two of them agree, and the other thing is that they are so foggy in what they say that it is almost impossible to figure out what they mean. It is jargon; absolute jargon." Once Roosevelt remarked to Keynes of Leon Henderson, "Just look at Leon. When I got him, he was only an economist." (Keynes could hardly wait to repeat this to Henderson.) Roosevelt dealt proficiently with practical questions of government finance, as he showed in his press conferences on the budget; but abstract theory left him cold.

Considering the state of economic theory in the nineteen thirties, this was not necessarily a disabling prejudice. Roosevelt had, as J. K. Galbraith has suggested, what was more important than theory, and surely far more useful than bad theory, a set of intelligent economic attitudes. He believed in government as an instrument for effecting economic change (though not as an instrument for doing everything: in 1934, he complained to the National Emergency Council, "There is the general feeling that it is up to the Government to take care of everybody . . . they should be told all the different things the Government can not do"). He did not regard successful businessmen as infallible repositories of economic wisdom. He regarded the nation as an estate to be improved for those who would eventually inherit it. He was willing to try nearly anything. And he had a sense of the complex continuities of history—that special intimacy with the American past which, as Frances Perkins perceptively observed, signified a man who had talked with old people who had talked with older people who remembered many things back to the War of the Revolution.

From this perspective, Roosevelt could not get excited about the debate between the First and Second New Deals. No one knew what he really thought about the question of the organic economy versus the restoration of competition. Tugwell, perhaps the most vigilant student of Roosevelt's economic ideas, could in one mood pronounce Roosevelt "a progressive of the nineteenth century in economic matters" (1946) who "clung to the Brandeis-Frankfurter view" (1950) and "could be persuaded away from the old progressive line only in the direst circumstances" (1950); in another, he could speak of Roosevelt's "preference for a planned and disciplined business system" (1957) and for "overhead management of the whole economy" (1940), and question whether he ever believed in Brandeis (1957). Corcoran and Cohen, who helped persuade Roosevelt to the Second New Deal, thought he never really abandoned the NRA dream of directing the economy through some kind of central economic mechanism. Roosevelt himself, confronted with a direct question, always wriggled away ("Brandeis is one thousand per cent right in principle but in certain fields there must be a guiding or restraining hand of Government because of the very nature of the specific field"). He never could see why the United States has to be all one way or all the other. "This country is big enough to experiment with several diverse systems and follow several different lines," he once remarked to Adolf Berle. "Why must we put our economic policy in a single systemic strait jacket?"

Rejecting the battle between the New Nationalism and the New Freedom which had so long divided American liberalism, Roosevelt equably defined the New Deal as the "satisfactory combination" of both. Rejecting the platonic distinction between "capitalism" and "socialism," he led the way toward a new society which took elements from each and rendered both obsolescent. It was this freedom from dogma which outraged the angry, logical men who saw everything with dazzling certitude. Roosevelt's illusion, said Herbert Hoover, was "that any economic system would work in a mixture of others. No greater illusions ever mesmerized the American people." "Your President," said Leon Trotsky with contempt, "abhors 'systems' and 'generalities.' . . . Your philosophic method is even more antiquated than your economic system." But the American President always resisted ideological commitment. His determination was to keep options open within the general frame of a humanized democracy; and his belief was that the very diversity of systems strengthened the basis for freedom.

Without some critical vision, pragmatism could be a meaningless technique; the flight from ideology, a form of laziness; the middle way, an empty conception. For some politicians, such an approach meant nothing more than splitting the difference between extremes; the middle of the road was thus determined by the clamor from each side. At times it appeared to mean little more than this to Roosevelt. But at bottom he had a guiding vision with substantive content of its own. The content was not, however, intellectual; and this was where he disappointed more precise and exacting minds around him. It was rather a human content, a sense of the fortune and happiness of people. In 1936 a Canadian editor asked him to state his objectives. Roosevelt's off-the-cuff reply defined his goal in all its naïveté and power:

> . . . to do what any honest Government of any country would do; try to increase the security and the happiness of a larger number of people in all occupations of life and in all parts of the country; to give them more of the good things of life, to give them a greater distribution not only of wealth in the narrow terms, but of wealth in the wider terms; to give them places to go in the summer time—recreation; to give them assurance that they are not going to starve in their old age; to give honest business a

> chance to go ahead and make a reasonable profit, and to give everyone a chance to earn a living.

The listing was neither considered nor comprehensive, but the spirit was accurate. "The intellectual and spiritual climate," said Frances Perkins, "was Roosevelt's general attitude that *the people mattered.*" Nothing else would count until ordinary people were provided an environment and an opportunity "as good as human ingenuity can devise and fit for children of God."

Developed against the backdrop of depression, his philosophy of compassion had a particular bias toward the idea of security —"a greater physical and mental and spiritual security for the people of this country." "Security," he once said.

> means a kind of feeling within our individual selves that we have lacked all through the course of history. We have had to take our chance about our old age in days past. We have had to take our chance with depressions and boom times. We have had to take chances on buying our homes. I have believed for a great many years that the time has come in our civilization when a great many of these chances should be eliminated from our lives.

The urgencies of depression carried the concern for security to a degree which later generations, who thought they could assume abundance and move on to problems of opportunity and self-fulfillment, would find hard to understand. The old American dream, Roosevelt told a collection of young people in 1935, was the dream of the golden ladder—each individual for himself. But the newer generation would have a different dream: "Your advancement, you hope, is along a broad highway on which thousands of your fellow men and women are advancing with you." In many ways this was a dispiriting hope. In the longer run, security, while indispensable as a social minimum, might be cloying and perhaps even stultifying as a social ideal.

But this was a nuance imposed by depression. His essential ideals had an old-fashioned flavor. He was unconsciously seeing America in the Jeffersonian image of Dutchess County and Hyde Park. He hoped, as he said, to extend "to our national life the old principal of the local community, the principle that no individual, man, woman or child, has a right to do things that hurt his neighbors." "Our task of reconstruction does not require the creation of new and strange values. It is rather the finding of the way once more to known, but to some degree forgotten ideals." He wanted to make other people happy as he had been happy himself. Lifting his right hand high, his left hand only a little, he would say, "This difference is too big, it must become smaller—like this. . . . Wasn't I able to study, travel, take care of my sickness? The man who doesn't have to worry about his daily bread is securer and freer." He spoke of his philosophy as "social-mindedness." He meant by this essentially the humanization of industrial society.

A viewpoint so general provided no infallible guide to daily decision. Roosevelt therefore had to live by trial and error. His first term had its share of error: the overextension of NRA; the fumbling with monetary policy; the reluctant approach to spending; the waste of energy in trying to achieve the communitarian dream; the bungling of the London Economic Conference; the administrative confusion and conflict; the excessive reliance on ballyhoo and oratory. At times Roosevelt seemed almost to extemporize for the joy of it; his pragmatism appeared an addition to playing by ear in the nervous conviction that any kind of noise was better than silence. "Instead of being alarmed by the spirit of improvisation," wrote George Creel, "he seemed delighted by it, whooping on the improvisers with the excitement of one riding to hounds."

The chronic changing of front exposed the New Deal to repeated charges that it had no core of doctrine, that it was improvised and opportunistic, that it was guided only by circumstance. These charges were all true. But they also represented the New Deal's strength. For the advantage enjoyed by the pragmatists over the ideologists was their exceptional sensitivity to social and human reality. They measured results in terms not of conformity to *a priori* models but of concrete impact on people's lives. The New Deal thus had built-in mechanisms of feed-back, readjustment, and self-correction. Its incoherences were considerably more faithful to a highly complicated and shifting reality than any preconceived dogmatic system could have been. In the welter of confusion and ignorance, experiment corrected by compassion was the best answer.

Roosevelt's genius lay in the fact that he recognized—rather, rejoiced in—the challenge to the pragmatic nerve. His basic principle was not to sacrifice human beings to logic. Frances Perkins describes him as "in full revolt against the 'economic man.' " He had no philosophy save experiment, which was a technique; constitutionalism, which was a procedure; and humanity, which was a faith.

The depression, the Social Science Research Council Committee on Studies in Social Aspects of the Depression declared in unwontedly nonacademic language, "was like the explosion of a bomb dropped in the midst of society." It shook and strained the American community in a multitude of ways and profoundly challenged the nation's will to survive. The American people, in recording in 1936 so astonishing a vote of confidence in the New Deal, were by no means endorsing everything that had taken place in the tumultuous years since March 4, 1933. But they were voting unmistakably for the capacity of a representative democracy under strong leadership to produce energetic, resourceful, and free government in the face of an economic holocaust. And their vote came at a time when, throughout the west, faith in government by the people—faith in free society itself—was flickering and fading. While the men of Washington wrote their laws and established their agencies and set out to make America over, other men in Berlin and in Moscow looked confidently forward to the collapse of free institutions—and too few in free countries dared say them nay. In a real sense, the New Deal was testing the resources of democracy, not just for Americans, but for all mankind. Roosevelt's victory, said *The Times* of London, "is a matter of supreme importance at the moment when English-speaking nations are becoming more isolated as the champions of democracy in a world 'blown about by all the winds of doctrine.' "

Could the pragmatic experiment possibly work? Would not its failure hurtle the nation—and perhaps the western world—into darker and more desperate experiments? "I can hardly describe," said Winston Churchill, "with what eagerness, not only our working people, but all those who think about social problems in this island are watching the results of President Roosevelt's valiant effort to solve the riddle of the sphinx." "My whole impression," wrote Sir Stafford Cripps after visiting Roosevelt in 1935, "is of an honest anxious man faced by an impossible task—humanising capitalism and making it work." "It takes an opportunist and a moderate liberal to wreck capitalism in an hour of crisis and to prepare the way for the radical dictator," said Lawrence Dennis hopefully, adding, "Mr. Roosevelt is the Kerensky of American capitalism." Roosevelt sometimes used to make the Kerensky joke himself. No one can guess to what extent such jokes ventilated the interior doubts and fears which might well surge up in rare moments of solitude, when the shouting died away and he could not longer evade the ultimates. But Roosevelt had had private agonies before, and had conquered doubts and fears. There were historical consolations, too: Tugwell has compared the ordeal of Roosevelt's struggle against depression with the ordeal of Lincoln's struggle against disunion—the generals tried and dismissed, the strategic plans adopted and discarded, the troubles with Congress and the Supreme Court, the resistance of the faint of heart and the stubborn of mind, the waste and the tears, until at last national energies came into focus and produced victory.

Whatever might haunt Roosevelt in the dark of night, he showed nothing in the daylight but confidence and decision. He well knew that more was at stake than America—that the challenge of achieving economic security within a framework of freedom offered civilized society a decisive test. No one stated the challenge more exactly than John Maynard Keynes in his letter to Roosevelt at the end of 1933.

"You have made yourself," Keynes said, "the trustee for those in every country who seek to mend the evils of our condition by reasoned experiment within the framework of the existing social system.

"If you fail, rational choice will be gravely prejudiced throughout the world, leaving orthodoxy and revolution to fight it out.

"But, if you succeed, new and bolder methods will be tried everywhere, and we may date the first chapter of a new economic era from your accession to office."

He was apparently succeeding; and people could start to believe again in the free state and its capacity to solve problems of economic stability and social justice. Free society, in consequence, might not yet be finished; it had a future; it might have the strength and steadfastness to surmount the totalitarian challenge. Franklin Roosevelt and Adolf Hitler had come to power together in 1933. Four years later their two images were more sharply juxtaposed than ever, symbolizing a conflict between profoundly different views of society and humanity.

When Roosevelt was re-elected in 1936, the French Chamber of Deputies passed, without dissent, a resolution of congratulations. "Henceforth democracy has its chief!" said *Paris-Soir.* "After his brilliant triumph President Roosevelt has become the statesman on whom every hope is to be pinned if the great liberal and democratic civilization of the west is one day threatened, either by Bolshevism or by autocracy." "No dictator, whether Fascist or Communist," said *The Times* of London, "can challenge the solid basis of his backing. None can afford so securely to take the course which he believes to be right without regard for any need of a spell-bound popularity."

In England, Winston Churchill, roused from his pessimism of 1930, took a new look at the prospects of freedom. "His impulse," Churchill wrote of Roosevelt, "is one which makes toward the fuller life of the masses of the people in every land, and which, as it glows the brighter, may well eclipse both the lurid flames of German Nordic self-assertion and the baleful unnatural lights which are diffused from Soviet Russia."

For all his absorption in the struggle for American recovery during these years, Roosevelt had watched the spread of fascism and aggression with increasing apprehension. The only answer, he felt, was the strengthened vitality of democracy. When he accepted renomination at Franklin Field on June 27, 1936, he seemed also to accept a larger challenge. There were, he said, people in other lands who had once fought for freedom, but who now appeared too weary to carry on the fight, who had "sold their heritage of freedom for the illusion of a living."

"I believe in my heart," Roosevelt said, "that only our success can stir their ancient hope. They begin to know that here in America we are waging a great and successful war. It is not alone a war against want and destitution and economic demoralization. It is more than that: it is a war for the survival of democracy. We are fighting to save a great and precious form of government for ourselves and for the world.

"I accept the commission you have tendered me. I join with you. I am enlisted for the duration of the war."

James MacGregor Burns

FDR: UNSUCCESSFUL IMPROVISER

JAMES MACGREGOR BURNS, Professor of Political Science at Williams College, like Arthur Schlesinger, Jr., has long been active in liberal politics. One of his special concerns has been the analysis of those American political institutions which have blocked progressive reforms, a problem he has discussed in *Congress on Trial* (1949) and *The Deadlock of Democracy* (1963). This concern pervaded his superb political biography, *Roosevelt: The Lion and the Fox,* and resulted in the first important critique of FDR by a liberal historian.

Burns argues, first of all, that Roosevelt failed to end the depression despite the fact that the formula for doing so, Keynesian economic policy, was available and was being urged upon the President by its brilliant creator. Burns believes that Roosevelt's mind was too undisciplined, too unsystematic, to accept even a program which so perfectly embodied the "middle way" between individualistic capitalism and socialism. Keynesian economics called for a complete commitment; the depression could be ended if the government were willing to inject enough money into the economy, but a little bit of deficit spending, while it might improve economic conditions, could not bring complete recovery. FDR could not grasp this point. His idea of the middle way was a compromise between diametrically opposed solutions. Consequently, the New

From *Roosevelt: The Lion and the Fox* by James MacGregor Burns, pp. 328–336, 375–380, 400–404. Copyright © 1956 by James MacGregor Burns. Reprinted by permission of the publishers, Harcourt, Brace & World, Inc.

Deal never undertook the program of massive spending which the nation needed, and its inability to end the depression was "a major failure of American democracy."

Even more critical was Roosevelt's failure to reorganize the party system and establish the Democratic party as a positive liberal force in American politics. During the years when his prestige was at its peak, he worked with a regular party organization dominated by Southern conservatives and non-ideological city bosses. He made no effort to undertake the difficult but necessary job of rebuilding the party structure from the bottom up. By 1938, when he attempted to "purge" several leading conservatives in Democratic party primary elections, it was too late. (A subsequent effort in the fall of 1944 to attract Wendell Willkie and his liberal Republican following into the party was aborted by Willkie's sudden death.) As a result, the Democratic party remained a loose coalition of conflicting groups incapable of continuing and enlarging the New Deal.

Unable to make basic commitments at key moments, "captive to his habit of mediating among pressures rather than reshaping them," FDR "was less a great creative leader than a skillful manipulator and a brilliant interpreter." Whatever his successes, "he failed to achieve that combination of tactical skill and strategic planning that represents the acme of political leadership."

Burns actually has a large degree of sympathy for Roosevelt; nevertheless, his critique is a harsh one. Those who disagree would argue that the author undervalues the many accomplishments of the New Deal, underestimates the many problems and pressures which diverted Roosevelt from party realignment, fails to grasp the novelty of Keynesian economics in the 1930's, and exaggerates the powers of the Presidency. Still, *Roosevelt: The Lion and the Fox* expresses the most important and convincing critique of its subject yet made. It is securely established as one of the great books on FDR and the New Deal.

ROOSEVELT AS AN ECONOMIST

One day late in Roosevelt's second term Marriner Eccles reported at the White House to raise some pressing economic questions with the President. He had been promised an hour-long luncheon engagement—a prize that an administrator might spend weeks conniving for. To his dismay, he found that Senator McAdoo was cutting into his time. When Eccles finally got into the President's study the burly old Californian was standing over Roosevelt and declaiming about the political situation back home.

"Bring up a chair, Marriner," the President said. To McAdoo he added: "Marriner and I are just about to have lunch."

McAdoo was too engrossed in his problems to take the hint. "Oh, that's all right," he said, "you two boys go right ahead—I'll talk while you eat."

Reaching to a warming oven next to his chair, Roosevelt pulled out a plate. It was burning hot. Juggling it awkwardly, he managed to place it before Eccles. While the President shook his scorched fingers and Eccles burned inside, McAdoo continued to talk. He finally wound up:

"Now, remember, Franklin. I want to leave one last thought with you. When it comes to appointing any of those federal judges in California, I wish you would take the matter up with me instead of with that son-of-a-bitch Downey. . . ."

McAdoo finally left. Marveling at Roosevelt's good humor through all this, Eccles leaned forward to talk. But as the waiter rolled away the tray there was a new diversion. Fala bounded in, Roosevelt took a ball out of his desk, and for several minutes the dog played retriever for his master, while Eccles feebly voiced words of praise.

"That's enough now," Roosevelt said to Fala. "I've got to get back to work." Eccles started talking, but after a few minutes he saw that he had lost his audience. Roosevelt was looking around the room for Fala. Suddenly the President burst out: "Well, I'll be God-damned! Marriner, do you see what I see?"

Eccles did. Over in a corner Fala was committing an indiscretion on the rug. Several more minutes elapsed while Roosevelt summoned a guard, had Fala's nose rubbed in the mess, and delivered a post mortem. By now Eccles' time was almost up. He left in a blind rage. To his associates awaiting him expectantly at the Federal Reserve Building he could report only on California politics and on the doings of Fala.

This sort of thing happened many times. People were amazed at Roosevelt's governmental habits—at his way of running through a series of wholly unrelated conferences like a child in a playroom turning from toy to toy, at his ability seemingly to put one matter out of his head when he turned to another, above all at his serenity and even gaiety under the pitiless pressures of men and events. The methods, of course, reflected the man. Roosevelt's mental agility and flexibility were well suited to the experimental phase of the New Deal. In 1938 Roosevelt was still the improviser, still the pragmatist.

Was practicality enough? Roosevelt's fumbling and indecisiveness during the recession showed his failings as an economist and thinker. His distrust of old and doctrinaire theories freed him from slavery to ideas that would have been risky in the 1930's. But at the same time, that distrust helped cut him off from the one economist and the one economic idea that might have provided a spectacular solution to Roosevelt's chief economic, political, and constitutional difficulties.

The man was the noted British economist John Maynard Keynes. An academician who was yet a leader in the bizarre Bloomsbury set, an economist who had won and lost fortunes as a speculator, a Cambridge don who also ran insurance companies, a prickly intellectual who was close to men of affairs throughout the world, a reformer who believed in liberal capitalism, Keynes for two decades had been provoking British opinion with his unorthodox views of economics, industry, and international affairs. In 1936 he had published the capstone of his economic thought, *The General Theory of Employment, Interest, and Money.* Bristling with critical references to cherished theories and honored names, filled with strange terms and equations, punctuated by lengthy appendixes, the *General Theory* had been read by few. But its impact on liberal economists in America was already making itself felt.

For, out of all the complexities and involutions of Keynes's writings, there emerged a central idea that was dazzling in its stark simplicity. Classical economics dictated that in bad times governments must permit if not encourage lower wages, lower prices, and rigorously balanced budgets. Purged and cleansed by this stringent process, the economy could then right itself and once again march up the long foothills to the mountain peaks of the business cycle. Keynes boldly assaulted this notion. The nub of his advice to government in time of depression was to unbalance the budget deliberately by heavy spending and low taxes. Only through heavy spending by consumers and investing by government or private capitalists could the economy right itself.

To call any single doctrine a "solution" is, of course, dangerous business. Keynesianism, moreover, is still a highly controversial topic among economists and policy makers; its usefulness is sharply limited depending on the nature of an economy, the people, the condition, and the time. Yet it seems clear that if ever the idea of deficit financing had urgent applicability, it was to the America of the 1930's, with its huge army of unemployed, its vast raw materials, and the state of its industrial arts.

In the first place, deficit spending was constitutional. When at a social gathering Justice Stone whispered to Miss Perkins, "My dear, the taxing power is sufficient for everything you want and need," he was in effect reminding the administration of its plenitude of power in the whole fiscal realm as compared with other avenues that could be blocked off by judicial action. Indeed, a great authority on the Constitution, Professor Edward S. Corwin of Princeton, had predicted the "twilight of the Supreme Court" because the Court, by making difficult a legal challenge to federal appropriations, had left to Congress power over spending and taxing.

Massive deficit spending was politically feasible too. Despite the ceaseless talk of economy on the Hill, Congress, at least during Roosevelt's first five years, was eager to spend. It is an old political bromide that congressmen want to vote for all spending bills and against all taxing bills—which happens to be just the right combination for deficit spending. The President often had to throw his weight *against* the congressional spenders, as in the case of the veterans' bonus. If Roosevelt had urged spending programs on Congress rather than the court plan and certain reform measures in 1937, he probably could have both met his commitments to the one-third ill-housed, ill-fed, and ill-clothed and achieved substantial re-employment.

Deficit spending was ideally suited to Roosevelt's ideology and program. He was no doctrinaire capitalist; twenty years before his presidency he was a New Deal state senator favoring a host of governmental controls and reforms, and he had stood for progressivism as a Wilson lieutenant and as governor. He was no doctrinaire socialist; he had never embraced the idea of central state ownership of the means of production. Rejecting both doctrinaire solutions, Keynesian economics was a true middle way—at a time when New Dealers were groping for a middle way that worked.

As a practical man, Roosevelt liked to apply the test, "Will it work?" Deficit spending *had* worked in 1935 and 1936 with the huge relief programs, veterans' bonus payments, and monetary expansion. Then had come a shift to the opposite policy: relief spending had been cut, reserve requirements for commercial banks raised, holdings of securities by banks reduced, and the growth of loans slowed. This shift from deficit spending had *not* worked. Both experiments had been fairly conclusive, each in its way; Roosevelt might have wanted the chance to experiment further, but a nation can hardly be expected to serve indefinitely as a laboratory.

Why did this most practical of men miss out on what probably would have been the ideal solution for his economic, political, and judicial problems?

Not because Keynes had failed to reach him. The Englishman had corresponded with the President, and he had talked with him in 1934. The two men liked each other, but the intellectual and the politician were cut from different cloth: Roosevelt was dubious about Keynes's "rigmarole of figures" and seemed surprised to find him a mathematician rather than a political economist; for his part Keynes was disappointed that the President was not more literate in economics.

From England, Keynes had watched the sharp decline of late 1937 with mounting anxiety. On February 1, 1938, he had written the President a long and eloquent letter. "You received me so kindly when I visited you some three years ago that I make bold to send you some bird's eye impressions. . . ." After a disclaimer of omniscience, Keynes delivered a polite but candid attack on the administration's recent economic policies. There had been an "error of optimism," he said, in 1936. Recovery was possible only through a large-scale recourse to public works and other investments. The administration had had an unexampled opportunity to organize increased investment in durable goods such as housing, public utilities and transport.

Could the administration, asked Keynes, escape criticism for the failure of increased investment? "The handling of the housing problem has been really wicked," and housing could be the best aid to recovery. As for utilities, their litigation against the government was senseless. But as for the allegedly wicked holding companies, no one had suggested a way to unscramble the eggs. The President should either make peace with the utilities or be more drastic. Keynes leaned toward nationalizing them, but if public opinion was not yet ripe for that, what was the point of "chasing the utilities around the lot every other week"? As for railroads, either take them over or have pity on the overwhelming problems of the managers.

Keynes even tried to educate the President on the nature of businessmen. They had a different set of delusions from politicians, he warned, and thus required different handling. "They are, however, much milder than politicians, at the same time allured and terrified by the glare of publicity, easily persuaded to be 'patriots,' perplexed, bemused, indeed terrified, yet only too anxious to take a cheerful view, vain perhaps but very unsure of themselves, pathetically responsive to a kind word. You could do anything you liked with them, if you would treat them (even the big ones), not as wolves and tigers, but as domestic animals by nature, even though they have been badly brought up and not trained as you would wish."

It was a mistake, Keynes went on, to think that businessmen were more immoral than politicians. "If you work them into the surly, obstinate, terrified mood of which domestic animals, wrongly handled, are so capable, the nation's burden will not get carried to market; and in the end, public opinion will veer their way. . . ."

"Forgive the candour of these remarks," Keynes had concluded. He listed half a dozen administration policies he supported with enthusiasm. "But I am terrified lest progressive causes in all the democratic countries should suffer injury, because you have taken too lightly the risk to their prestige which would result from a failure measured in terms of immediate prosperity. There *need* be no failure. But the maintenance of prosperity in the modern world is extremely *difficult;* and it is so easy to lose precious time."

The eloquent appeal had not moved the President. He asked Morgenthau to write a reply to Keynes for him, and the President signed as written the banal little letter that Morgenthau produced. Two months later Roosevelt did resume spending, of course, but it was not the kind of massive spending that Keynes was calling for.

Part of the reason for Roosevelt's failure to exploit Keynes and his ideas lay in the web of political circumstances. Lacking a coherent economic philosophy in 1932, Roosevelt had opportunistically pummeled Hoover from both right and left, attacking him both for do-nothing government *and* for unbalancing the budget. Roosevelt had thus committed himself to a balanced budget, at least in the long run, and during his presidential years he mired himself further in this swamp. The more he unbalanced the budget, the more—literally scores of times—he insisted that eventually he would balance it. The more he promised, the more he gave hostages to the conservatives on the Hill and in his party. His personal stand became party policy in both the 1932 and 1936 platforms.

Another reason for the failure lay with Roosevelt's advisers. Some of them, of course, opposed any type of heavy spending; but even those who leaned toward a new economic program were unable to exploit the full potential of Keynes's idea. Some of them were mainly concerned about price rigidity—so concerned, indeed, that they wished to make this the main basis of a campaign against big business. Some were more worried about inflation than continuing unemployment. Some wanted to penalize business by raising taxes—good politics, perhaps, but a contradiction of the Keynesian idea of lowering taxes while increasing spending. Some, lacking faith in the long-term prospects of capitalism in America, believed in a theory of secular stagnation that did not admit that Keynesian economics was a basic solution. Some were believers only in pump priming; the government could pour heavy doses of purchasing power into the economy, as it had in 1935 and 1936, but after that business was supposed to man the pumps.

These splits even among his liberal advisers reflected to some extent the haphazard fashion in which Roosevelt had assembled his brain trust. Even so, there were few out-and-out Keynesians in the government, and most of these were in the lower echelons and lacked access to the President. And Keynesian theory was so new that certain statistical and analytical tools were lacking.

The main reason for Roosevelt's failure in the economic sphere, however, lay neither in the political situation nor in his divided advisers. With his immense political resourcefulness and volatility Roosevelt could always have broken out of the party and congressional web, at least in 1936 and early 1937. He could always have changed his advisers. His main trouble was intellectual. Roosevelt was simply unable as a thinker to seize the opportunity that Keynesian economics gave him. His failure as an economist was part of a broader intellectual failure.

What was the nature of this failure? Roosevelt's mind was an eminently operative one, quick, keen, fast, flexible. It showed in his intellectual habits. He disdained elaborate, fine-spun theories; he paid little attention to the long and abstract briefs that academic people were always sending him on ways of improving administration, on strengthening the cabinet as an institution, on dealing with Congress. He hated abstractions. His mind yearned for the detail, the particular, the specific. Invariably he answered general questions in terms of examples —in terms of an individual business, of a farmer in Kansas, of a problem in Hyde Park, of a situation during the Wilson administration. He had a passion for the concrete.

His working habits bespoke his mind. From the start of his day to the end, from his skimming through a half-dozen newspapers at breakfast through a schedule of quick conferences on a score of different subjects to his playing with his stamps before bedtime, his mind sped from topic to topic, picking them up, toying with them, and dropping them. His intellectual habits were not disorderly; they were staccato.

Roosevelt's mental way of life was nourished by its own successes. He liked to outwit the reporters in fast repartee. He liked to show off the incredible knowledge of a wide variety of specific matters that he carried in his head. Sometimes there was a touch of fakery in this, for the President could steer a conversation toward a subject on which he was newly briefed. But to an extraordinary extent he grasped an immediate, specific situation in all its particulars and complexity. He knew, for example, the tangled political situations and multitude of personalities in each of the states; he could talk for hours about the housing, roads, people, and history of Hyde Park; he could describe knowledgeably the activities and problems of a host of businesses and industries; he could pull out of his head hundreds of specific prices, rents, wages; he could identify countless varieties of fish, birds, trees; he could not be stumped on geography.

His self-esteem as a practical man must have been fed, too, by the ignorance of so many of his critics. Many men of affairs were slaves to the theories of defunct economists, and Roosevelt could puncture their pretensions with his knowledge of their own business and its relation to the rest of the world. His indignant complaints to his friends about the businessmen's failure to advance specific constructive suggestions was the lament of the practitioner against the theorist. Undoubtedly Roosevelt's emphasis on his own practicality had an element of overcompensation too. Cartoonists in 1938 were still picturing him as a fuzzy theorist surrounded by bemused brain trusters; and a friend who had romped with him as a child in the Hyde Park nursery, and who had evidently learned little since those days, rebuked him with the words: "You are not an essentially practical person."

And now, by a supreme irony, fate placed before this man of practicality an economic theory that seemed to embody only uncommon sense. The idea of boosting spending and holding down taxes and of doing this year after year as a deliberate policy, the idea of gaining prosperity by the deliberate creation of huge debts—this idea in its full dimensions seemed but another fanciful academic theory, and Roosevelt by 1938 had had a bellyful of such theories. Pump priming as a temporary emergency measure he could understand—but not deficit spending as the central, long-term approach to full-scale economic recovery.

Deficit spending posed a special intellectual problem for the President. If there had been consistency in his handling of economic affairs, it was his habit of trying to make economic decisions by combining opposites. "Lock yourself in a room and don't come out until you agree," he would say blithely to people who differed hopelessly in their economic premises—to free traders and nationalists, to deflationists and inflationists, to trust busters and collectivists, to spenders and economizers. The trouble with deficit spending was that halfway application did not work. It had utility only through full and determined use; otherwise it served only to antagonize and worry business by increasing the public debt without sufficiently raising spending and investment.

A Keynesian solution, in short, involved an almost absolute commitment, and Roosevelt was not one to commit himself absolutely to any political or economic method. His mind was a barometric reflection of the personal and policy pressures around him. "We are at one of those uncommon junctures of human affairs," Keynes said in the 1930's, "when we can be saved by the solution of intellectual problems and in no other way." But Roosevelt's mind was attuned to the handling of a great variety of operational and tactical matters, not to the solving of intellectual problems.

Roosevelt's deficiencies as an economist were as striking as his triumphs as a politician. It was a major failure of American democracy that it was not able in the late 1930's to show that a great nation could provide jobs for its workers and food, clothes, and houses for its people. What Roosevelt could not achieve World War II would achieve as a by-product enabling Republicans to charge later that the New Deal could end depression only through war. It was a personal failure for Roosevelt too. Halfway through his second term the man who had ousted Hoover on the depression issue knew that eight or nine million people were walking the streets. He knew that millions were still living in shanties and tenements, and that some were not far from starvation. Would the great promise of January 1937 become a mockery?

ROOSEVELT AS A PARTY LEADER

The New Deal, wrote historian Walter Millis toward the end of 1938, "has been reduced to a movement with no program, with no effective political organization, with no vast popular party strength behind it, and with no candidate." The passage of time has not invalidated this judgment. But it has sharpened the question: Why did the most gifted campaigner of his time receive and deserve this estimate only two years after the greatest election triumph in recent American history?

The answer lay partly in the kind of political tactics Roosevelt had used ever since the time he started campaigning for president. In 1931 and 1932, he had, like any ambitious politician, tried to win over Democratic leaders and groups that embraced a great variety of attitudes and interests. Since the Democratic party was deeply divided among its sectional and ideological splinter groups, Roosevelt began the presidential campaign of 1932 with a mixed and ill-assorted group backing. Hoover's unpopularity with many elements in his own party brought various Republican and independent groups to Roosevelt's support. Inevitably the mandate of 1932 was a highly uncertain one, except that the new President must do something —anything—to cope with the Depression.

Responding to the crisis, Roosevelt assumed in his magnificent way the role of leader of all the people. Playing down his party support he mediated among a host of conflicting interest groups, political leaders, and ideological proponents. During the crisis atmosphere of 1933 his broker leadership worked. He won enormous popularity, he put through his crisis program, he restored the morale of the whole nation. The congressional elections of 1934 were less a tribute to the Democratic party than a testament of the President's wide support.

Then his ill-assorted following began to unravel at the edges. The right wing rebelled, labor erupted, Huey Long and others stepped up their harrying attacks. As a result of these political developments, the cancellation of part of the New Deal by the courts, and the need to put through the waiting reform bills, Roosevelt made a huge, sudden, and unplanned shift leftward. The shift put him in the role of leader of a great, though teeming and amorphous, coalition of center and liberal groups; it left him, in short, as party chief. From mid-1935 to about the end of 1938 Roosevelt deserted his role as broker among all groups and assumed the role as party leader commanding his Grand Coalition of the center and left.

This role, too, the President played magnificently, most notably in the closing days of the 1936 campaign. During 1937 he spoke often of Jefferson and Jackson and of other great presidents who, he said, had served as great leaders of popular majorities. During 1938 he tried to perfect the Democratic party as an instrument of a popular majority. But in the end the effort failed—in the court fight, the defeat of effective recovery measures, and the party purge.

That failure had many causes. The American constitutional system had been devised to prevent easy capture of the government by popular majorities. The recovery of the mid-1930's not only made the whole country more confident of itself and less dependent on the leader in the White House, but it strengthened and emboldened a host of interest groups and leaders, who soon were pushing beyond the limits of New Deal policy and of Roosevelt's leadership. Too, the party system could not easily be reformed or modernized, and the anti-third-term custom led to expectations that Roosevelt was nearing the end of his political power. But the failure also stemmed from Roosevelt's limitations as a political strategist.

The trouble was that Roosevelt had assumed his role as party or majority leader not as part of a deliberate, planned political strategy but in response to a conjunction of immediate developments. As majority leader he relied on his personal popularity, on his *charisma* or warm emotional appeal. He did not try to build up a solid, organized mass base for the extended New Deal that he projected in the inaugural speech of 1937. Lacking such a mass base, he could not establish a rank-and-file majority group in Congress to push through his program. Hence the court fight ended as a congressional fight in which the President had too few reserve forces to throw into the battle.

Roosevelt as party leader, in short, never made the strategic commitment that would allow a carefully considered, thorough, and long-term attempt at party reorganization. The purge marked the bankruptcy of his party leadership. For five years the President had made a fetish of his refusal to interfere in "local" elections. When candidates—many of them stalwart New Dealers—had turned desperately to the White House for support, McIntyre or Early had flung at them the "unbreakable" rule that "the President takes no part in local elections." When the administration's good friend Key Pittman had faced a coalition of Republicans and McCarran Democrats in 1934, all Roosevelt could say was "I wish to goodness I could speak out loud in meeting and tell Nevada that I am one thousand per cent for you!" but an "imposed silence in things like primaries is one of the many penalties of my job." When cabinet members had asked during the 1934 elections if they could make campaign speeches, Roosevelt had said, No, except in their own states.

After all this delicacy Roosevelt in 1938 completely reversed himself and threw every ounce of the administration's political weight—money, propaganda, newspaper influence, federal jobholders as well as his own name—into local campaigns in an effort to purge his foes. He mainly failed, and his failure was due in large part to his earlier policy. After five years of being ignored by the White House, local candidates and party groups were not amenable to presidential control. Why should they be? The White House had done little enough for them.

The execution of the purge in itself was typical of Roosevelt's improvising methods. Although the problem of party defections had been evident for months and the idea of a purge had been taking shape in the winter of 1938, most of the administration's efforts were marked by hurried, inadequate, and amateurish maneuvers at the last minute. In some states the White House interfered enough to antagonize the opponent within the party but not enough to insure his defeat. Roosevelt's own tactics were marked by a strange combination of rashness and irresolution, of blunt face-to-face encounters and wily, backscene stratagems.

But Roosevelt's main failure as party leader lay not in the purge. It involved the condition of the Democratic party in state after state six years after he took over as national Democratic chief. Pennsylvania, for example, was the scene of such noisy brawling among labor, New Dealers, and old-line Democrats that Roosevelt himself compared it to Dante's Inferno. A bitter feud wracked the Democracy in Illinois. The Democrats in Wisconsin, Nebraska, and Minnesota were still reeling under their ditchings by the White House in 1934 and 1936. The party in California was split among organization Democrats, $30 every Thursday backers, and a host of other factions.

In New York the condition of the Democratic party was even more significant, for Roosevelt had detailed knowledge of politics in his home state and had no inhibitions about intervening there. He intervened so adroitly and indirectly in the New York City mayoralty elections of 1933 that politicians were arguing years later as to which Democratic faction he had aided, or whether he was intent mainly on electing La Guardia. In 1936 he encouraged the formation of the Labor party in New York State to help his own re-election, and he pooh-poohed the arguments of Farley, Flynn, and other Democrats that the Labor party would some day turn against the state Democracy—as indeed it later did. By 1938 the Democratic party in New York State was weaker and more faction-ridden than it had been for many years.

It was characteristic of Roosevelt to interpret the 1938 election setbacks largely in terms of the weakness of local Democratic candidates and leaders. Actually the trouble lay much deeper. The President's failure to build a stronger party system at the grass roots, more directly responsive to national direction and more closely oriented around New Deal programs and issues, left a political vacuum that was rapidly filled by power groupings centered on state and local leaders holding office or contending for office. Roosevelt and his New Deal had vastly strengthened local party groups in the same way they had organized interest groups. And just as, nationally, the New Deal jolted interest groups out of their lethargy and mobilized them into political power groups that threatened to disrupt the Roosevelt coalition, so the New Deal stimulated local party groups to throw off the White House apron strings.

"If our beloved leader," wrote William Allen White to Farley early in the second term, "cannot find the least common multiple between John Lewis and Carter Glass he will have to take a maul and crack the monolith, forget that he had a party and build his policy with the pieces which fall under his hammer." The perceptive old Kansan's comment was typical of the hopes of many liberals of the day. The President had pulled so many rabbits out of his hat. Could he not produce just one more?

The purge indicated that he could not. The hat was empty. But White's suggestion posed the cardinal test of Roosevelt as party leader. How much leeway did the President have? Was it ever possible for him to build a stronger party? Or did the nature of the American party system, and especially the Democratic party, preclude the basic changes that would have been necessary to carry through the broader New Deal that the President proclaimed in his second-term inaugural?

On the face of it the forces of inertia were impressive. The American party system does not lend itself easily to change. In its major respects the national party is a holding company for complex and interlacing clusters of local groups revolving around men holding or contending for innumerable state and local offices—governors, sheriffs, state legislators, mayors, district attorneys, United States senators, county commissioners, city councilmen, and so on, all strung loosely together by party tradition, presidential leadership, and, to some extent, common ideas. As long as the American constitutional system creates electoral prizes to hold and contend for in the states and localities, the party is likely to remain undisciplined and decentralized.

Long immersed in the local undergrowth of American politics, Roosevelt was wholly familiar with the obstacles to party change. His refusal to break with some of the more unsavory local bosses like Hague and Kelly is clear evidence that he had no disposition to undertake the most obvious kind of reform. Perhaps, though, the President underestimated the possibility of party invigoration from the top.

Some New Dealers, worried by the decay of the Democratic party as a bulwark for progressive government, wanted to build up "presidential" factions pledged to the New Deal, factions that could lift the party out of the ruck of local bickering and orient it toward its national program. Attempts to build such presidential factions were abortive. They might have succeeded, however, had the President given them direction and backing. The New Deal had stimulated vigorous new elements in the party that put programs before local patronage, that were chiefly concerned with national policies of reform and recovery. By joining hands with these elements, by exploiting his own popularity and his control over the national party machinery, the President could have challenged anti-New Deal factions and tried to convert neutralists into backers of the New Deal.

Whether such an attempt would have succeeded cannot be answered because the attempt was never made. Paradoxically enough, however, the purge itself indicates that a long-run, well-organized effort might have worked in many states. For the purge did succeed under two conditions—in a Northern urban area, where there was some planning rather than total improvisation, and in those Southern states where the White House was helping a well-entrenched incumbent rather than trying to oust a well-entrenched opponent. The first was the case of O'Connor, the second the cases of Pepper and of Barkley.* Indeed, the results of the purge charted a rough line be-

* John J. O'Connor, a conservative New York Democrat who chaired the House Rules Committee, was successfully "purged" in the 1938 Democratic primary. Pro-New Deal Senators Claude Pepper (Florida) and Alben Barkley (Kentucky) received White House assistance in their successful campaigns for renomination.—Ed.

tween the area within the presidential reach and the area beyond it. Undoubtedly the former area would have been much bigger had Roosevelt systematically nourished New Deal strength within the party during his first term.

But he did not. The reasons that the President ignored the potentialities of the great political organization he headed were manifold. He was something of a prisoner of the great concessions he had made to gain the 1932 nomination, including the admission of Garner and other conservatives to the inner circle. His first-term success had made his method of personal leadership look workable; overcoming crisis after crisis through his limitless resourcefulness and magnetism, Roosevelt did not bother to organize the party for the long run. As a politician eager to win, Roosevelt was concerned with his own political and electoral standing at whatever expense to the party. It was much easier to exploit his own political skill than try to improve the rickety, sprawling party organization.

The main reason, however, for Roosevelt's failure to build up the party lay in his unwillingness to commit himself to the full implications of party leadership, in his eternal desire to keep open alternative tactical lines of action, including a line of retreat. The personal traits that made Roosevelt a brilliant tactician—his dexterity, his command of a variety of roles, his skill in attack and defense, above all his personal magnetism and *charisma*—were not the best traits for hard, long-range purposeful building of a strong popular movement behind a coherent political program. The latter would have demanded a continuing intellectual and political commitment to a set strategy—and this kind of commitment Roosevelt would not make.

He never forgot the great lesson of Woodrow Wilson, who got too far ahead of his followers. Perhaps, though, he never appreciated enough Wilson's injunction that "if the President leads the way, his party can hardly resist him." If Roosevelt had led and organized the party toward well-drawn goals, if he had aroused and tied into the party the masses of farmers and workers and reliefers and white-collar workers and minority religious and racial groups, if he had met the massed power of group interests with an organized movement of his own, the story of the New Deal on the domestic front during the second term might have been quite different.

Thus Roosevelt can be described as a great party leader only if the term is rigidly defined. On the one hand he tied the party, loosely perhaps, to a program; he brought it glorious victories; he helped point it in new ideological directions. On the other hand, he subordinated the party to his own political needs; he failed to exploit its full possibilities as a source of liberal thought and action; and he left the party, at least at its base, little stronger than when he became its leader.

ROOSEVELT AS A POLITICAL LEADER

No leader is a free agent. Even Hitler had to cope with grumbling and foot dragging among the military; even Stalin had to deal with backward peasants and with party rivals grasping for power. Roosevelt's plight was far more difficult. He was captain of the ship of state, but many hands reached for the tiller, and a rebellious crew manned the sails. It was only natural that this vessel should move ahead by hugging the shore, threading its way past shoal and reef, putting into harbor when the storm roared. The test of great political leadership is not whether the leader has his way; it is, first, whether the leader makes the most of existing materials he has to work with, and, second, whether he creates new materials to help him meet his goals.

At the end of 1939, as Roosevelt neared the last year of his second term, it was time to apply to him both tests of leadership. His goal had always been clear in broad outline—a prosperous people in a secure nation. By the end of 1939 this goal was still far off. Economic conditions had improved since the recession, but not back to the uncertain levels of the mid-1930's, with millions out of work. And as the President himself saw more clearly than most Americans, the nation was in grave peril.

The ship of state had not reached port; neither had it foundered. How had the captain done?

Undeniably the reefs and shoals were formidable. Any attempt to chart a clear course to port—in this case to build a liberal program for New Deal objectives—ran head on into the absence of a cohesive liberal tradition in America. Any effort to shape long-term economic programs ran up against limited understanding of economic problems. Any effort to build a consistent foreign policy that would throw the country's weight toward peace and against the aggressors encountered the fierce isolationism of most Americans. The political and governmental means to these ends were equally hard to forge. Attempts to build a stronger "presidential party" behind the New Deal fell afoul of the federal, factional make-up of the existing party system. Any effort to establish a cohesive rank-and-file group for New Deal policies in Congress splintered against the entrenched power of seniority. Even the attempt to fashion a more cohesive executive branch ran into the centrifugal tendencies of the American system and the pervasive popular fear of executive power.

But what was the factor of creative leadership in these lost battles? Could it be said that Roosevelt had tried and failed? Was it bad luck, or a rebellious crew, or a flimsy ship that had kept him from reaching port? Or was the blame his alone?

There is an important difference between the politician who is simply an able tactician, and the politician who is a creative political leader. The former accepts political conditions as given and fashions a campaign and a set of policies best suited to the existing conditions. The latter tries consciously to change the matrix of political forces amid which he operates, in order that he may better lead the people in the direction he wants to go. The former operates within slender margins; the latter, through sheer will and conviction as well as political skill, tries to widen the margins within which he operates. He seeks not merely to win votes but consciously to alter basic political forces such as public opinion, party power, interest-group pressure, the governmental system.

There were times—most notably in 1935—when Roosevelt brilliantly capitalized on every opportunity to convert New Deal aims into law. There were times—most notably in the court fight—when he tested and found the outer limits of his power. But sometimes he made no effort at all—especially in gaining lasting influence in Congress. Sometimes he tried too little and too late. And sometimes—as in the case of party consolidation and realignment and of economic program—he seemed to lack the intellectual qualities necessary to the task.

During his second term Roosevelt seemed to forget the great lesson of his inaugural speech of 1933—that courageous affirmation in itself changes the political dimensions of a situation.

That speech was more than a speech—it was an act that loosened a tidal wave of support behind the new administration. The most important instrument a leader has to work with is himself—his own personality and its impact on other people. When the people's opinions are vaguely directed the way the leader is headed but lack depth and solidity, action by the leader can shift opinion in his own favor. In the parallelogram of forces in which the leader operates, such action alters the whole equation. To be sure, more than speeches was needed after 1937, for the feeling of crisis had gone and popular attitudes had hardened. But the inaugural speech of 1933 stood as an index of the leader's influence when he takes a posture of bold affirmation.

Roosevelt's failure to build a liberal coalition and a new party behind the New Deal is a further case in point. For here the materials were available for the right shaping and mixing. To be sure, most Americans during the mid-1930's as an abstract matter opposed realigning the parties along liberal and conservative lines. But when confronted in 1938 with the question of following "President Roosevelt's" proposal that old party lines be disregarded and that liberals of all parties unite to support liberal candidates for Congress, twice as many people favored as opposed the idea. The missing key was long-term and effective organization by Roosevelt of firmer support for realignment. Despite its failure, the purge showed the great potential of party realignment in the North and in the border states.

As for foreign policy, at potential turning points of public opinion—most notably in 1935 and 1936, when the people's fear of war might have been directed toward internationalist policies rather than isolationist ones—the President had failed to give the cue the people needed. Roosevelt did not exploit his superior information about the foreign situation and his understanding of foreign policy in order to guide popular attitudes.

Indeed, Roosevelt to a surprising degree was captive to the political forces around him rather than their shaper. In a democracy such must ever be the case. But democracy assigns a place for creative political leadership too. The forces handcuffing Roosevelt stemmed as much from his own actions and personality as from the unyielding political environment. He could not reshape his party, reorient foreign policy attitudes, reorganize Congress and the bureaucracy, or solve the economic problem largely because he lacked the necessary intellectual commitment to the right union of ends and means.

A test of Roosevelt's creative leadership, of his willingness to alter the environment—the pressures working on him—when he had the capacity to do so, was provided by the inner circle of his advisers. Haphazardly brought together, embracing conservatives and liberals, isolationists and internationalists, his brain trust helped him mediate among opposing policies and ideas during his first term. But, despite the comings and goings of individuals, the brain trust remained an amorphous and divided group during Roosevelt's later period of party leadership, at a time when he needed program guidance more directly and clearly pointed toward the aims of an expanded New Deal at home and toward firmer action abroad. Instead of compelling his advisers to serve his new needs, he allowed them unduly to define his own purposes. Fearing commitment to any one adviser or faction, he became overly involved in the divisions among all of them.

Roosevelt, in a sense, was captive to himself as well as to his political environment. He was captive to his habits of mediating among pressures rather than reshaping them, of responding eclectically to all the people around him, of balancing warring groups and leaders against one another, of improvising with brilliance and gusto. Impatient of theory, insatiably curious about people and their ideas, sensitively attuned to the play of forces around him, he lacked that burning and almost fanatic conviction that great leadership demands.

Roosevelt was less a great creative leader than a skillful manipulator and a brilliant interpreter. Given the big, decisive event—depression at home or naked aggression abroad—he could dramatize its significance and convey its import to the American people. But when the crisis was less striking but no less serious, and when its solution demanded a union of intellectual comprehension and unified and continuing strategic action, Roosevelt saw his efforts turn to dust, as in the cases of court packing, the purge, and putting his country behind efforts toward collective security. He was always a superb tactician, and sometimes a courageous leader, but he failed to achieve that combination of tactical skill and strategic planning that represents the acme of political leadership.

THE POLITICS OF THE NEW DEAL

Samuel Lubell

THE ROOSEVELT COALITION

SAMUEL LUBELL, a noted political analyst who supplements statistical study with personal interviewing, has done more than any other student of American politics to explain the ways in which the New Deal affected American voting patterns. His important book, *The Future of American Politics,* originally published in 1951, is still the major point of departure for historians who seek to understand the nature of the overwhelming electoral support which sustained Franklin D. Roosevelt and the New Deal.

The Roosevelt coalition, as Lubell sees it, began to take shape in the 1920's as urban immigrant groups, unable to identify with the leadership or ideology of the Republican party, moved away from the GOP. The magnetic appeal of Al Smith brought these minorities to the Democratic party in 1928 and gave it a solid majority in the twelve largest cities. Consolidating this support, Roosevelt added to the coalition old-stock Americans from the lower and lower-middle classes and vast numbers of Negroes. These elements, normally antagonistic, could unite behind the New Deal because of the benefits it distributed to them. Its job programs for the unemployed and its mortgage programs for hard-pressed homeowners, if not as spectacular as the NRA or the AAA, were more crucial to the lives of many. Equally important was the

---

From *The Future of American Politics* by Samuel Lubell, 3d rev. ed. (Colophon), pp. 43–68. Copyright © 1951, 1952, 1956, 1965 by Samuel Lubell. Reprinted by permission of Harper & Row, Publishers.

New Deal's encouragement of labor, and the new Congress of Industrial Organizations, whose membership largely reflected the new coalition, assumed an active role in politics and became a major rallying point for New Deal supporters.

World War II, as Lubell observes, somewhat altered the Roosevelt coalition. Americans of German and Italian descent tended to fall away from the Democratic party, but other groups, such as Jews and Polish-Americans, gave Roosevelt heavier support than ever. The author's analysis is a reminder that deeply-held ethnic loyalties may be as important as rational individual self-interest in determining political commitments.

Lubell agrees with several other writers that beginning about 1935 there was an important shift in the tone and emphasis of the New Deal—one which he defines as a shift from concentration on simple economic recovery to the promotion of far-reaching reforms. It was this change which assured the emergence of the Roosevelt coalition in 1936. Lubell also argues that it was the war, not the New Deal, which brought back prosperity. Despite the defection of some German- and Italian-Americans, the defense boom and FDR's third-term campaign of 1940 essentially solidified the new political divisions which the New Deal had brought into being.

Lubell's assertion that important population shifts necessarily lead to political realignments seems somewhat simplistic, but whatever the shortcomings of his general theory, no writer has told us more about the politics of the New Deal.

A LITTLE MATTER OF BIRTH RATES

In the winter of 1910 Congress received the longest report ever submitted by a government investigating body up to that time. From early 1907 a special commission had been studying almost every imaginable aspect of immigration, filling forty-two fat volumes with its findings. Buried in that statistical mountain was at least one table of figures which was to prove peculiarly prophetic for our own times.

This table showed that a majority of the children in the schools of thirty-seven of the nation's leading cities had foreign-born fathers. In cities like Chelsea, Fall River, New Bedford, Duluth, New York and Chicago more than *two out of every three* school children were the sons and daughters of immigrants.

Viewed in today's perspective, it is clear that those figures forecast a major political upheaval some time between 1930 and 1940. By then all of these children, plus baby brothers and sisters not enrolled in school, would have grown to voting age. Massed as they were in the states commanding the largest electoral vote, their sheer numbers would topple any prevailing political balance.

No matter what else had happened, the growing up of these children of the 13,000,000 immigrants who poured into the country between 1900 and 1914 was bound to exert a leveling pull on American society. As it was, the Great Depression—striking when most of them had barely entered the adult world—sharpened all their memories of childhood handicaps. When Roosevelt first took office, no segment of the population was more ready for "a new deal" than the submerged, inarticulate urban masses. They became the chief carriers of the Roosevelt Revolution.

The real revolutionary surge behind the New Deal lay in this coupling of the depression with the rise of a new generation, which had been malnourished on the congestion of our cities and the abuses of industrialism. Roosevelt did not start this revolt of the city. What he did do was to awaken the climbing urban masses to a consciousness of the power in their numbers. He extended to them the warming hand of recognition, through patronage and protective legislation. In the New Deal he supplied the leveling philosophy required by their sheer numbers and by the hungers stimulated by advertising. In turn, the big-city masses furnished the votes which re-elected Roosevelt again and again—and, in the process, ended the traditional Republican majority in this country.

In the elections that followed this same big-city generation would stand like a human wall between the Republicans and their past dominance. It was this generation—now grown to parenthood and in many cases to home-owning, but still bound by common underdog attitudes—which the Republicans had to crack to win and hold the Presidency.

Twice before in American history a majority party has been

transformed into a minority party. Each time the change was prefaced by a dramatic reshuffling of population. Jacksonian democracy tramped in to the echoes of the oxcarts which had rolled westward in the twenty years before. In 1800 only one of twenty Americans lived west of the Appalachians; when Jackson was inaugurated the transmountain country claimed one of every three Americans.

Similarly, the formation of the Republican party was preceded by a tremendous westward expansion into the Great Lakes and Midwest regions. Between 1840 and 1860 the nation's population almost doubled, swelling another 60 per cent by 1880. If it is true that the pre-Civil War parties were overwhelmed by their inability to dam back the passions stirred by the slavery controversy, it is also true that they were unable to channel the flood of new voters.

There were two population currents which cleared the way for the New Deal:

Between 1910 and 1930 for the first time a majority of the American people came to live in cities. The second population shift might be described as the triumph of the birth rates of the poor and underprivileged over those of the rich and well-born.

Searching for families of five or more, the U.S. Immigration Commission's investigators found two-and-a-half times as many among unskilled laborers as among businessmen. In Minneapolis, for example, the second generation of English stock—the backbone of Republican strength—celebrated a blessed event on the average of one every five years. Among the foreign born a new baby arrived every three years.

As late as 1925 wives of miners and laborers were still having twice as many children as the wives of bankers.

Nor was it the birth rates of the immigrants alone which were threatening the Republican majority. The other prolific baby patches were in the farming areas, particularly in the Appalachian hills and in the South. When World War One shut off the flow of European immigrants, it was into these areas of high human fertility and low living standards that industry sent its recruiting agents searching for cheap labor. Whites and Negroes were sucked north into the cities, especially after 1920 when immigration was curtailed sharply.

Between 1920 and 1930 more than 6,500,000 persons were

drawn off the farms and hills; 4,500,000 came into New York, Chicago, Detroit and Los Angeles alone. They hit the cities at roughly the same time that the children of the immigrants were growing up and bestirring themselves. The human potential for a revolutionary political change had thus been brought together in our larger cities when the economic skies caved in.

Through the entire Roosevelt era the Republicans labored on the wrong side of the birth rate. Nor was there anything they could do about it, since the birth rates frustrating them were those of 1910 to 1920. During the last years of Republican victory, from 1920 through 1928, roughly 17,000,000 potential new voters passed the age of twenty-one. From 1936 through 1944, the number ran over 21,000,000, most of them coming from poorer, Democratically inclined families.

Whatever inroads into Roosevelt's popularity the Republicans made was offset largely by these new voters. In 1936, for example, nearly 6,000,000 more ballots were cast than in 1932. While the Republicans gained just under 1,000,000, Roosevelt's vote swelled by almost 5,000,000.

Except for the Polish-Americans and Italo-Americans, the wave of new voters among the immigrant groups passed its crest by 1945. Not until the late 1960's will the record number of births of recent years register politically. Until then the nation's basal political metabolism is likely to remain more sluggish than during the Roosevelt years. The issues of realignment will have to be fought out primarily among existing population elements, whose instinctive voting attitudes are already largely formed.

This prospect, of no abrupt change in the make-up of the electorate, re-emphasizes the decisive importance of the big-city generation, which came of age through the Roosevelt years. Without their overwhelming urban pluralities the Democrats would not have won in either 1940, 1944 or 1948. The 1948 election was so close because Truman's vote in the twelve largest cities fell nearly 750,000 below Roosevelt's 1944 plurality.

Not only does this generation hold the balance of political power in the nation. It also constitutes a radically new political force in American history. The old Republican dominance was rooted in the Civil War and the transcontinental expansion which followed. Most of the immigrants who peopled our larger cities came to these shores long after the Civil War, even after the exhaustion of free lands in the West. To their children and grandchildren the loyalties of Appomattox and the Homestead Act were details in history books rather than a family experience passed down from grandfather to grandson.

Never having known anything but city life, this new generation was bound to develop a different attitude toward the role of government from that of Americans born on farms or in small towns. To Herbert Hoover the phrase "rugged individualism" evoked nostalgic memories of a rural self-sufficiency in which a thrifty, toiling farmer had to look to the marketplace for only the last fifth of his needs. The Iowa homestead on which Hoover grew up produced all of its own vegetables, its own soap, its own bread. Fuel was cut and hauled from the woods ten miles away, where one could also gather walnuts free. "Sweetness" was obtained from sorghums. Every fall the cellar was filled with jars and barrels which, as Hoover observes in his memoirs, "was social security in itself."

To men and women who regulated their labors by the sun and rain, there was recognizable logic in talking of natural economic laws—although even among farmers the murmur for government intervention grew louder, as their operations became more commercialized and less self-sufficient.

In the city, though, the issue has always been man against man. What bowed the backs of the factory worker prematurely were not hardships inflicted by Mother Nature but by human nature. He was completely dependent on a money wage. Without a job, there were no vegetables for his family, no bread, no rent, no fuel, no soap, so "sweetness." Crop failures, plagues of grasshoppers or searing drought could be put down as acts of God. Getting fired or having one's wages cut were only too plainly acts of the Boss.

A philosophy that called for "leaving things alone" to work themselves out seemed either unreal or hypocritical in the cities, where nearly every condition of living groaned for reform. The wage earner had to look to the government to make sure that the milk bought for his baby was not watered or tubercular; he had to look to government to regulate the construction of tenements so all sunlight was not blocked out. If only God could make a tree, only the government could make a park.

Neither the Republicans nor the New Dealers seem to have

appreciated how sharp a wrench from the continuity of the past was involved in the rise of this big-city generation. G.O.P. leaders persisted in regarding Roosevelt's popularity as a form of hero worship, abetted by the radio. Only Roosevelt's personal magnetism and political skill were holding together the varied Democratic elements, reasoned the Republicans. With "that voice" quieted, the coalition would fall apart. The nation would then return to safe and sane Republicanism. What this reasoning overlooked was that the Roosevelt generation had no tradition of Republicanism to go back to. For them the weight of tradition was such that if they were undecided about rival Presidential candidates, they instinctively would give the Democrats preference.

The basic weakness of the Republican party stems from this fact, that it has remained rooted in an earlier historical era in which it was dominant. The resilient Democratic strength springs from being so alive—clumsily perhaps, but definitely alive—to the problems with which the newer generation has grown up.

Between the Republican and Democratic appeals, as we shall see, the issue has been less one of conservatism versus liberalism than one of timeliness.

THE FORGOTTEN WARRIOR

At the height of Roosevelt's popularity, Republicans used to lament over the youthfulness of so many of the nation's voters. Since they had come of age after 1928, the complaint ran, the only Presidents they knew were Roosevelt and Hoover, who was hopelessly linked with the depression. Still, it would be a mistake to regard the Roosevelt coalition as strictly a product of the depression.

The startling fact—generally overlooked—is that through the booming twenties Republican pluralities in the large industrial centers were dropping steadily. Even when the stock market tickers were clicking most gratifyingly the forces of urban revolt were gathering momentum.

Consider the waning Republican strength revealed in the table below which totals the vote in our twelve largest cities (New York, Chicago, Philadelphia, Pittsburgh, Detroit, Cleveland, Baltimore, St. Louis, Boston, Milwaukee, San Francisco and Los Angeles). In 1920 the Republicans had 1,638,000 more votes than the Democrats in these twelve cities. This net Republican plurality dropped in 1924 and was turned into a Democratic plurality by 1928.

Year	*Net Party Plurality*
1920	1,540,000 Republican
1924	1,308,000 Republican
1928	210,000 Democratic
1932	1,791,000 Democratic
1936	3,479,000 Democratic
1940	2,112,000 Democratic
1944	2,230,000 Democratic
1948	1,481,000 Democratic

Two things stand out from those figures. First, it was not the depression which made Roosevelt the champion of the urban masses but what he did after he came to the Presidency. Between 1932 and 1936 the Democratic plurality in these cities leaped 80 per cent, the biggest change in any single election. Second, the Republican hold on the cities was broken not by Roosevelt but by Alfred E. Smith. Before the Roosevelt Revolution there was an Al Smith Revolution.

In many ways, Smith's defeat in 1928, rather than Roosevelt's 1932 victory, marked off the arena in which today's politics are being fought. The Happy Warrior and four-time governor of New York first hacked out the rural-city cleavage which generates so much of the force behind the present struggle between Congress and the President. It was Smith who first slashed through the traditional alignments that had held so firmly since the Civil War, clearing the way for the more comprehensive realignment which came later.

Smith split not only the Solid South but the Republican North as well. While Hoover was carrying more than 300 Southern and border state counties which had not gone Republican since Reconstruction, Smith was swinging 122 Northern counties out of the G.O.P. column.

Seventy-seven of these counties are predominantly Catholic. But more than religious sympathy inspired their support of Smith. This is shown clearly by the way these counties have voted since. Fifty-seven have remained staunchly Democratic in every Presidential election from 1928 through 1948. Included are some of our heaviest voting areas—New York, Boston, Providence, St. Louis, San Francisco, Cleveland, Milwaukee and St. Paul, also Butte, Montana, and Burlington, Vermont.

Of the sixty-two Smith counties whose allegiance has wavered, most are German-American in background and therefore broke against Roosevelt in 1940 because of the war. In 1948 Truman gained over Roosevelt in fifty of these counties, with eighteen returning to the Democratic party.

Smith may be today's "Forgotten Warrior" but the line he drew across the map of American politics has never been erased.

How profound a social upheaval stirred beneath the Smith vote can be seen most clearly in the industrial East, where one finds the heaviest concentration of counties which have been Democratic since 1928. Before Smith, no other part of the country was more religiously Republican. None had a heavier proportion of foreign born. Nor were these two factors unrelated.

During the twenty years of heaviest immigration, from 1890 to 1910, coal production tripled and steel output multiplied seven times. It was in the cities with the most immigrants that Bryan's free silver crusade was beaten. To a considerable extent, in short, both the expansion of industry and Republican political dominance rested on the immigrant.

The conditions under which these immigrants worked and lived hardly requires description here. Coming to this country after the free lands were gone, they were thrust into the sectors of the economy with the sorest tensions, into the sweatiest jobs, where wages were not much above subsistence level and where labor unions were feeble. The foreign born made up 60 per cent of the workers in the packing-house plants described by Upton Sinclair's *The Jungle;* 57 per cent of those in iron and steel, 61 per cent of our miners, nearly 70 per cent of those toiling in textiles or clothing.

Probably of greater long-run political significance than their low wages was the segregation in which they lived. In one-industry coal and steel towns the separation of laborers and managers was as complete as that between serfs and lord on a feudal manor. In the larger cities, even where Gold Coast and slum were hardly a block apart, they still constituted two separate worlds. Roosevelt has often been accused of ranging class against class, as if class antagonism did not exist before the New Deal. Yet, certainly since the turn of the century our urban social structure had been a class structure.

For a long time, though, the resentment of the "other half" against those on top merely smoldered submissively. Even had the immigrants been inclined to political activity, they would have found it difficult. In 1910 one of every five among the foreign born spoke no English. Until 1920 the twelve-hour working day, still the rule in iron and steel, left little leisure time. As late as 1933, when the N.R.A. codes were being considered, Secretary of Labor Frances Perkins had to go out into the mill towns to drum up interest among the steel workers. At Homestead a Catholic priest arranged a meeting with some Polish-American workers, all of whom came scrupulously scrubbed. They spoke no English, and the meeting had to be conducted through an interpreter. Mrs. Perkins was visibly touched when several workers rose and spoke and it developed they were asking God to bless the President, much as peasants in Russia might have blessed the czar.

The rise in the educational level is a revealing index to the quickening political pulse of the urban masses. At the turn of the century only one of every fifteen youngsters was going beyond the elementary school. By 1930 every second child of high school age was in high school.

At first, this rising generation found little real identification with either of the major parties. In exchange for a favor or a two-dollar bill the newly naturalized voter would vote the way the political machine instructed. But he was as likely to follow the dictates of a Republican boss in Philadelphia as of Tammany Hall in New York. None of the Republican Presidents stirred that most vital of all political assets: vicarious identification. It was not a matter of postwar disillusionment. Far from feeling like a lost generation, the children of the immigrants were intensely idealistic. But with whom could they identify this idealism? Harding was a dirty story. Calvin Coolidge might be untouched by scandal, but the same Puritanical, small-town qualities which endeared him to Main Street made "Silent Cal" a chilling, pedagogic figure to city kids.

On the Democratic side, Woodrow Wilson had captured the

imagination of some of these underdog elements through favorable labor legislation, through his dream of peace and by championing the cause of Europe's minorities. For years afterward, in appealing to Czechs and Poles, Democratic politicians found it effective to invoke Wilson's memory. But this enthusiasm did not carry over to either James M. Cox, an Ohio publisher, or John W. Davis, a Wall Street lawyer. As for William Jennings Bryan, his revivalist oratory might inflame the Bible belt—but in the city he was a repellent, even comic figure. When the "Great Commoner" rose before the 1924 Democratic Convention in New York to oppose denouncing the Ku Klux Klan by name, contending "We can exterminate Ku Kluxism better by recognizing their honesty and teaching them that they are wrong," he was hissed and booed by the galleries.

By 1924, "the enemy's country," as Bryan called the East, had flung up its own Great Commoner in Al Smith. Prohibition and the Klan were the immediate weapons in the duel Smith and Bryan fought; but behind each antagonist were ranged the habits and prejudices, hopes and frustrations, prides and hatreds of two different cultures and two historical eras.

The very eccentricities and mannerisms of the two men were symbolic. The brown derby and rasping East Side accent, which stamped Smith as "one of our boys" to the sidewalk masses, sent shivers down the spine of Protestant respectability. In turn, the traits which made Bryan seem like the voice of pious morality to his Prohibitionist, rural, Protestant following—the liberal use of Biblical phrases, the resonant Chautauqua tones, the heaven-stomping energy—made him sound like the voice of bigotry to the urban masses.

Both men were mouthpieces of protest—Bryan of the overmortgaged Bible belt, Smith of the underpaid melting pot. Whether either was understood in the other's country is doubtful. Could the factory worker really share the despair of the farmer watching a sheriff tack a foreclosure notice on the barn door? Could the farmer feel the vicarious terror of the factory masses reading of a shirtwaist-factory fire in which 145 women were trapped and burned alive?

The year of this Triangle factory fire, 1911, was the year Smith first went to Albany. It marked the beginning of his fight to improve factory conditions, reduce the hours of labor for women and for other social legislation. After his relations with

Roosevelt had curdled, Smith came to denounce the New Deal's "socialism." But during the 1920's he was the means by which the Democratic party absorbed the agitations—and votes—of the Socialists and their sympathizers.

What Smith really embodied was the revolt of the underdog, urban immigrant against the top dog of "old American" stock. His Catholicism was an essential element in that revolt. The so-called "old" immigration which settled the farms was drawn largely from Protestant countries, England, Norway, Sweden and Germany. The "new" immigrant after 1885 which crowded the teeming cities, came mainly from Italy, Poland, Russia, Greece and the disintegrating Hapsburg Empire. The larger part of these new immigrants were Catholic. They also included perhaps 1,500,000 Jews.

Because they came to this country late, these immigrants and their children were concentrated in the lower economic rungs. Moreover, they resented what seemed to them efforts to force conformity to an Anglo-Saxon, Protestant culture, through Sunday Blue Laws, prohibition and the Klan.

Throughout the industrialized East, the make-up of society was such that Protestantism coincided largely with the Republican party, with millowners and financiers, with the snobbish members of exclusive clubs—in short, with the upper class. Catholicism, in turn, coincided largely with discrimination and sweated labor, with immigrant minorities who were looked down upon as inferior beings—in short, the lower class.

In his campaign Smith did not draw the line of class conflict. His campaign manager, John S. Raskob, was a millionaire. So were other ardent supporters like Pierre Du Pont, Herbert Lehman and William F. Kenny, who was reputed to have made $30,000,000 as a contractor. Still, the class and cultural cleavage was there, like a deep fault, in the granite of our national life. Smith's candidacy unavoidably split the rock along that fault.

Before Smith the Democrats were little more of an urban party than were the Republicans. In Pennsylvania, for example, the three counties the Democrats won in 1920 and 1924—Columbia, Green and Monroe—were largely rural and native born. These counties swung for Hoover in 1928. In their place, the Democrats captured three mining and industrial counties—

Elk, Lucerne and Lackawanna—which had not gone Democratic since 1892. In Pennsylvania, Smith pushed the Democratic vote above the million mark for the first time. Throughout New England, whole voting elements such as the French-Canadian and Italo-Americans were swung out of the Republican party never to return.

Smith also made women's suffrage a reality for the urban poor. In better income families, women started voting in 1920 as soon as they were granted the privilege; but among the urban masses the tradition that a woman's place was in the home still held strong until 1928. That year in Massachusetts (which Smith carried along with Rhode Island) the outpouring of women lifted the number of voters by 40 per cent over 1924. The turnout in Boston was 44 per cent heavier.

Although the issues of 1928 have long passed off, the cleavage which Smith's candidacy laid bare persisted. If New England remained the most Republican of the major regions, it was also where the line between unwaveringly Republican and unwaveringly Democratic voters was most rigidly drawn. Between 1932 and 1944, New England's Democratic vote did not shift by more than 2 per cent in any election, while other parts of the country were fluctuating by 5 and 10 per cent.

There were Catholic Republicans, of course, as there were Yankee Democrats, but the bedrock cleavage in the East remains a Catholic-Protestant one. . . .

But if Smith lifted the Democratic vote to new heights in some cities, he lost such Democratic strongholds as Oklahoma City, Atlanta, Birmingham, Dallas, Houston. In virtually all the Southern cities, Smith's vote fell off, as well as in cities with heavy Scandinavian populations, reflecting Lutheran distrust of Catholicism; he also lost ground wherever the population was mainly native born or Ku Klux in sympathy.

To sum up, by 1928 the masses in the cities with the most foreign born were already in political revolt. But that part of the urban population which was drawn from native American stock had still to be roused.

THE YEAR OF DECISION

Bowls of red roses graced the speakers' table while American flags and tricolored bunting draped the walls of the banquet hall. The occasion was the first annual dinner of the Muncie, Indiana, Chamber of Commerce since the depression. Its immediate inspiration had been the news that General Motors, which had stripped its local plant three years before, was moving back. Mindful that the company was returning to escape a strike in Toledo, the Mayor assured the banqueters that "the citizens of Muncie are in no mood for outsiders to come in and agitate."

Returning to the city that June week in 1935 to begin their study of "Middletown in Transition," Robert and Helen Lynd were struck by the eagerness with which Muncie's community leaders were hailing the return of the "good old days."

But if Muncie's businessmen were ready to forget the depression as "just a bad bump in the road," that was not the feeling across the railroad tracks "in the other world of wage-earners." Predominantly native born, drawn mainly from nearby farms, Muncie's "corn-feds," as the local workers were called, had seen no point in labor unions before the depression. Out of a working force of 13,000, hardly 700 had carried union cards, fewer than joined the Klan. Al Smith won a lone precinct in the city, losing one of the two precincts which went Democratic in 1924. With every fourth Muncie worker jobless in 1932, Roosevelt carried thirteen precincts, but still lost the city.

As in so many other communities, the N.R.A. brought a rush among Muncie's workers to join labor unions. At the Ball glass factory and the automotive plants—Muncie's two strongest antiunion citadels—the American Federation of Labor was petitioned to send in organizers. But the A. F. of L. was fumbling and inept, while the business community was militantly efficient. The local police force was secretly increased. Persons distributing handbills advertising a union meeting were picked up. One local newspaper front-paged a photograph of a picket in Oregon being dragged through the streets under the caption, THIS PICKET HAD REAL "DRAG" WITH COPS.

By the time the 1936 Presidential campaign opened, the drive to unionize Muncie had been broken. But the workers still had the ballot. To the Lynds the 1936 campaign "witnessed perhaps the strongest effort in the city's history by the local big businessmen (industrialists and bankers) to stampede local opinion in behalf of a single Presidential candidate." When the ballots were in, Muncie had gone for a Democratic President for the first time since the Civil War. Exulted one worker to the Lynds, "We certainly licked the big bosses."

Muncie was not the only Republican citadel which resisted Roosevelt in 1932 but fell in 1936. Twenty-three other counties, which the Republicans held in 1932, swung four years later and —like Muncie—stayed Democratic. Among these was "Bloody" Harlan in southeast Kentucky, where efforts to organize the miners in the 1930's exploded in assassinations and pitched battles; also the cities of Philadelphia and Wilmington, the home of the Du Ponts. To defeat Roosevelt, various members of the Du Pont clan contributed more than $500,000 to the Republicans, in addition to their donations to the American Liberty League. The net effect seems only to have advertised more sharply who was on whose side.

So overwhelming was Roosevelt's 1936 victory, that its political decisiveness is often overlooked. With only Maine and Vermont remaining Republican, Roosevelt's re-election seemed primarily a vote of gratitude for lifting the country out of a desperate economic crisis. Certainly many people favored him for that reason. But 1936 was also the year of realignment in which the Democrats became the nation's normal majority party. The traditional dominance which the Republicans had enjoyed since the Civil War was washed away and a new era in American politics began.

The depression vote of 1932 still mirrored the orbit of conflict of the old Republican order. The G.O.P. cleavage had been mainly a struggle between the "progressives" of the Midwest and Far West against the industrial East. Roosevelt's first campaign was directed primarily toward splitting off this "progressive" vote. His best showing came in the Western and Mountain states. All six states he lost—Pennsylvania, Delaware, Connecticut, Vermont, New Hampshire and Maine—were in the East.

The shift in the basis of Roosevelt's appeal "from acreage to population," to use Raymond Moley's phrase, occurred in 1935. Moley credits the change to Huey Long's "Share Our Wealth" agitation and to Roosevelt's ire over the Supreme Court's declaring the N.R.A. unconstitutional. To steal Long's thunder, Roosevelt proposed a "soak the rich" tax bill, which, Moley feels, marked the beginning of the conservative-liberal split inside the Democratic party. Whatever the exact turning point,

1935 saw more social legislation enacted than in any other year in the nation's history—the "wealth tax," the Wagner Labor Relations Act, the Social Security Law, the creation of WPA, the Public Utilities Holding Law, the start of the Rural Electrification Administration.

Not only in Washington but throughout the country 1935 was the year of decision. To go back to the old order or to move forward to something different? That was the question posed for decision in 1935, in countless different ways, in every phase of life.

In the early New Deal days how things were done had been less important than getting the stalled economy going again. By 1935 recovery had progressed to the point where there no longer was any question that the country would be saved. The new issue was: Would the "good old days" of unchallenged business dominance be restored? Or was America to be reshaped?

The more articulate business groups had one answer. As in Muncie, they were ready to resume their annual Chamber of Commerce dinners as if there never had been a depression. But the same processes of recovery which restored the courage of businessmen also enabled the leaders of organized labor to recover their nerve. Early in 1933 John L. Lewis, Phil Murray and Tom Kennedy lamented to Roosevelt that the United Mine Workers had barely enough members to pay the union's expenses. "Go home and have a good night's sleep," Roosevelt consoled them. "If I don't do anything else in my administration I am going to give the miners an opportunity to organize in the United Mine Workers of America."

Taking Roosevelt at his word, Lewis nearly emptied the UMW treasury to hire organizers, sending them out to tell the miners, "The President wants you to join a union." By 1934 Lewis could stand before the A. F. of L. convention and boast that the UMW was again a fighting force of 400,000 miners. By 1935 he was ready to demand that the A. F. of L. embrace the principle of industrial unionism or let a new labor movement organize the mass production industries.

When the first sit-down strike broke in November 1935, it came—significantly—not among workers of immigrant origin, but among the rubber workers of Akron. That city had drawn so many hillbillies from near-by states that it was often jokingly called "the capital of West Virginia." Before taking their place in the picket line, some rubber workers knelt in prayer. After the last "Amen," they picked up their baseball bats and lead pipes and moved into formation around the factories.

This fervor for unions which swept the native American workers—some observers likened it to a religious revival—was of crucial political importance. Al Smith, as we have seen, stirred a new sense of political consciousness among workers of immigrant and Catholic origin. But the native workers of the farms and hills had always held suspiciously aloof from those of immigrant stock.

The hillbillies had their own sense of group solidarity. Flint, Michigan, had its "Little Missouri" and "Little Arkansas" residential settlements. In Akron, the West Virginia State Society had 25,000 members and put on an annual West Virginia day picnic. Marked off from the older inhabitants by their accents, manners and dress, the "snake-eaters" were the butt of ridicule and jokes, which were fiercely resented. A judge in Akron suspended sentence on one man on condition that he return to West Virginia. A newspaper reporter wrote up the incident, "Judge Sentences Man to West Virginia for Life." At the next election the hapless judge was badly beaten by the votes of outraged mountaineers.

The formation of the CIO marked the fusing of the interests of the immigrant and native-stock workers, both Negro and white. That, I believe, is perhaps the most telling accomplishment of the CIO. Its political importance can hardly be exaggerated. The mass production industries had been the ones in which racial and religious antagonisms among the workers were most divisive. Carnegie, Illinois, had sprinkled clusters of different nationalities in each of its mines, reasoning correctly that a Balkanized working force would be more difficult to unionize. In some industries immigrants and Negroes had first been introduced as strikebreakers or because they would work for lower wages than native-born workers. The failure of the Knights of Labor in the 1880's was largely a failure to unite the immigrant working groups. Much of the A. F. of L.'s reluctance to embark on a real organizing drive in the mass production industries reflected the dislike of the "aristocrats of labor" in the skilled crafts for the immigrant "rubbish."

By 1935, of course, the immigrants had made considerable progress toward Americanization. But the key to the change was the rise of a common class consciousness among all workers. The depression, in making all workers more aware of their economic interests, suppressed their racial and religous antagonisms. Put crudely, the hatred of bankers among the native American workers had become greater than their hatred of the Pope or even of the Negro.

This struggle between the old nativist prejudices and the newer class consciousness still remains one of the crucial behind-the-scenes battles in the mass production unions. Class feeling or racial-religious feeling? The future of American labor rests largely on which holds the ascendancy.

The rise in class consciousness among native-American workers was a nation-wide development. In Muncie the Lynds reported the first evidences of class-feeling among the workers, stirred by the sense that the government could do something for them. In "Yankee City" (Newburyport, Mass.) W. Lloyd Warner tells of a similar change among the so-called "Riverbrookers," the proud, clannish, Yankee-stock workers who had always refused to join unions with immigrant workers. When the new shoe union staged the first successful strike in Yankee City's history, the Riverbrookers supplied the leadership.

Negroes were another voting element which was determined to go forward rather than back. In some cities as many as four out of five Negro families were on relief. "Don't Buy Where You Can't Work" campaigns were being pressed to force white storeowners to hire Negroes. In Harlem the accumulated tensions of the depression years were exploded suddenly by a trivial incident.

On March 19, 1935, a sixteen-year-old boy snatched a ten-cent bread knife from a five-and-ten-cent counter—"just for fun" he later told the police. Two white clerks and the white manager chased the boy to the rear of the store. When they grabbed him, he bit their hands and broke away.

The boy was a Puerto Rican, yet the rumor spread that a Negro had been lynched in the store. Pickets appeared. A soapbox orator on one street corner attracted a growing crowd. When a funeral hearse happened to drive by a woman shrieked, "They've come to take the boy's body!" The Negro mob went on a rampage. When the riot was over, one man was dead—

three others died later of injuries—and a hundred or more whites and Negroes had been shot, stabbed or stoned.

The grisly tragedy was lightened only by the action of a Chinese laundryman. When he saw the mob surging through the streets, heaving stones into store windows, he hastily thrust a sign into his window, "Me colored too."

New York City had four previous race riots, without anything much happening afterward. The 1935 riot, however, set off a series of far-reaching changes. Harlem's shopowners hastily put on Negro employees. Before the year was out Tammany Hall had named its first Negro district leader. Mayor Fiorello La Guardia had appointed the first Negro magistrate. In 1932 most Negro voters in the country were still Republican. In 1936, in many cities two of every three Negro voters were for Roosevelt.

And so it went all through the country. It would be impossible to trace in full all the different ways in which the question —whether to go back or forward—was being asked of the American people. Sometimes the query was put bluntly in so many words. More often it was implicit in the logic of events or in reminders of the depression. At the end of 1935, more than $780,000,000 was still tied up in closed banks, 3,000,000 persons were still on relief; one survey of a group of garment workers showed that half of them had not bought a new coat for four years.

Lifelong Socialists had to ask themselves—did they return to the ivory tower of a futile third party or did they defend their immediate interests by rallying behind Roosevelt? Sidney Hillman and David Dubinsky, whose unions had been saved by the N.R.A., formed a new American Labor party to enable New Yorkers to vote for Roosevelt and still remain independent of the Democrats. Norman Thomas poled 884,000 Socialist votes nationally in 1932 but only 187,000 votes four years later.

On the other side of the political barricades the realignment was equally sharp. In 1932 one fourth of the Democratic campaign funds was contributed by bankers. In 1936 bankers accounted for a mere 3 per cent of the Democratic party's war chest. (Their total contributions to the Democrats were only about a third of the $750,000 spent by organized labor.)

Particularly in rural areas, the 1936 vote showed that sizable numbers of voters were ready to return to the Republicanism of their ancestors. Winston County, which had seceded from Alabama during the Civil War to remain loyal to the union, swung back to the Republican party in 1936; so did thirty-two counties in Missouri, all but eight bone-dry by tradition. Less than a dozen wheat counties in the whole country had stayed Republican in 1932. Four years later, most of the wheat counties were on their way back to the Republican party.

In the industrial centers, however, the political allegiances that had grown out of the Civil War were uprooted for good. In New York, New Jersey and Pennsylvania, alone, the Democratic vote leaped by roughly 1,800,000. Despite the depression, in 1932, Roosevelt failed to carry a dozen cities with 100,000 or more population—Philadelphia, Scranton and Reading in Pennsylvania; Canton, Youngstown and Columbus in Ohio; Gary, Duluth, Des Moines, Grand Rapids and Springfield, Massachusetts. Every one swung for Roosevelt in 1936 and except for Grand Rapids have remained Democratic since.

A dramatic glimpse into the nature of this hidden political revolution will be found by comparing the 1928 and 1936 vote in our major cities. While Smith won six of every ten voters in some cities, in others he drew only three out of ten. This disparity had narrowed by 1932, but wide divergences in voting still prevailed in different parts of the country. With the 1936 election, as the facing table shows, the voting of nearly all our major cities hit a common level.

Whether the cities are heavily foreign born or native American in make-up, Catholic or Protestant, with large numbers of Negroes or of whites up from the South, did not make too much difference in their 1936 vote. Nor whether the city had a strong labor tradition like San Francisco or an open shop tradition like Los Angeles, nor whether it was located on the East or West coast or in the Midwest.

A new nationalizing force had clearly been injected into American politics. In the past American political realignments have always followed sectional lines. The Revolt of the City, however, had drawn the same class-conscious line of economic interest across the entire country, overriding not only regional distinctions but equally strong cultural differences.

This development was not without its irony. In drawing the line of cleavage between worker and "economic royalists," Roosevelt unquestionably sharpened the sense of class division

CITIES HIGH SMITH		
City	Dem. % 1928	Dem. % 1936
Lawrence	71	73
Boston	67	63
Lowell	64	61
Fall River	64	67
New York	60	75
New Haven	57	65
Milwaukee	53	76
New Bedford	52	65
Cleveland	52	76
St. Louis	51	66
San Francisco	49	72
Chicago	48	65
Pittsburgh	47	67
Baltimore	47	67

CITIES LOW SMITH		
City	Dem. % 1928	Dem. % 1936
Flint	19	72
Wichita, Kan.	24	64
Los Angeles	28	67
Akron	31	71
Des Moines	31	55
San Diego	32	65
Seattle	32	64
Duluth	32	71
Canton	34	66
Spokane	35	71
Detroit	37	65
Indianapolis	39	57
Philadelphia	39	60
Youngstown	39	74

in American society. Yet, in doing so, he subordinated the old nativistic prejudices of race and religion, which had divided the lower half of American society for so long, bringing to these lower income elements a greater degree of social unity than they had ever shared before. Was Roosevelt dividing or unifying the country? . . .

BY FIRE AND WATER

If the 1936 vote marked the emergence of the new Roosevelt coalition, the third term election brought the crucial trial by fire and water which demonstrated the coalition's durability.

In both 1932 and 1936 Roosevelt would still have been elected without his heavy urban pluralities. In 1940, however, with the war and the third-term issue cutting heavily into his rural strength, the margin of victory that accounted for at least 212 electoral votes was supplied by the dozen largest cities in the country.

In every city I visited while doing a postelection survey I found that the Roosevelt vote broke at virtually the same economic level, between $45 and $60 a month rent. Below that line his pluralities were overwhelming. Above it, they faded away. In Pittsburgh, for example, Roosevelt got three fourths of the vote in wards whose rentals averaged under $40 a month and only four tenths of the vote where rentals were above $65 a month. Minneapolis, whose social make-up contrasts sharply with Pittsburgh, showed much the same results —about 40 per cent of the vote for Roosevelt in the highest income ward, but seven of every ten voters in the lower rental areas.

The sharpness with which the balloting stratified in city after city—Chicago, Boston, St. Louis, Seattle, Cleveland—left little room for any appreciable shift of votes because of the campaign put on by Wendell Willkie. When I asked one auto unionist in Detroit why the third-term issue had made so little difference he replied, "I'll say it even though it doesn't sound nice. We've grown class conscious." With other unions there may have been less bitterness but the division between worker and "economic royalist" was as sharply drawn. In a Minneapolis ward, inhabited largely by teamsters, the pastor of one church had been outspoken in condemning the third term. He admitted bitterly, "I don't suppose I changed a single vote." John Lewis, who had endorsed Willkie, could have echoed him.

This class consciousness, it should be noted, was not confined to workers. The balloting revealed as much class feeling among the higher income Republicans. If Roosevelt solidified the lower classes, he also welded the upper class.

The one sharp break from "economic voting" came on the basis of ethnic background, reflecting the varying impact upon different groups of Hitler's War. Roosevelt's heaviest losses came in German-American and Italo-American wards, where resentment was strong against his "stab in the back" reference to Mussolini's attack on France. The highest income areas voting for Roosevelt were Jewish. In Brooklyn he carried streets with $15,000 homes—a comfortable valuation in 1940— and apartment houses with doormen. Where low income status coincided with the nationality background of a country invaded by Germany, the vote for Roosevelt was prodigious. Polish-American wards in Buffalo went Democratic nine to one, with individual precincts running as high as twenty to one, his heaviest pluralities in the whole country.

Curiously, the ethnic elements most bitterly antagonized by Hitler were largely those contributing the heaviest numbers of new voters. In Buffalo, in 1940, the Polish-Americans mustered enough votes to elect a Polish-American judge for the first time. One Democratic ward leader, John Kryzinski, a tavern keeper, was foaming with enthusiasm at the significance of this victory.

"Out in ritzy Humboldt Park they get two voters to a family," he snorted contemptuously. "I get six out of my house. I got neighbors who give me eight. We elected a judge this year. The way things are going in eight years we'll elect a mayor."

Nine years later Buffalo did elect Joseph Mruc its first Polish-American mayor.

In every city one could see the same inexorable spread of numbers and the same leveling pressures. Almost it seemed, in fact, that the Republicans had decided to abandon the cities to the Democratic masses, taking refuge in the suburbs. In St. Louis the Twenty-eighth Ward had stayed Republican in 1932. By 1940 this G.O.P. stronghold had been reduced to three precincts. Along Lindell Boulevard and Skinker Road, "For Sale" signs were propped in front of mansionlike homes with graveled driveways, flagstone walks and antique-fabricated lampposts. Some of the more imposing residences were being razed to make way for apartment houses. In the old days at the Pageant, the neighborhood movie house, seats were reserved. When I saw it, the lobby was placarded with handbills advertising double features on Wednesday and Thursdays, with three features for a quarter on Fridays and Saturdays.

In Harlem, as well, the spirit of 1936 had quickened. Along 125th Street Negroes were working in hundreds of establishments which as late as 1935 had been manned completely by whites. Garment workers, janitors, bartenders, waiters and waitresses, Pullman porters, laundry workers, newspaper men, retail clerks and redcaps were flocking into labor unions with a sense of deliverance. To the Negro, unionism promised more than a wage boost. It also seemed the trumpet which would eventually tumble the Jericho walls of discrimination. Some Harlem unions were holding daily classes to teach Negroes selling, typing and stenography, to be able to rebuff employers who protested, "I can't hire Negroes, they're not experienced."

Probably 50 per cent of Harlem's Negroes were still getting relief of some kind. Older Negroes, clinging to the Republican party, might shake their graying heads and mutter, "Our people are selling their birthrights for a mess of pottage." Younger Negroes had a different slant on WPA. "The really important thing about WPA is that it is a guarantee of a living wage," explained Carl Lawrence, a reporter on the *Amsterdam News.* "It means Negroes don't have to work for anything people want to give them. This helps lift the standards of all Negroes, even those not on WPA."

The fall of France in 1940 had spurted the armament program, and the defense boom had been building up steadily in the months before the election. With the boom in employment, a highly significant thing was happening. Older people, who had been thrown out of work during the depression, were not being re-employed. The jobs were going to their children, while the older folk stayed on relief or lived on their savings, plus some help from their children. It hardly had been planned that way, but the New Deal was cushioning a wholesale shift in the working population, by easing the older generation of depression casualties out of the way to make room for a new generation.

In the Charlestown area of Boston one half of the voters were under forty. The ward leader himself, William Galvin, was thirty-six. Two younger brothers had got out of high school during the depression and had gone into the CCC camps. When employment in the Boston Navy Yard expanded, they got jobs as electrician's and pipe fitter's helpers. From the CCC to the Navy Yard—to these two youths, the government had brought advancement as real as any they could have achieved under a private employer.

As a reporter in Washington I had shared the general belief that the New Deal was hastily improvised and animated by no coherent philosophy. When one translated its benefits down to what they meant to the families I was interviewing in 1940, the whole Roosevelt program took on a new consistency.

The depression had thrown grave strains upon lower income families. Many family heads had lost their jobs, never to be employed regularly again. In some instances, the children were old enough to take over the bread-winning, which often robbed the deposed patriarch of his self-respect. In other families the parents had to struggle along until the children grew of age and took over.

In varied ways the New Deal eased these family strains. Through the HOLC * a million homes were saved. Many home-owners were too old to have been able to buy a new home, if they had lost their old ones. With their children grown older, I found, many were renting out part of the house, often to a married son or daughter.

Into the CCC camps went 2,750,000 sons of the cities. No longer a drain on the family larder, they even sent some money back home. Children in high school might get NYA † aid. Those who went to work usually did so in low-wage industries where the effects of the wage-hour law were most noticeable.

These and other New Deal benefits did not solve all the family problems by any means. They did ease the adjustments that had to be made as the unfortunates of one generation grew unemployable and another generation finally found its opportunity in defense employment.

The recovery from the depression low helped Roosevelt politically with all groups. It was particularly important in the cities because that recovery coincided with the hatching out of the birth rates of 1910 to 1920 and the rise of a new generation. The very size of the Democratically inclined families helped knit them to the New Deal. Even persons who had done rather well for themselves were likely to have a less fortunate family member lower down the economic ladder being benefited by the New Deal. Old-age pensions and other aid eased the burden of having to care for parents too old to work. Instead of being dragged by family burdens, the rising generation was able to solidify its gains.

How much of all this was "planned that way" and how much of it just happened can be speculated upon endlessly. One can also speculate about what might have happened if Roosevelt had not run for a third term and if the war in Europe had not broken out when it did.

Both Garner and Farley have written that they opposed a third term to keep the Democratic party from degenerating into a personal vehicle for Roosevelt and Roosevelt alone. If Roosevelt runs again, Garner told Bascom Timmons, his bi-

* Home Owners Loan Corporation.—Ed.
† National Youth Administration.—Ed.

ographer, "after he is off the ticket the Democratic party will fall to pieces." Despite Garner's deserved reputation for political shrewdness, he seems to have misjudged the forces at work. But for the third term, it is questionable whether many of the elements who had thrown their strength to the Democrats for the first time in 1936 would have solidified in the party. Early in 1940, for example, Ralph Bunche was still writing of the Negro vote as being "essentially Republican."

Paradoxically, the New Deal also appears to have grown stronger politically after it was abandoned. The outbreak of the war put an end to social reform. But the war boom made unnecessary any additional New Deal measures. In fact, the war succeeded in doing what the New Deal never could accomplish; it brought the country out of the depression.

Unemployment never fell below eight million in 1939 and growing numbers of people wondered whether there ever would be full employment. In the "little steel" strike of 1937 organized labor suffered a serious setback. If the recession of 1938 had dragged on, labor might have had to retreat, instead of entrenching itself as a permanent force in the mass production industries. All through the 1930's surplus sons and daughters had been held back on the farms because of a lack of opportunity in the cities.

The defense boom sparked anew the migration from farm to city. It also sparked new vigor into the marriage rate. In the middle 1930's one of four youths in their late teens and early twenties had never had regular work. By 1939 the marriage rate had risen from the depression low of eight to nearly eleven per thousand population. In 1941 it leaped to almost thirteen per thousand.

Economically speaking, then, the defense boom was the happy ending which saved the New Deal and made it a success story. The years of full employment which followed the outbreak of Hitler's War solved the economic problem of the Roosevelt generation, solidifying them in the Democratic party. But in the process this generation changed markedly. Not only had it aged and taken on new responsibilities, but much of this generation had climbed from poverty into the middle class. . . .

James T. Patterson

THE CONSERVATIVE COALITION

JAMES T. PATTERSON, Associate Professor of History at Indiana University, studied at Williams College with James MacGregor Burns and at Harvard with Frank Freidel. His book, *Congressional Conservatism and the New Deal,* winner of the 1966 Prize Studies award of the Organization of American Historians, was the first effort to explore in depth the nature of the conservative coalition which stalemated the New Deal and largely dominated congressional politics until 1964. This article is a concise presentation of Professor Patterson's findings.

The coalition, he asserts, was not made up of old men living in the past, though its leaders did have considerable congressional seniority. It was never well organized, and its membership shifted from issue to issue. Generally, however, its most consistent participants came from "safe" districts and tended to represent rural areas. The coalition crystallized as Roosevelt's prestige dropped because of the court-packing plan, the sit-down strikes, the recession of 1937–1938, and the President's failure to "purge" key conservatives in 1938. At the same time, a partial economic recovery reduced the sense of urgency which had impelled many Congressmen to vote for New Deal measures earlier in the decade. Finally,

From "A Conservative Coalition Forms in Congress, 1933–1939" by James T. Patterson, *Journal of American History,* LII (March, 1966), 757–772.
Copyright © 1966 by the Organization of American Historians. Reprinted by permission of the Editor of the *Journal of American History.*

Roosevelt's urban coalition by its own excesses and lack of unity helped bring the conservative coalition into being. As the author sees it, the coalition grew out of a series of uncontrollable circumstances, not bad presidential leadership. The result in any case was a rebirth of the urban-rural antagonism which had disrupted the Democratic party in the 1920's and which now brought an effective end to the New Deal.

Few political developments in recent American history have been more significant than the creation of a conservative coalition in Congress. Formed by Republicans and conservative Democrats to combat the New Deal, this "unholy alliance" operated effectively as early as 1937, and by 1939 it was strong enough to block extensions of the administration's program. It has functioned with varying degrees of success since that time, harassing and alarming Presidents of both parties.

Certain aspects of the coalition are well known and open to little question. Undoubtedly, both houses of Congress were more cantankerous in President Franklin D. Roosevelt's second term than they had been in his first, and most of the uncooperative congressmen were conservative on key issues. They tended to favor balanced budgets, to oppose welfare programs, to be suspicious of organized labor, and to speak favorably of states rights and limited government.

But historians have seldom ventured beyond these generalizations. They have not identified the members of the coalition. They have not tried to generalize about them as a group. They have not probed into the questions of why or when the coalition began. Finally, they have not shown whether the coalition was consciously organized, well disciplined, or coherent on crucial roll calls. These matters deserve attention.

Actually, the conservative leaders were well known. In the House the focus of conservative strength was the Rules Committee, dominated after 1938 by Edward E. Cox, a fiery Georgian who was a ranking Democratic member, and by Howard W. Smith, a Jeffersonian Democrat from Virginia. These two men, with three other southern Democrats and four Republicans, composed a majority of the fourteen-man committee after 1936. Cox was friendly with Joseph W. Martin, Jr. of Massachusetts, the leading Republican member of the committee in 1937-1938 who became House minority leader in 1939. When controversial issues arose, Cox and Martin usually conferred. If they agreed —which was often—Martin instructed his Republican colleagues on the committee to vote with Cox and the southern Democrats. Martin said later that he and Cox were the "principal points of contact between the northern Republicans and the southern Democratic conservatives."

Conservative leadership in the Senate was more diverse. The official Republican leader was Charles L. McNary of Oregon. The popular McNary was neither an orator nor a conservative by nature; indeed, he had voted for most New Deal measures before 1937. Though McNary participated in GOP strategy conferences, the most aggressive Republican senator after 1936 was the moderately conservative Arthur H. Vandenberg of Michigan. Other well-known Republicans who usually voted against major administration proposals included Henry Cabot Lodge, Jr. of Massachusetts, Warren R. Austin of Vermont, and Hiram W. Johnson of California, who became one of the most vitriolic foes of the New Deal after 1936.

Democratic conservatives in the Senate were a varied group. On the extreme right was a cluster of irreconcilables who had voted against most New Deal programs since 1933. These included Carter Glass and Harry F. Byrd of Virginia and Josiah W. Bailey of North Carolina. Bailey was particularly pungent in his criticism of Roosevelt. The President, he wrote,

> figures on hard times and does not wish for recovery. He would perish like a rattlesnake in the sun under conditions of prosperity. Pardon the illustration. Mr. Roosevelt is not a rattlesnake. He rattles a great deal, but that is all I am willing to say. Perhaps you know the rattlesnake must stay in the swamp for the reason that he does not have any means of sweating or panting. His heat accumulates. Mr. Roosevelt belongs to that type of man who lives on hard times and discontent.

Other Democrats, equally irreconcilable, joined Bailey in 1935-1936. These included Edward R. Burke of Nebraska, Peter G. Gerry of Rhode Island, Walter F. George of Georgia, and Ellison D. ("Cotton Ed") Smith of South Carolina. Such powerful veterans as Byron ("Pat") Harrison of Mississippi and James F. Byrnes of South Carolina, early supporters of the New Deal, also voted consistently against New Deal spending, tax, and labor programs after 1937. Vice-President John N. Garner of Texas, an influential figure in both houses, was another Democrat who by 1937 was counselling Roosevelt to move in a conservative direction.

While these men were unquestionably the most prominent congressional conservatives, it is not easy to generalize about them as a group. In the main they were not simply old men who had outlived their times. True, some like "Cotton Ed" Smith and Glass undoubtedly had. "Perhaps I am a relic of constitutional government," Glass admitted in 1938. "I entertain what may be the misguided notion that the Constitution of the United States, as it existed in the time of Grover Cleveland, is the same Constitution that exists today. . . ." But others, such as Byrd, Martin, and Howard Smith, were relatively young men. The average age of the most conservative Democratic senators in 1937 was precisely that of the Senate as a whole, while the most conserative Democratic representatives in 1937 averaged fifty years of age, two years less than the entire House.

Furthermore, the conservatives were by no means all veterans whose congressional service preceded the New Deal. Glass, George, and some others fitted this category, but many more first served in 1933 or thereafter, and the percentage of veteran and "coat-tail" Democrats who opposed the New Deal on most crucial roll calls was very much the same. Moreover, the most senior Republicans after 1935 included the moderately progressive McNary, William E. Borah of Idaho, and Arthur Capper of Kansas, while newcomers Austin of Vermont and H. Styles Bridges of New Hampshire tended to be among the most consistent opponents of the New Deal. Democratic veterans included not only conservatives of the Glass variety but New Deal regulars Alben W. Barkley of Kentucky, Hugo L. Black of Alabama, and Robert F. Wagner of New York. As Arthur S. Link has pointed out, the Congresses of the 1920s contained many relics of the progressive era; some of these veteran congressmen became reliable supporters of the New Deal in the 1930s.

Similarly, it is not entirely accurate to say that conservative strength in Congress derived from chairmanships of key committees. In the House, committee chairmen John J. O'Connor of New York and Hatton W. Sumners of Texas occasionally blocked administration proposals. So did "Cotton Ed" Smith,

Glass, and Harrison in the Senate. But these men were counterbalanced by such liberal chairmen as Senators Black, Wagner, and Elbert D. Thomas of Utah and Representatives Sam Rayburn of Texas, Adolph J. Sabath of Illinois, and Sol Bloom of New York. More often than not, committee chairmen cooperated with the administration.

Roosevelt's congressional troubles after 1936 stemmed not so much from uncooperative committee chairmen as from more widespread opposition to his programs. In the House, for example, his three most painful defeats on domestic legislation from 1937 through 1939 were the recommittal of the fair labor standards bill in 1937, the recommittal of executive reorganization in 1938, and the defeat of his lending program in 1939. All three came at the hands of the entire House. In the Senate he lost three successive battles for increased relief expenditures in 1939, and each time the reason was the adverse vote of the entire Senate. It is too easy—and too misleading—to blame the seniority rule for Roosevelt's congressional problems.

At first glance it would appear that the conservative bloc was composed of Republicans and southern Democrats, but such was not always the case. It is undeniable that Republicans, especially in the House, opposed the administration with remarkable solidarity after 1936, but the stance of southerners was less easy to determine. Occasionally, it seemed that Cox and Bailey were representative southern spokesmen. For instance, when the House recommitted the fair labor standards bill by a vote of 216-198 in December 1937, 81 of the 99 southern Democrats voted for recommittal, as opposed to but 51 of the remaining 230 Democrats in the House. And when the Senate in August 1937 adopted, 44-39, the so-called Byrd amendment aimed at damaging the Wagner housing bill, 10 of the 22 southern Democrats supported the amendment, while only 19 of the remaining 54 Senate Democrats were with the majority.

Two factors dispel much of this seeming clarity. First, voting alignments depended upon the issue. The labor bill, by proposing to destroy southern competitive wage advantages, upset southerners of all persuasions. Walter Lippmann, in fact, called the bill "sectional legislation disguised as humanitarian reform." On other crucial votes in the House, however, such as those which recommitted reorganization in 1938 and defeated the death sentence provision of the utility holding company bill in 1935, representatives from the South divided as did

Democrats from other sections. Secondly, southerners were seldom united. As V. O. Key put it, "while individual southern Senators may frequently vote with the Republicans, a majority rarely does; and when it does, the group as a whole is badly split more than half the time." The New Deal Congresses had their Glasses and Baileys, but they also had their Blacks and Rayburns. Except on race legislation, southern congressmen were never "solid."

Three things, nonetheless, were generally true of the congressional conservatives as a group. First of all, most of the vocal conservatives came from safe states or districts. The Glass-Byrd machine in Virginia, for instance, was able not only to keep veterans like Glass in the Senate but to send new conservatives to the House throughout the period. With all his power and prestige Roosevelt was too often unable to influence congressional nominations; the result was the nomination and election of many conservative Democrats during the New Deal years. In 1935 alone, new Senate Democrats included Rush D. Holt of West Virginia, Gerry of Rhode Island, and Burke of Nebraska, all of whom were soon to become staunch foes of the New Deal. That such men could be nominated in a year of unusually restive and liberal politics indicates both the limitations of presidential political power and the continuing strength of local political organizations.

Second, most of the effective Democratic conservatives, though not committee chairmen, were ranking or near-ranking members of important committees. Cox was the most strategically placed of these men, but there were several others. In the House they included Martin Dies, Jr. of Texas on the Rules Committee and Clifton A. Woodrum of Virginia on appropriations. In the Senate Bailey, George, William H. King of Utah, and many others comprised this group. Those conservative Democrats without responsibility, it seemed, often felt free to act as they pleased.

Thirdly, most conservative congressmen after 1936 were from rural districts or states. Too much should not be made of this fact: so, too, were many liberals. There were also many conservative Democrats from urbanized states, such as Senators Gerry of Rhode Island and Millard E. Tydings of Maryland. The nature of opposition to administration programs depended greatly upon the type of issue: New Deal farm bills, for example, often aroused considerable hostility among urban congressmen. Generally, however, rural congressmen voted against New Deal programs more consistently than did urban congressmen. The coalition was composed not so much of Republicans and southern Democrats as of Republicans and rural Democrats; urban southerners were often more favorably disposed to administration programs than their rural counterparts.

The existence of this urban-rural split upon many economic issues after 1936 was indisputable. Democratic votes in the House against administration measures in the 1937-1939 period were: investigation of sit-downs, 82 percent rural; recommit fair labor standards, 74 percent rural; investigate National Labor Relations Board, 77 percent rural; lending bill, 69 percent rural; and housing bill, 83 percent rural. Since the percentage of Democrats who represented rural districts was 54 in 1937 and 57 in 1939, it is clear that the Democratic opposition on these bills was heavily rural in character.*

It is difficult to say that any given issue or year "created" the conservative group. Rather, different groups of inherently conservative men switched at different times from unhappy allegiance to the New Deal to open hostility. In most cases these men changed their positions because they discovered that they could oppose the administration without fear of electoral extinction. The state of the President's prestige, as much as the nature of his program, determined the kind of reception he received on Capitol Hill.

Roosevelt's great popularity before 1937 was undeniable. Even Republicans bowed before it. "There can be no doubt," wrote one Republican senator in 1933, "that at the moment the President has an extraordinary support throughout the country and is able to do with the Congress as he wills. I suppose prudence dictates that one should not attempt to swim against the tide." Thus, Republicans through 1936 split sharply on final votes on major pieces of legislation. Cautious men like Vandenberg supported part of the administration program; others, not

* An urban congressman is one who represented a district in which 50 percent or more of its inhabitants lived in areas identified as urban by the *Sixteenth Census of the United States, 1940, Population,* I (Washington, 1942), 10. This definition admittedly does not differentiate among the different types of urban districts nor does it take into account the fact that some urban districts were represented by men with rural backgrounds and values—or vice versa. But it seems the fairest way to deal with the often rather haphazardly defined concepts of "rural" and "urban."

so astute, lost in 1934 or 1936. Many congressmen of both parties were unhappy with the New Deal well before 1937, but few dared to publicize their discontent with adverse votes.

Nevertheless, Democratic disaffection in Congress grew ominously as early as 1935. In that year the House three times defeated the death sentence clause of the utility holding company bill, and in the Senate the "wealth tax" bill antagonized not only the Democratic irreconcilables but also moderates like Harrison and Byrnes. Roosevelt's success with his 1935 Congress was indeed remarkable, but it cost him some political capital. Even if he had not thrown Congress into turmoil in 1937 with his court reform plan, he probably would have had great difficulty with the many congressmen who had already chafed at his relentless leadership and who considered the reform era at an end.

The court reform plan, presented in February 1937, provided these fractious congressmen with the ideal occasion for open rebellion. While Harrison and some other leaders remained outwardly loyal, the plan caused many formerly dependable Democrats to oppose the President openly. In addition, it united progressive and conservative Republicans, created intense personal rancor, and left all but the "100 percent New Dealers" suspicious of the President's motives. Above all, it emboldened congressmen who had not dared speak out before.

Other events after 1936 increased congressional courage. The wave of sit-down strikes in 1937 caused many to blame the New Deal for the growth of labor "radicalism." The recession of 1937-1938 convinced others that the New Deal had failed. The President's plan to reorganize the executive branch, a divisive issue in 1938, provided another occasion for successful coalition effort. And Roosevelt's unsuccessful attempt to purge his conservative opponents in 1938 encouraged disenchanted congressmen to become still more outspoken.

The election of 1938 solidified this trend. Republicans gained 80 seats in the House and 8 in the Senate, increasing their numbers to 169 and 23 respectively. Since unreliable Democrats already numbered some 40 in the House and 20 in the Senate, the administration faced a divided Congress before the session began. The President's achievements in 1939 were negligible; the domestic New Deal, for all intents and purposes, made no more striking gains.

These external events, however, were not the only causes of

Roosevelt's difficulties, nor should the President receive all the blame for the change. Two other developments—the changing nature of the liberal coalition and improved economic conditions—also contributed materially to the growth of congressional conservatism after 1936.

Roosevelt's liberal coalition had changed dramatically from the largely southern-western alliance of 1932 to a congeries of politically conscious pressure groups. Composed of labor unions, underprivileged ethnic groups, Negroes, and relief recipients, this aggregation was essentially northern-urban in character. Enormously encouraged by the 1936 election, these groups pressed relentlessly for their objectives in ensuing sessions, often without Roosevelt's approval. The sit-downs, for instance, were not Roosevelt's idea, and he refused to take sides in the matter. Similarly, relief workers and Democratic mayors badgered the President for higher relief expenditures than he was willing to seek. The fair labor standards bill, criticized by conservative southerners, faced even more serious opposition from AFL spokesmen fearful of government interference with collective bargaining. The President did not press either for housing or antilynching legislation, but liberal congressmen insisted upon introducing them, and bitter struggles ensued. Except for the court plan, unquestionably a major presidential blunder, Roosevelt made few tactically serious errors after 1936. But the well organized elements of his predominantly northern-urban coalition were demanding more aid at the same time that many other congressmen, not so dependent upon these elements for political survival, were convinced of the need for retrenchment. And many rural congressmen, while friendly to much of the New Deal, believed these urban elements were preempting funds or favors which might otherwise have benefited rural areas. The result was a largely urban-rural split within the unwieldy coalition which was the Democratic party.* No amount of presidential flattery could have prevented it.†

* It was also true that rural overrepresentation in both houses aided the conservative cause. Yet since this overrepresentation also existed before 1936, emphasis here is placed upon other factors.

† James M. Burns, *Roosevelt*, 347-49, 375-80, suggests that if Roosevelt had committed himself earlier to developing a strong progressive element in Congress, he would have escaped many of his congressional dilemmas after 1936. Such an effort, however, would have required far too much time even to consider during the emergency years of the early New Deal. Moreover, Burns presents insufficient evidence to show that such an

It is also worth noting that the changed emphasis of the New Deal in 1935—such as it was—was not nearly so disturbing to many congressmen as the pressure generated by urban elements in 1937. Southerners, Harrison and Byrnes for instance, had in 1935 approved social security, banking reform, and moderate tax reform. And men like Cox, hostile to abuses by private utilities, had even found it possible to vote for the death sentence clause of the utility bill. But none of these men favored the more urban liberalism espoused by liberal congressmen in 1937-1939. Prior to 1936 the economic emergency, together with the administration's emphasis upon measures benefiting all areas of the nation, had temporarily obscured the urban-rural fissures so apparent in the Democratic party in the 1920s. But when the urban wing of the party, awakened and dominant, sought to gain beneficial legislation in 1937-1939, the split reappeared to plague the New Deal and subsequent liberal administrations.

Improved economic conditions were of great significance to this split, for if one examines executive-congressional relations in the twentieth century, he finds that congressmen were never so tractable as in the desperate years from 1933 through 1935. Without detracting from Roosevelt's able congressional leadership in these years, it is certain that the emergency provided ideal conditions for the success of his program in Congress. Practically every congressman, besieged for relief by his constituents, responded with alacrity to the President's activist leadership. By 1937 this sense of crisis had diminished. Thus many of the same moderate congressmen who had so gratefully supported the administration through 1935 became unreliable two and three years later. And the recession of 1937-1938, far from reviving this sense of crisis, served instead to suggest that Roosevelt was not the magician he had previously seemed to be. Indeed, to many hostile congressmen the period was the "Roosevelt recession." In a sense, the economic state of the nation was the President's greatest ally before 1936, his greatest adversary thereafter.

The sit-down strikes, the defeat of the court plan and the purge, and the recession gave considerable confidence to many

---

effort could have succeeded in overcoming entrenched party organizations in the states. Roosevelt, in working with rather than against the pressure groups from 1933 through 1936, was pursuing the only sensible course possible.

inherently conservative congressmen who had already been uneasy or restive with the New Deal in 1935-1936. The beginning of effective conservative opposition in Congress, accordingly, can be set in 1937. But the roots stemmed at least to 1935, and in retrospect it seems that the court plan merely hastened the development of an inevitable division among the disparate elements of the dominant Democratic party.

One major problem remains: how did the conservative bloc function as a group? Was it a well organized conspiracy, or was it simply a loose combination of the moment?

At a glance, the coalition appears to have been well organized. In the Senate fight against the court plan, Burton K. Wheeler of Montana led a bipartisan team against the President. Senators from both parties not only cooperated but met from time to time in private homes to plan joint strategy. And Republicans agreed to keep quiet lest their partisan charges antagonize moderate Democrats. As Vandenberg admitted later, there was a "bipartisan high command. . . . Only a coalition could succeed—a preponderantly Democratic coalition. This was frankly recognized. There was no secret about it. . . . Republicans voluntarily subordinated themselves and withdrew to the reserve lines. . . ."

Many of the senators who opposed the court plan remained at odds with the administration in the 1938 and 1939 sessions, and Wheeler led quite similar blocs against executive reorganization. And in the House, 1937 was the year when the conservative bloc in the Rules Committee first began to operate against the administration, refusing three times between August 1937 and May 1938 to report out the fair labor standards bill. Unquestionably, conservatives in both houses developed networks of personal communications across party lines in 1937 and 1938. On crucial roll call votes it was safe to predict that an all but unanimous group of Republicans in both houses would be joined by at least 20 Democrats in the Senate and from 40 to 110 in the House.

Such evidence, however, does not prove the existence of a coordinated group functioning as a team on all—or even most—issues. Wheeler, for example, was not so reactionary as liberals insisted, and he continued after 1937 to back many administration relief, labor, and farm bills. Conversely, Harrison and Byrnes remained loyal to the administration during both the court and reorganization battles, while stridently opposing the fair labor standards bill, increased spending for relief, and the undistributed profits tax. And foreign policy questions created completely different alignments.

That the type of issue determined the composition of the conservative bloc was especially clear in the 1939 session. In the Senate, conservative alliances defeated the administration in struggles over relief spending in January and temporarily over reorganization in March. The crucial votes were 47-46 and 45-44 respectively. On both occasions Republicans voted solidly against the administration; of the 23 in the Senate, 20 voted against relief and 22 against reorganization. Of the 69 Democrats, 26 opposed relief and 21 reorganization. But the bloc was not monolithic. Eleven of the 26 Democrats against the relief bill supported the President on reorganization; 7 Democrats who had backed the President on relief deserted him on reorganization. A conservative nucleus of 20 Republicans and 15 Democrats opposed the administration on both bills. The others shifted in and out at will. For partisan reasons Republicans were remarkably united, but conservative Democrats were seldom able to work together in either house.

Furthermore, even the predictable core of very conservative Democrats ordinarily voted with Republicans because there was a meeting of the minds, not because they had conferred secretly with them in advance of crucial votes. The fate which befell the one serious effort in the direction of long-range conservative planning revealed the insuperable problems involved in developing such bipartisan agreement. This effort occurred in the fall of 1937.

After the Supreme Court's "switch in time that saved nine" in the spring of 1937, Bailey realized that the Senate must replace the court as the bulwark of conservative strength in the country, and he became anxious to form a more cohesive bloc against the New Deal. "What we have to do," he wrote Byrd in September, "is to preserve, if we can, the Democratic Party against his [Roosevelt's] efforts to make it the Roosevelt Party. But above this we must place the preservation of Constitutional Representative Government. We must frame a policy and maintain it—and this must be done in the next Congress. We must ascertain on whom we may rely—get them together and make our battle, win or lose."

When Bailey and his fellow conservatives returned for a special session in November they determined to put their coalition into effect. On December 2 ten conservative Democrats and two Republicans feasted on quail in a Senate dining room and laid plans for the future. As Vandenberg, one of the participants, put it privately, the group "informally resolved upon attempting a coalition statement to the country." For the next ten days this group, led by Vandenberg, Bailey, and Gerry, worked diligently at consulting conservative colleagues and trying to draft a statement of principles. They sought to present Roosevelt with a show of bipartisan strength and to persuade him to adopt a program more conciliatory to business. But their plan was also "replete with the possibility of open coalition upon the floor of the Senate." Senators who subscribed to the principles enunciated in the statement—broad phrases covering tax, spending, and labor policy—were expected to vote accordingly when these issues arose in subsequent congressional sessions.

Bailey's effort failed dismally. To begin with, moderately conservative Democrats like Harrison and Byrnes refused to participate. As southerners they did not relish formal associations with Republicans, nor did they wish to antagonize the President for no good purpose. Others naturally preferred to maintain their freedom of action in the future. And still others feared that such a challenge would drive Roosevelt, then pursuing an uncertain course in dealing with the recession, into the hands of the spenders. Before Bailey and his cohorts had time to circulate the finished document, McNary secured a copy and gave it to the press, which published it without delay on December 16. The surprised conservatives fumed silently. "Premature publicity—*thanks to treachery*—ended the episode," Vandenberg noted in his scrapbook. "The next time we want to plan a patriotically dramatic contribution to the welfare of the country, we shall let no one in who is not *tried and true.*" Bailey added that the "premature publicity was brought about wholly because this man [McNary] and some of his associates took a partisan view that the declaration of principles would help the Democratic cause and hurt the Republican cause." As both men realized, McNary's action ended the frail hopes for a resounding, well-timed demonstration of conservative strength.

McNary's thinking was indeed partly partisan. At that time he was conferring with Alfred M. Landon, Frank Knox, and other Republican leaders in the Capitol. Encouraged by Roosevelt's declining prestige, these men believed that Republicans could survive without seeking coalitions with conservative Democrats. The idea of a bipartisan statement of conservatism seemed to them considerably less attractive than it did to Vandenberg. Yet McNary's chief motivation was ideological; like other progressive Republicans, he frankly disagreed with the views of the conservatives involved. If Republicans associated with men like Bailey, he believed, they would give the GOP an even more reactionary coloring than it already wore. McNary's "treachery" was evidence both of the power of partisanship and of the divisions within his party.

Neither Bailey nor his fellow conservatives again pressed seriously for the plan. Republicans became increasingly partisan, driving Democrats of all persuasions into uneasy unity for the coming campaign. Despite the attempted purges which followed, both Republicans and Democrats in the ensuing primaries acted along partisan rather than conservative-liberal lines, and the flimsy chances for bipartisan conservative cooperation in the Senate faded quickly. Conservatives continued to vote together in 1938 and 1939 if there was a meeting of the minds; otherwise, as Bailey had feared, they voted apart. As a newsman close to the scene explained at the close of the 1939 session,

> in both houses, when a pro- and anti-New Deal issue is squarely presented, a shifting population of conservative Democrats can be counted upon to join the Republicans to vote against the President. The arrangement is not formal. There is nothing calculated about it, except the Republican strategy originated . . . by McNary of refraining from arousing the Democrats' partisan feelings by inflammatory oratory.

A conservative bipartisan bloc was often able by 1939 to block major legislative extensions of the New Deal. But it was not united, and it followed no blueprint. Conservative congressmen, representing widely differing states and districts, faced widely differing political exigencies. They refused to be chained to a "conspiracy." More important, most congressmen were first of all partisans. For all but a few the party organizations of their constituencies were the chief facts of their political careers, and few of these organizations, in 1937 or at any time, wished bipartisanship to operate for long.

THE NEW DEAL AND THE PROGRESSIVE TRADITION

Carl N. Degler

THE THIRD AMERICAN REVOLUTION

CARL N. DEGLER, Professor of History at Stanford University, is one of the strongest advocates of the argument that the New Deal departed in fundamental ways from past American political practices and traditions. It was not until the 1930's, he believes, that the nation unequivocally abandoned laissez-faire. The economic disaster of the Great Depression led to a national mood which refused to accept the idea that the business cycle was beyond human control. The result was positive, dynamic government participation in economic life, even occasional forays into socialism, on a scale unparalleled in American history. President Roosevelt may have been "at heart a conservative," but he was also an extremely flexible experimentalist who sensed the demand for change and responded to it. Reformers of the past had worked to establish a state which would be an impartial policeman, a regulator. Roosevelt and the New Deal represented a government which went beyond regulation to distribute positive benefits to underprivileged groups and assure minimum levels of well-being to all, a "guarantor state."

Degler's conclusions are extremely controversial. Some historians argue with his characterization of previous progressive reform movements; others doubt that the New Deal established a guarantor state in any meaningful sense and point to the present-day

---

Abridgment of pp. 379, 384–391, 412–416 from *Out of Our Past* by Carl N. Degler. Copyright © 1959 by Carl N. Degler. Reprinted by permission of Harper & Row, Publishers.

existence of mass poverty as proof. One might also quarrel with Degler's depiction of Roosevelt. In seeking to come to grips with Degler's arguments, the reader clearly must find satisfactory definitions for such key terms as "laissez-faire," "guarantor state," and "conservative."

Twice since the founding of the Republic, cataclysmic events have sliced through the fabric of American life, snapping many of the threads which ordinarily bind the past to the future. The War for the Union was one such event, the Great Depression of the 1930's the other. And, as the Civil War was precipitated from the political and moral tensions of the preceding era, so the Great Depression was a culmination of the social and economic forces of industrialization and urbanization which had been transforming America since 1865. A depression of such pervasiveness as that of the thirties could happen only to a people already tightly interlaced by the multitudinous cords of a machine civilization and embedded in the matrix of an urban society.

In all our history no other economic collapse brought so many Americans to near starvation, endured so long, or came so close to overturning the basic institutions of American life. It is understandable, therefore, that from that experience should issue a new conception of the good society.

THE END OF LAISSEZ FAIRE

Perhaps the most striking alteration in American thought which the depression fostered concerned the role of the government in the economy. Buffeted and bewildered by the economic debacle, the American people in the course of the 1930's abandoned, once and for all, the doctrine of laissez faire. This beau ideal of the nineteenth-century economists had become, ever since the days of Jackson, an increasingly cherished shibboleth of Americans. But now it was almost casually discarded. It is true, of course, that the rejection of laissez faire had a long history; certainly the Populists worked to undermine it. But with the depression the nation at large accepted the government as a permanent influence in the economy.

Almost every one of the best-known measures of the federal government during the depression era made inroads into the hitherto private preserves of business and the individual. Furthermore, most of these new measures survived the period, taking their places as fundamental elements in the structure of American life. For modern Americans living under a federal government of transcendent influence and control in the economy, this is the historic meaning of the great depression.

Much of what is taken for granted today as the legitimate function of government and the social responsibility of business began only with the legislation of these turbulent years. Out of the investigation of banking and bankers in 1933, for example, issued legislation which separated commercial banking from the stock and bond markets, and insured the bank deposits of ordinary citizens. The stock market, like the banks, was placed under new controls and a higher sense of responsibility to the public imposed upon it by the new Securities and Exchange Commission. The lesson of Black Tuesday in 1929 had not been forgotten; the classic free market itself—the Exchange—was hereafter to be under continuous governmental scrutiny.

The three Agricultural Adjustment Acts of 1933, 1936, and 1938, while somewhat diverse in detail, laid down the basic lines of what is still today the American approach to the agricultural problem. Ever since the collapse of the boom after the First World War, American agriculture had suffered from the low prices born of the tremendous surpluses. Unable to devise a method for expanding markets to absorb the excess, the government turned to restriction of output as the only feasible alternative. But because restriction of output meant curtailment of income for the farmer, it became necessary, if farm income was to be sustained, that farmers be compensated for their cut in production. Thus was inaugurated the singular phenomenon, which is still a part of the American answer to the agricultural surplus, of paying farmers for *not* growing crops. The other device introduced for raising farm prices, and still the mainstay of our farm policy, came with the 1938 act, which provided that the government would purchase and store excess farm goods, thus supporting the price level by withdrawing the surplus from the competitive market. Both methods constitute a subsidy for the farmer from society at large.

Though the Eisenhower administration in the 1950's called for a return to a free market in farm products—that is, the removal of government supports from prices—very few steps have been taken in that direction, and probably very few ever will. A free market was actually in operation during the twenties, but it succeeded only in making farmers the stepchildren of the golden prosperity of that decade. Today the farm bloc is too powerful politically to be treated so cavalierly. Moreover, the depression has taught most Americans that a free market is not only a rarity in the modern world but sometimes inimical to a stable and lasting prosperity.

Perhaps the most imaginative and fruitful of these innovations was the Tennessee Valley Authority, which transformed the heart of the South. "It was and is literally a down to earth experiment," native Tennesseean Broadus Mitchell has written, "with all that we know from test tube and logarithm tables called on to help. It was a union of heart and mind to restore what had been wasted. It was a social resurrection." For the TVA was much more than flood and erosion control or even hydroelectric power—though its gleaming white dams are perhaps its most striking and best-known monuments. It was social planning of the most humane sort, where even the dead were carefully removed from cemeteries before the waters backed up behind the dams. It brought new ideas, new wealth, new skills, new hope into a wasted, tired, and discouraged region.

At the time of the inception of the TVA, it was scarcely believable that the "backward" South would ever utilize all the power the great dams would create. But in its report of 1956, the Authority declared that the Valley's consumption of electricity far exceeded that produced from water sites: almost three quarters of TVA's power is now generated from steam power, not from waterfall. In large part it was the TVA which taught the Valley how to use more power to expand its industries and to lighten the people's burdens. Back in 1935, Drew and Leon Pearson saw this creation of consumer demand in action. "Uncle Sam is a drummer with a commercial line to sell," they wrote in *Harper's Magazine*. "He sold liberty bonds before, but never refrigerators."

Measured against textbook definitions, the TVA is unquestionably socialism. The government owns the means of production and, moreover, it competes with private producers of electricity. But pragmatic Americans—and particularly those living in the Valley—have had few sleepless nights as a consequence of this fact. The TVA does its appointed job and, as the recent fight over the Dixon and Yates contract seemed to show, it is here to stay. It, too, with all the talk of "creeping socialism," has been absorbed into that new American Way fashioned by the experimentalism of the American people from the wreckage of the Great Depression.

Undoubtedly social security deserves the appellation "revolutionary" quite as much as the TVA; it brought government into the lives of people as nothing had since the draft and the income tax. Social security legislation actually comprises two systems: insurance against old age and insurance in the event of loss of work. The first system was completely organized and operated by the federal government; the second was shared with the states—but the national government set the standards; both were clear acknowledgment of the changes which had taken place in the family and in the business of making a living in America. No longer in urban America could the old folks, whose proportion in the society was steadily increasing, count on being taken in by their offspring as had been customary in a more agrarian world. Besides, such a makeshift arrangement was scarcely satisfying to the self-respect of the oldsters. With the transformation of the economy by industrialization, most Americans had become helpless before the vagaries of the business cycle. As a consequence of the social forces which were steadily augmenting social insecurity, only collective action by the government could arrest the drift.

To have the government concerned about the security of the individual was a new thing. Keenly aware of the novelty of this aim in individualistic America, Roosevelt was careful to deny any serious departure from traditional paths. "These three great objectives—the security of the home, the security of livelihood, and the security of social insurance," he said in 1934, constitute "a minimum of the promise that we can offer to the American people." But this, he quickly added, "does not indicate a change in values."

Whether the American people thought their values had

changed is not nearly as important as the fact that they accepted social security. And the proof that they did is shown in the steady increase in the proportion of the population covered by the old-age benefit program since 1935; today about 80 per cent of nonfarm workers are included in the system. Apart from being a minimum protection for the individual and society against the dry rot of industrial idleness, unemployment insurance is now recognized as one of the major devices for warding off another depression.

It is true, as proponents of the agrarian life have been quick to point out, that an industrialized people, stripped as they are of their economic self-reliance, have felt the need for social insurance more than people in other types of society. But it is perhaps just as important to recognize that it is only in such a highly productive society that people can even dare to dream of social security. Men in other ages have felt the biting pains of economic crisis, but few pre-industrial people have ever enjoyed that surfeit of goods which permits the fat years to fill out the lean ones. But like so much else concerning industrialism, it is not always easy to calculate whether the boons it offers exceed in value the burdens which it imposes.

For the average man, the scourge of unemployment was the essence of the depression. Widespread unemployment, permeating all ranks and stations in society, drove the American people and their government into some of their most determined and deliberate departures from the hallowed policy of "hands off." But despite the determination, as late as 1938 the workless still numbered almost ten million—two thirds as great as in 1932 under President Hoover. The governmental policies of the 1930's never appreciably diminished the horde of unemployed—only the war prosperity of 1940 and after did that—but the providing of jobs by the federal government was a reflection of the people's new conviction that the government had a responsibility to alleviate economic disaster. Such bold action on the part of government, after the inconclusive, bewildered approach of the Hoover administration, was a tonic for the dragging spirits of the people.

A whole range of agencies, from the Civil Works Administration (CWA) to the Works Progress Administration (WPA), were created to carry the attack against unemployment. It is true that the vast program of relief which was organized was not "permanent" in the sense that it is still in being, but for two reasons it deserves to be discussed here. First, since these agencies constituted America's principal weapon against unemployment, some form of them will surely be utilized if a depression should occur again. Second, the various relief agencies of the period afford the best examples of the new welfare outlook, which was then in the process of formation.

Though in the beginning relief programs were premised on little more than Harry Hopkins' celebrated dictum, "Hunger is not debatable," much more complex solutions to unemployment were soon worked out. The relief program of the WPA, which after 1935 was the major relief agency, was a case in point. In 1937, *Fortune* magazine commented on "the evolution of unemployment relief from tool to institution"—a recognition of the importance and duration of relief in America. "In 1936, the federal government was so deeply involved in the relief of the unemployed," *Fortune* contended, "that it was not only keeping them alive, but it was also giving them an opportunity to work; and not only giving them an opportunity to work but giving them an opportunity to work at jobs for which they were peculiarly fitted; and not only giving them an opportunity to work at jobs for which they were peculiarly fitted, but creating for them jobs of an interest and usefulness which they could not have expected to find in private employment." The statement somewhat distorts the work of the WPA, but it sums up the main outlines of the evolution of the relief program.

The various artistic and cultural employment programs of the WPA are excellent examples of how relief provided more than employment, though any of the youth agencies like the Civilian Conservation Corps or the National Youth Administration (it subsidized student work) would serve equally well. At its peak, the Federal Writers' Project employed some 6,000 journalists, poets, novelists, and Ph. D.'s of one sort or another; unknowns worked on the same payroll, if not side by side, with John Steinbeck, Vardis Fisher, and Conrad Aiken. The $46 million expended on art—that is, painting and sculpture—by the WPA in 1936–37 exceeded the artistic budget of any country outside the totalitarian orbit—and there art was frankly propagandistic. *Fortune,* in May, 1937, found the American government's sponsorship of art singularly free of censorship or propaganda. The magazine concluded that "by and large the

Arts Projects have been given a freedom no one would have thought possible in a government run undertaking. And by and large that freedom has not been abused." During the first fifteen months of the Federal Music Project, some fifty million people heard live concerts; in the first year of the WPA Theater, sixty million people in thirty states saw performances, with weekly attendance running to half a million. T. S. Eliot's *Murder in the Cathedral,* too risky for a commercial producer, was presented in New York by the Federal Theater to 40,000 people at a top price of 55 cents.

"What the government's experiments in music, painting, and the theater actually did," concluded *Fortune* in May, 1937, "even in their first year, was to work a sort of cultural revolution in America." For the first time the American audience and the American artist were brought face to face for their mutual benefit. "Art in America is being given its chance," said the British writer Ford Madox Ford, "and there has been nothing like it since before the Reformation. . . ."

Instead of being ignored on the superficially plausible grounds of the exigencies of the depression, the precious skills of thousands of painters, writers, and musicians were utilized. By this timely rescue of skills, tastes, and talents from the deadening hand of unemployment, the American people, through their government, showed their humanity and social imagination. Important for the future was the foresight displayed in the conserving of artistic talents and creations for the enrichment of generations to come.

The entrance of the federal government into a vast program of relief work was an abrupt departure from all previous practice, but it proved enduring. "When President Roosevelt laid it down that government had a social responsibility to care for the victims of the business cycle," *Fortune* remarked prophetically in 1937, "he set in motion an irreversible process." The burden of unemployment relief was too heavy to be carried by local government or private charities in an industrialized society; from now on, the national government would be expected to shoulder the responsibility. "Those who are on relief and in close contact otherwise with public matters realize that what has happened to the country is a bloodless revolution," wrote an anonymous relief recipient in *Harper's* in 1936. The government, he said, has assumed a new role in depressions, and only the rich might still be oblivious to it. But they too "will know it by 1940. And in time," they will "come to approve the idea of everyone having enough to eat." Few people escaped the wide net of the depression: "Anybody sinks after a while," the anonymous reliefer pointed out. "Even you would have if God hadn't preserved, without apparent rhyme or reason, your job and your income." That the depression was a threat to all was perhaps the first lesson gained from the 1930's.

The second was that only through collective defense could such a threat be met. By virtue of the vigorous attacks made upon the economic problems of the thirties by the government, the age-old conviction that dips in the business cycle were either the will of God or the consequence of unalterable economic laws was effectively demolished. As recently as 1931, President Hoover had told an audience that some people "have indomitable confidence that by some legerdemain we can legislate ourselves out of a world-wide depression. Such views are as accurate as the belief that we can exorcise a Caribbean hurricane." From the experience of the depression era, the American people learned that something could and ought to be done when economic disaster strikes. No party and no politician with a future will ever again dare to take the fatalistic and defeatist course of Herbert Hoover in 1929–33.

THE GUARANTOR STATE

In the thirties, as now, the place of the New Deal in the broad stream of American development has been a matter of controversy. Historians and commentators on the American scene have not yet reached a firm agreement—if they ever will—as to whether the New Deal was conservative or radical in character, though it does appear that the consensus now seems to lean toward calling it conservative and traditional. Certainly if one searches the writings and utterances of Franklin Roosevelt, his own consciousness of conservative aims is quickly apparent. "The New Deal is an old deal—as old as the earliest aspirations of humanity for liberty and justice and the good life," he declared in 1934. "It was this administration," he told a Chicago audience in 1936, "which saved the system of private profit and free enterprise after it had been dragged to the brink of ruin. . . ."

But men making a revolution among a profoundly conservative people do not advertise their activity, and above all Franklin Roosevelt understood the temper of his people. Nor should such a statement be interpreted as an insinuation of high conspiracy—far from it. Roosevelt was at heart a conservative, as his lifelong interest in history, among other things, suggests. But he was without dogma in his conservatism. He did not shy away from new means and new approaches to problems when circumstances demanded it. His willingness to experiment, to listen to his university-bred Brains Trust, to accept a measure like the TVA, reveal the flexibility in his thought. Both his lack of theoretical presuppositions and his flexibility are to be seen in the way he came to support novel measures like social security and the Wagner Act. Response to popular demand was the major reason. "The Congress can't stand the pressure of the Townsend Plan unless we have a real old-age insurance system," he complained to Frances Perkins, "nor can I face the country without having . . . a solid plan which will give some assurance to old people of systematic assistance upon retirement." In like manner, the revolutionary NLRA was adopted as a part of his otherwise sketchy and rule-of-thumb philosophy of society. Though ultimately Roosevelt championed the Wagner bill in the House, it was a belated conversion dictated by the foreshadowed success of the measure and the recent invalidation of the NRA. In his pragmatic and common-sense reactions to the exigencies of the depression, Roosevelt, the easygoing conservative, ironically enough became the embodiment of a new era and a new social philosophy for the American people.

"This election," Herbert Hoover presciently said in 1932, "is not a mere shift from the ins to the outs. It means deciding the direction our nation will take over a century to come." The election of Franklin Roosevelt, he predicted, would result in "a radical departure from the foundations of 150 years which have made this the greatest nation in the world." Though Hoover may be charged with nothing more than campaign flourishing, it is nevertheless a fact that his speech was made just after Roosevelt's revealing Commonwealth Club address of September. Only in this single utterance, it should be remembered, did Roosevelt disclose in clear outline the philosophy and program which was later to be the New Deal. "Every man has a right to life," he had said, "and this means that he has also a right to make a comfortable living. . . . Our government, formal and informal, political and economic," he went on, "owes to everyone an avenue to possess himself of a portion of that plenty [from our industrial society] sufficient for his needs, through his own work." Here were the intimations of those new goals which the New Deal set for America.

Accent as heavily as one wishes the continuity between the reforms of the Progressive era and the New Deal, yet the wide difference between the goals of the two periods still remains. The Progressive impulse was narrowly reformist: it limited business, it assisted agriculture, it freed labor from some of the shackles imposed by the courts, but it continued to conceive of the state as policeman or judge and nothing more. The New Deal, on the other hand, was more than a regulator—though it was that too, as shown by the SEC and the reinvigoration of the antitrust division of the Justice Department. To the old goals for America set forth and fought for by the Jeffersonians and the Progressives the New Deal appended new ones. Its primary and general innovation was the guaranteeing of a minimum standard of welfare for the people of the nation. WPA and the whole series of relief agencies which were a part of it, wages and hours legislation, AAA, bank deposit insurance, and social security,* each illustrates this new conception of the federal government. A resolution offered by New Deal Senator Walsh in 1935 clearly enunciated the new obligations of government. The resolution took notice of the disastrous effects of the depression "upon the lives of young men and women . . ." and then went on to say that "it is the duty of the Federal Government to use every possible means of opening up opportunities" for the youth of the nation "so that they may be rehabilitated and restored to *a decent standard of living* and ensured proper development of their talents. . . ."

But the guarantor state as it developed under the New Deal

* Social security is an excellent example of how, under the New Deal, reform measures, when they conflicted with recovery, were given priority. In siphoning millions of dollars of social security taxes from the purchasing power of the workers, social security was a deflationary measure, which must have seriously threatened the precariously based new economic recovery. For this reason and others, Abraham Epstein, the foremost authority in America on social security, denounced the act as a "sharing of poverty."

was more active and positive than this. It was a vigorous and dynamic force in the society, energizing and, if necessary, supplanting private enterprise when the general welfare required it. With the Wagner Act, for example, the government served notice that it would actively participate in securing the unionization of the American worker; the state was no longer to be an impartial policeman merely keeping order; it now declared for the side of labor. When social and economic problems like the rehabilitation of the Valley of the Tennessee were ignored or shirked by private enterprise, then the federal government undertook to do the job. Did private enterprise fail to provide adequate and sufficient housing for a minimum standard of welfare for the people, then the government would build houses. As a result, boasted Nathan Straus, head of the U.S. Housing Authority, "for the first time in a hundred years the slums of America ceased growing and began to shrink."

Few areas of American life were beyond the touch of the experimenting fingers of the New Deal; even the once sacrosanct domain of prices and the valuation of money felt the tinkering. The devaluation of the dollar, the gold-purchase program, the departure from the gold standard—in short, the whole monetary policy undertaken by F. D. R. as a means to stimulate recovery through a price rise—constituted an unprecedented repudiation of orthodox public finance. To achieve that minimum standard of well-being which the depression had taught the American people to expect of their government, nothing was out of bounds.

But it is not the variety of change which stamps the New Deal as the creator of a new America; its significance lies in the permanence of its program. For, novel as the New Deal program was, it has, significantly, not been repudiated by the Eisenhower administration, the first Republican government since the reforms were instituted. Verbally, it is true, the Republican administration has had to minimize its actual commitments to the New Deal philosophy, and it tends to trust private business more than the New Dealers did—witness, for example, its elimination of the minor governmental manufacturing enterprises which competed with private firms. But despite this, the administration's firm commitment to the guaranteeing of prosperity and averting depression at all costs is an accurate reflection of the American people's agreement with the New Deal's diagnosis of the depression. Nor has the Republican party dared to repeal or even emasculate the legislation which made up the vitals of the New Deal: TVA, banking and currency, SEC, social security, the Wagner Act, and fair treatment of the Negro. The New Deal Revolution has become so much a part of the American Way that no political party which aspires to high office dares now to repudiate it.

It may or may not be significant in this regard (for apothegms are more slippery than precise) but it is nonetheless interesting that Roosevelt and Eisenhower have both been impressed with the same single sentence from Lincoln regarding the role of government. "The legitimate object of Government," wrote Lincoln, "is to do for a community of people whatever they need to have done but cannot do at all or cannot do so well for themselves in their separate or individual capacities." Twice, in 1934 and again in 1936, F. D. R. in public addresses used this expression to epitomize his own New Deal, and Robert Donovan in his officially inspired book on the Eisenhower administration writes that this same "fragment of Lincoln's writing . . . Eisenhower uses time and again in describing his own philosophy of government." Between Lincoln and Eisenhower there was no Republican President, except perhaps Theodore Roosevelt, who would have been willing to subscribe to such a free-wheeling description of the federal power; in this can be measured the impact of the New Deal and the depression.

The conclusion seems inescapable that, traditional as the words may have been in which the New Deal expressed itself, in actuality it was a revolutionary response to a revolutionary situation. In its long history America has passed through two revolutions since the first one in 1776, but only the last two, the Civil War and the depression, were of such force as to change the direction of the relatively smooth flow of its progress. The Civil War rendered a final and irrevocable decision in the long debate over the nature of the Union and the position of the Negro in American society. From that revolutionary experience, America emerged a strong national state and dedicated by the words of its most hallowed document to the inclusion of the black man in a democratic culture. The searing ordeal of the Great Depression purged the American people of their belief in the limited powers of the federal government and convinced them of the necessity of the guarantor state. And as the Civil War constituted a watershed in American thought, so the depression and its New Deal marked the crossing of a divide from which, it would seem, there could be no turning back.

Richard Hofstadter

THE NEW DEPARTURE AND THE NEW OPPORTUNISM

RICHARD HOFSTADTER, DeWitt Clinton Professor of History at Columbia University, is in essential agreement with Carl Degler's argument that the New Deal represented a great divide in the history of American reform. In this selection from his Pulitzer Prize-winning volume, *The Age of Reform,* Hofstadter presents a sophisticated, if highly impressionistic, analysis of the differences between the New Deal and the progressive movement. The New Dealers, he argues, unlike previous reformers, had to devote most of their energies to combating a serious depression; they could not concentrate on such progressive hobgoblins as the city machines or the trusts. The New Deal, moreover, was "social-democratic" rather than "entrepreneurial" in outlook. The progressives had been interested mainly in creating opportunities for aspiring business and professional groups; the New Dealers were centrally concerned with social welfare legislation. The New Deal was opportunistic, experimental, politically amoral, and, by implication, practical; the progressive movement rigidly moralistic and, by implication, unrealistic and impractical.

Hofstadter's interpretation raises many of the same questions as Degler's. In addition, one might ask whether the New Deal approach to the question of monopoly provides evidence of a new

---

From *The Age of Reform: From Bryan to F. D. R.* (Vintage ed.) by Richard Hofstadter, pp. 302–328. Copyright © 1955 by Richard Hofstadter. Reprinted by permission of Alfred A. Knopf, Inc.

departure in American reform or whether it indicates that on this problem the New Deal was simply caught up in the same dilemma as the progressive movement. One might also disagree that Hofstadter's major example, Thurman Arnold, embodied New Deal thought to the extent that the author believes. Whatever one's reservations, however, it is undeniable that Hofstadter's subtle interpretation is a major contribution to New Deal historiography.

THE NEW DEPARTURE

The Great Depression, which broke the mood of the twenties almost as suddenly as the postwar reaction had killed the Progressive fervor, rendered obsolete most of the antagonisms that had flavored the politics of the postwar era. Once again the demand for reform became irresistible, and out of the chaotic and often mutually contradictory schemes for salvation that arose from all corners of the country the New Deal took form. In the years 1933–8 the New Deal sponsored a series of legislative changes that made the enactments of the Progressive era seem timid by comparison, changes that, in their totality, carried the politics and administration of the United States farther from the conditions of 1914 than those had been from the conditions of 1880.

It is tempting, out of a desire for symmetry and historical continuity, to see in the New Deal a return to the preoccupations of Progressivism, a resumption of the work of reform that had begun under Theodore Roosevelt and Woodrow Wilson, and a consummation of the changes that were proposed in the half-dozen years before the first World War. Much reason can be found for yielding to this temptation. Above all, the New Dealers shared with the Progressives a far greater willingness than had been seen in previous American history to make use of the machinery of government to meet the needs of the people and supplement the workings of the national economy. There are many occasions in its history when the New Deal, especially in its demand for organization, administration, and management from a central focus, seems to stand squarely in the tradition of the New Nationalism for which such Progressives as Herbert Croly had argued. Since it is hardly possible for any society to carve out a completely new vocabulary for every new problem it faces, there is also much in the New Deal rhetoric that is strongly reminiscent of Progressivism. Like the Progressives, the New Dealers invoked a larger democracy; and where the Progressives had their "plutocrats," the New Dealers had their "economic royalists." F. D. R., asserting in his first inaugural address that "The money changers have fled from their high seats in the temple of our civilization. We may now restore that temple to the ancient truths," sounds very much like almost any inspirational writer for *McClure's* in the old days.* On a number of particular issues, moreover, like the holding-company question, monopoly, and public power, one feels as though one is treating again, in the New Deal, with familiar problems—just as, in the crucial early days of 1933, the formation of a strong bloc of inflationist Senators from the West seemed to hark back to the Populist movement.

Still, granting that absolute discontinuities do not occur in history, and viewing the history of the New Deal as a whole, what seems outstanding about it is the drastic new departure that it marks in the history of American reformism. † The New Deal was different from anything that had yet happened in the United States: different because its central problem was unlike the problems of Progressivism; different in its ideas and its spirit and its techniques. Many men who had lived through Progressivism and had thought of its characteristic proposals as being in the main line of American traditions, even as being restoratives of those traditions, found in the New Deal an outrageous departure from everything they had known and valued, and so could interpret it only as an effort at subversion or as

* Naturally there was also some continuity in personnel, for F. D. R. himself was only one of a considerable number of American leaders who had been young Progressives before the war and were supporters of the major reforms of the thirties. However, one could draw up an equally formidable list—chiefly Republican insurgents of the Bull Moose era, but also many Democrats—who had supported Progressive measures and later became heated critics of the New Deal.

† Here I find myself in agreement with the view expressed by Samuel Lubell . . .: "The distinctive feature of the political revolution which Franklin D. Roosevelt began and Truman inherited lies not in its resemblance to the political wars of Andrew Jackson or Thomas Jefferson, but in its abrupt break with the continuity of the past."

the result of overpowering alien influences. Their opposition was all too often hysterical, but in their sense that something new had come into American political and economic life they were quite right.

Consider, to begin, the fundamental problem that the New Dealers faced, as compared with the problems of the Progressives. When Theodore Roosevelt took office in 1901, the country was well over three years past a severe depression and in the midst of a period of healthy economic development. Its farmers were more prosperous than they had been for about forty years, its working class was employed and gaining in living standards, and even its middle class was far busier counting the moral costs of success than it was worrying about any urgent problems of family finance. When F. D. R. took his oath of office, the entire working apparatus of American economic life had gone to smash. The customary masters and leaders of the social order were themselves in a state of near panic. Millions were unemployed, and discontent had reached a dangerous pitch on the farms and in the cities.

Indeed, the New Deal episode marks the first in the history of reform movements when a leader of the reform party took the reins of a government confronted above all by the problems of a sick economy. To be sure, the whole nineteenth-century tradition of reform in American politics was influenced by experience with periodic economic breakdowns; but its political leaders had never had to bear responsibility for curing them. Jefferson in 1801, Jackson in 1829, and after them T. R. and Wilson—all took over at moments when the economy was in good shape. While each of them had experience with economic relapse—Jefferson in 1807, as the consequence of his embargo policies, the Jacksonians briefly in 1834 and again after 1837, T. R. briefly during the "bankers' panic" of 1907, and Wilson with a momentary recession just before the wartime boom—their thinking, and the thinking of the movements they represented, was centered upon sharing an existing prosperity among the various social classes rather than upon restoring a lost prosperity or preventing recurrent slumps.

The earlier American tradition of political protest had been a response to the needs of entrepreneurial classes or of those who were on the verge of entrepreneurship—the farmers, small businessmen, professionals, and occasionally the upper caste of the artisans or the working class. The goal of such classes had generally been to clear the way for new enterprises and new men, break up privileged business, big business, and monopolies, and give the small man better access to credit. The ideas of this Progressive tradition, as one might expect, were founded not merely upon acceptance but even upon glorification of the competitive order. The Jeffersonians, the Jacksonians, and after them most of the Progressives had believed in the market economy, and the only major qualification of this belief they cared to make stemmed from their realization that the market needed to be policed and moralized by a government responsive to the needs of the economic beginner and the small entrepreneur. Occasionally, very occasionally, they had argued for the exercise of a few positive functions on the part of the national government, but chiefly they preferred to keep the positive functions of government minimal, and, where these were necessary, to keep them on the state rather than put them on the national level. Their conceptions of the role of the national government were at first largely negative and then largely preventive. In the Jeffersonian and Jacksonian days it was to avoid excessive expenditure and excessive taxation, to refrain from giving privileged charters. Later, in the corporate era, it was to prevent abuses by the railroads and the monopolists, to check and to regulate unsound and immoral practices. It is of course true that some of the more "advanced" thinkers of the Populist and Progressive movements began to think tentatively of more positive functions for government, but it was just such proposals—the subtreasury scheme for agricultural credits and the various public-ownership proposals—that provoked the greatest opposition when attempts were made to apply them on a national scale.

The whole reformist tradition, then, displayed a mentality founded on the existence of an essentially healthy society; it was chiefly concerned not with managing an economy to meet the problems of collapse but simply with democratizing an economy in sound working order. Managing an economy in such a way as to restore prosperity is above all a problem of organization,* while democratizing a well-organized economy

* The closest thing to an earlier model for the first efforts of the New Deal was not the economic legislation of Progressivism but the efforts of the Wilson administration to organize the economy for the first World War. Hugh Johnson in the NRA and George Peek in the AAA were in many ways recapitulating the experience they had had in the War Industries Board under Bernard Baruch.

had been, as we have seen, in some important respects an attempt to find ways of attacking or limiting organization. Hence the Progressive mind was hardly more prepared than the conservative mind for what came in 1929. Herbert Hoover, an old Bull Mooser, while more disposed to lead the country than any president had been in any previous depression, was unprepared for it, and was prevented from adjusting to it by a doctrinaire adherence to inherited principles. F. D. R.—a fairly typical product of Progressivism who had first won office in 1910—was also unprepared for it in his economic thinking, as anyone will see who examines his career in the 1920's, † but he was sufficiently opportunistic and flexible to cope with it somewhat more successfully.

Hoover, an engineer born in Iowa, represented the moral traditions of native Protestant politics. An amateur in politics who had never run for office before he was elected President in 1928, he had no patience with the politician's willingness to accommodate, and he hung on, as inflexibly as the situation would permit, to the private and voluntary methods that had always worked well in his administrative career.‡ F. D. R., a seasoned professional politician who had learned his trade straddling the terrible antagonisms of the 1920's, was thoroughly at home in the realities of machine politics and a master of the machine techniques of accommodation. Unlike Hoover, he had few hard and fast notions about economic principles, but he knew that it would be necessary to experiment and improvise. "It is common sense," he said in 1932, "to take a method and try it. If it fails, admit it frankly and try another. But above all, try something."

To describe the resulting flood of legislation as economic planning would be to confuse planning with interventionism. Planning was not quite the word for the New Deal: considered as an economic movement, it was a chaos of experimentation. Genuine planners like Rexford Guy Tugwell found themselves floundering amid the cross-currents of the New Deal, and ended in disillusionment. But if, from an economic standpoint, the New Deal was altogether lacking in that rationality or con-

† See Frank Freidel's *Franklin Roosevelt: the Ordeal* (Boston, 1954), and his forthcoming volume on F. D. R.'s governorship.

‡ Characteristically, also, Hoover accepted what might be called the nativist view of the Great Depression: it came from abroad; it was the product, not of any deficiencies in the American economy, but of repercussions of the unsound institutions of Europe.

sistency which is implied in the concept of planning, from a political standpoint it represented a masterly shifting equipoise of interests. And little wonder that some of the old Republican insurgents shuddered at its methods. If the state was believed neutral in the days of T. R. because its leaders claimed to sanction favors for no one, the state under F. D. R. could be called neutral only in the sense that it offered favors to everyone.

Even before F. D. R. took office a silent revolution had taken place in public opinion, the essential character of which can be seen when we recall how little opposition there was in the country, at the beginning, to the assumption of the New Dealers that henceforth, for the purposes of recovery, the federal government was to be responsible for the condition of the labor market as a part of its concern with the industrial problem as a whole. Nothing revolutionary was intended—but simply as a matter of politics it was necessary for the federal government to assume primary responsibility for the relief of the unemployed. And, simply as a matter of politics, if the industrialists were to be given the power to write enforceable codes of fair practice, labor must at least be given some formal recognition of its right of collective bargaining. Certainly no one foresaw, in the first year or two of the New Deal, that the immense infusions of purchasing power into the economy through federal unemployment relief would be as lasting or as vital a part of the economy of the next several years as they proved in fact to be. Nor did anyone foresee how great and powerful a labor movement would be called into being by the spirit and the promise of the New Deal and by the partial recovery of its first few years. But by the end of 1937 it was clear that something had been added to the social base of reformism. The demands of a large and powerful labor movement, coupled with the interests of the unemployed, gave the later New Deal a social-democratic tinge that had never before been present in American reform movements. Hitherto concerned very largely with reforms of an essentially entrepreneurial sort and only marginally with social legislation, American political reformism was fated henceforth to take responsibility on a large scale for social security, unemployment insurance, wages and hours, and housing.*

* As the counsel for the National Association of Manufacturers put it: "Regulation has passed from the negative stage of directing and con-

Still more imposing was the new fiscal role of the federal government. Again, none of this was premeditated. Large-scale spending and unbalanced budgets were, in the beginning, a response to imperative needs. While other schemes for recovery seemed to fall short of expectations, spending kept the economy going; and it was only when F. D. R. tried in 1937 to cut back expenditures that he learned that he had become the prisoner of his spending policies, and turned about and made a necessity into a virtue. His spending policy never represented, at any time before the outbreak of the war, an unambiguous or wholehearted commitment to Keynesian economics. Here only the war itself could consummate the fiscal revolution that the New Deal began. In 1940 Lord Keynes published in the United States an article in which he somewhat disconsolately reviewed the American experience with deficit spending during the previous decade. "It seems politically impossible," he concluded, "for a capitalistic democracy to organize expenditure on the scale necessary to make the grand experiment which would prove my case—except in war conditions." He then added that preparations for war and the production of armaments might teach Americans so much about the potentialities of their economy that it would be "the stimulus, which neither the victory nor the defeat of the New Deal could give you, to greater individual consumption and a higher standard of life." † How remarkably prophetic this was we can now see. There had been under peacetime conditions an immense weeping and wailing over the budgets of F. D. R.—which at their peak ran to seven billion dollars. Now we contemplate budgets of over eighty billion dollars with somewhat less anguish, because we know that most of this expenditure will be used for defense and will not be put to uses that are politically more controversial. But, above all, we have learned things about the possibilities of our economy that were not dreamed of in 1933,

---

trolling the character and form of business activity. The concept that the function of government was to prevent exploitation by virtue of superior power has been replaced by the concept that it is the duty of government to provide security against all the major hazards of life—against unemployment, accident, illness, old age, and death." Thomas P. Jenkin: *Reactions of Major Groups to Positive Government in the United States* (Berkeley, 1945), pp. 300–1.

† J. M. Keynes: "The United States and the Keynes Plan," *New Republic*, Vol. CIII (July 29, 1940), p. 158.

much less in 1903. While men still grow angry over federal fiscal and tax policies, hardly anyone doubts that in the calculable future it will be the fiscal role of the government that more than anything else determines the course of the economy.

And what of the old Progressive issues? They were bypassed, sidestepped, outgrown—anything but solved. To realize how true this was, one need only look at the New Deal approach to those two *bêtes noires* of the Progressive mind, the machines and the trusts.

Where the Progressives spent much of their energy, as we have seen, trying to defeat the bosses and the machines and to make such changes in the political machinery of the country as would bring about direct popular democracy and "restore government to the people," the New Deal was almost completely free of such crusading. To the discomfort of the old-fashioned, principled liberals who were otherwise enthusiastic about his reforms, F. D. R. made no effort to put an end to bossism and corruption, but simply ignored the entire problem. In the interest of larger national goals and more urgent needs, he worked with the bosses wherever they would work with him—and did not scruple to include one of the worst machines of all, the authoritarian Hague machine in New Jersey. As for the restoration of democracy, he seemed well satisfied with his feeling that the broadest public needs were at least being served by the state and that there was such an excellent rapport between the people and their executive leadership.*

The chief apparent exception to this opportune and managerial spirit in the field of political reform—namely, the attempt to enlarge the Supreme Court—proves on examination to be no exception at all. F. D. R.'s fight over the Supreme Court was begun, after all, not in the interest of some large "democratic" principle or out of a desire to reform the Constitutional machinery as such, but because the Court's decisions had made it seem impossible to achieve the managerial reorganization of society that was so urgently needed. His first concern was not that judicial review was "undemocratic" but

* Of course to speak of democracy in purely domestic terms is to underestimate the world-wide significance of the New Deal. At a time when democracy was everywhere in retreat, the New Deal gave to the world an example of a free nation coping with the problems of its economy in a democratic and humane way.

that the federal government had been stripped, as he thought, of its power to deal effectively with economic problems. Nor was this fight waged in the true Progressive spirit. The Progressives, too, had had their difficulties with the judiciary, and had responded with the characteristically principled but practically difficult proposal for the recall of judicial decisions. In short, they raised for reconsideration, as one might expect of principled men, the entire question of judicial review. F. D. R. chose no such method.* To reopen the entire question of the propriety of judicial review of the acts of Congress under a representative democracy would have been a high-minded approach to what he felt was a Constitutional impasse, but it would have ended perhaps even more disastrously than the tactic he employed. F. D. R. avoided such an approach, which would have involved a cumbersome effort to amend the Constitution, and devised a "gimmick" to achieve his ends—the pretense that the age of the judges prevented them from remaining abreast of their calendar, and the demand for the right to supplement the judiciary, to the number of six, with an additional judge for each incumbent who reached the age of seventy without retiring.

Students of the Court fight are fond of remarking that Roosevelt won his case, because the direction of the Court's decisions began to change while the fight was in progress and because Justice Van Devanter's retirement enabled the President to appoint a liberal justice and decisively change the composition of the Court.† It seems important, however, to point

* Indeed, in his message calling for reorganization Roosevelt declared that his proposal would make unnecessary any fundamental changes in the powers of the courts or in the Constitution, "changes which involve consequences so far-reaching as to cause uncertainty as to the wisdom of such a course." It remained for the leading senatorial opponent of the bill, Senator Burton K. Wheeler, to advocate an amendment to the Constitution permitting Congress to override judicial vetoes of its acts. Charles A. and Mary R. Beard: *America in Midpassage* (New York, 1939), Vol. I, p. 355.

† Presumably it will always be debated whether the new harmony between Congress and the Supreme Court that developed even while the Court fight was going on can be attributed to Roosevelt's Court reform bill. Merlo Pusey in his *Charles Evans Hughes* (Vol. II, pp. 766 ff.) argues that the change in the Court's decisions was not a political response to the legislative struggle. He points out, among other things, that the New Deal legislation that came before the Court after the NRA and AAA decisions was better drafted. It is beyond doubt, however, that the resignation of Van Devanter was precipitated by the Court fight. Ibid., Vol II,

out that a very heavy price had to be paid for even this pragmatic attempt to alter a great and sacrosanct conservative institution. The Court fight alienated many principled liberals and enabled many of F. D. R.'s conservative opponents to portray him to the public more convincingly as a man who aspired to personal dictatorship and aimed at the subversion of the Republic.

If we look at the second of the two great foes of Progressivism, big business and monopoly, we find that by the time of the New Deal public sentiment had changed materially. To be sure, the coming of the depression and the revelation of some of the less palatable business practices of the 1920's brought about a climate of opinion in which the leadership of business, and particularly of big business, was profoundly distrusted and bitterly resented. Its position certainly was, in these respects, considerably weaker than it had been twenty-five years before. Still, by 1933 the American public had lived with the great corporation for so long that it was felt to be domesticated, and there was far more concern with getting business life on such a footing as would enable it to provide jobs than there was with breaking up the larger units. The New Deal never developed a clear or consistent line on business consolidation, and New Dealers fought over the subject in terms that were at times reminiscent of the old battles between the trust-busters and the trust-regulators. What can be said, however, is that the subject of bigness and monopoly was subordinated in the New Deal era to that restless groping for a means to bring recovery that was so characteristic of Roosevelt's efforts. The New Deal began not with a flourish of trust-busting but rather, in the NRA, with an attempt to solve the problems of the business order through a gigantic system of governmentally underwritten codes that would ratify the trustification of society. One of the first political setbacks suffered by the New Deal arose from just this—for it had put the formation of its codes of fair practice so completely in the hands of the big-business interests that both small businessmen and organized labor were seriously resentful. Only five years

p. 761. The fact that advocates of both sides can go on arguing about who won the fight is the best evidence that the issue was satisfactorily settled. It aroused so much feeling that an unambiguous victory for either side would have been unfortunate.

from the date of its passage, after the NRA had failed to produce a sustained recovery and had been declared unconstitutional by the Supreme Court, did the administration turn off and take the opposite tack with its call for an inquiry into corporate consolidation and business power that led to the Temporary National Economic Committee's memorable investigation.* Although at the time many observers thought that the old Progressive trust-busting charade was about to be resumed, the New Deal never became committed to a categorical "dissection" of the business order of the sort Wilson had talked of in 1912, nor to the "demonstration" prosecutions with which T. R. had both excited and reassured the country. The New Deal was not trying to re-establish the competitive order that Wilson had nostalgically invoked and that T. R. had sternly insisted was no longer possible. Its approach, as it turned out, was severely managerial, and distinctly subordinated to those economic considerations that would promote purchasing power and hence recovery. It was, in short, a concerted effort to discipline the pricing policies of businesses, not with the problem of size in mind, nor out of consideration for smaller competitors, but with the purpose of eliminating that private power to tax which is the prerogative of monopoly, and of leaving in the hands of consumers vital purchasing power.

History cannot quite repeat itself, if only because the participants in the second round of any experience are aware of the outcome of the first. The anti-trust philosophers of the closing years of the New Deal were quite aware that previous efforts to enforce the Sherman Act had been ceremonial demonstrations rather than serious assaults upon big business. Thurman Arnold, who was put in charge of the anti-trust program, was well known for his belief that earlier interpretations of the Sherman Act had actually concealed and encouraged business consolidation. In his account of the contemporary function of anti-trust prosecution Arnold put his emphasis upon benefits for the consumer and repudiated the earlier use of the Sherman Act: "Since the consumers' interest was not emphasized, such enforcement efforts as existed were directed at the punishment of offenses rather than the achievement of economic objectives. Indeed, in very few antitrust prosecu-

* There had been in the meantime, however, the assault upon the holding companies embodied in the so-called "death sentence" of 1935.

tions was any practical economic objective defined or argued with respect to the distribution of any particular product. In this way the moral aspects of the offense, and that will-o'-the-wisp, corporate intent, became more important considerations than economic results. Antitrust enforcement, not being geared to the idea of consumers' interests, became a hunt for offenders instead of an effort to test the validity of organized power by its performance in aiding or preventing the flow of goods in commerce. The result was that although the economic ideal of a free competitive market as the cornerstone of our economy was kept alive, no adequate enforcement staff was ever provided to make that ideal a reality. Such, broadly speaking, was the state of the Sherman Act from 1890 down to the great depression." *

But if such a position as Thurman Arnold's can be legitimately distinguished from the Progressive type of antitrust, as I think it can, there are men today whose political thinking was forged in the service of the New Deal who go beyond him in repudiating anti-trust action as a mere attack upon size, and who take, on the whole, an acquiescent attitude toward big business. A few years ago John Kenneth Galbraith made quite a stir with his book *American Capitalism,* whose central thesis was that the process of business consolidation creates within itself a "countervailing power"—that is, that it brings about the organization not merely of strong sellers but of strong buyers as well, who distribute through large sectors of the economy their ability to save through organization.† In Galbraith's book, as in most recent literature in defense of bigness, it is not the effort at disorganization but the effects of counter-organization, in labor, agriculture, and government and within business itself, that are counted upon to minimize the evils of consolidation. More recently David Lilienthal, another graduate of the New Deal administrative agencies, has written a strong apologia for big business that followed Galbraith in stressing the technologically progressive character of large-scale industry in language that would have horrified Brandeis

* Thurman Arnold: *The Bottlenecks of Business* (New York, 1940), p. 263.
† This is a rather simplified statement of the thesis of Galbraith's *American Capitalism* (Boston, 1952). Students of the history of antitrust ideologies will be particularly interested in Galbraith's strictures on the TNEC Report (pp. 59–60).

and Wilson.* It is not clear whether the attitudes of men like Galbraith and Lilienthal represent dominant liberal sentiment today—though it may be pertinent to say that their books brought no outpouring of protest from other liberal writers. The spectacle of liberals defending, with whatever qualifications, bigness and concentration in industry suggests that that anti-monopoly sentiment which was so long at the heart of Progressive thinking is no longer its central theme. The generation for which Wilson and Brandeis spoke looked to economic life as a field for the expression of character; modern liberals seem to think of it quite exclusively as a field in which certain results are to be expected. It is this change in the moral stance that seems most worthy of remark. A generation ago, and more, the average American was taught to expect that a career in business would and should be in some sense a testing and proving ground for character and manhood, and it was in these terms that the competitive order was often made most appealing.† Contrariwise, those who criticized the economic order very commonly formed their appeals within the same mold of moral suasion: the economic order failed to bring out or reward the desired qualities of character, to reward virtue and penalize vice; it was a source of inequities and injustices. During the last fifteen or twenty years, however, as Galbraith observes, "the American radical has ceased to talk about inequality or exploitation under capitalism or even its 'inherent contradictions.' He has stressed, instead, the unreliability of its performance." ‡

* Galbraith argues that "the competition of the competitive model . . . almost completely precludes technical development" and that indeed "there must be some element of monopoly in an industry if it is to be progressive." Ibid., pp. 91, 93, and chapter vii, *passim.* Cf. David Lilienthal: *Big Business: a New Era* (New York, 1953), chapter vi. For another such friendly treatment by a former New Dealer, see Adolph A. Berle: *The Twentieth Century Capitalist Revolution* (New York, 1954).

† See, for instance, the touching letter quoted by Lilienthal (op. cit., p. 198), from a university graduate of the twenties: "We were dismayed at the vista of mediocre aspiration and of compartmentalized lives. The course of a big business career was predictable and foreclosed. It was also, as the personnel department pointed out, secure. The appeal of graduated salary raises and retirement on a pension was held out as the big lure. But in my high school days the appeal had been to ambition, a good deal was said about achievement and independence."

‡ Galbraith, op. cit., p. 70.

THE NEW OPPORTUNISM

The New Deal, and the thinking it engendered, represented the triumph of economic emergency and human needs over inherited notions and inhibitions. It was conceived and executed above all in the spirit of what Roosevelt called "bold, persistent experimentation," and what those more critical of the whole enterprise considered crass opportunism. In discussing Progressivism I emphasized its traffic in moral absolutes, its exalted moral tone. While something akin to this was by no means entirely absent from the New Deal, the later movement showed a strong and candid awareness that what was happening was not so much moral reformation as economic experimentation. Much of this experimentation seemed to the conservative opponents of the New Deal as not only dangerous but immoral.

The high moral indignation of the critics of the New Deal sheds light on another facet of the period—the relative reversal of the ideological roles of conservatives and reformers. Naturally in all ideologies, conservative or radical, there is a dual appeal to ultimate moral principles and to the practical necessities of institutional life. Classically, however, it has been the strength of conservatives that their appeal to institutional continuities, hard facts, and the limits of possibility is better founded; while it has usually been the strength of reformers that they arouse moral sentiments, denounce injustices, and rally the indignation of the community against intolerable abuses. Such had been the alignment of arguments during the Progressive era. During the New Deal, however, it was the reformers whose appeal to the urgent practical realities was most impressive—to the farmers without markets, to the unemployed without bread or hope, to those concerned over the condition of the banks, the investment market, and the like. It was the conservatives, on the other hand, who represented the greater moral indignation and rallied behind themselves the inspirational literature of American life; and this not merely because the conservatives were now the party of the opposition, but because things were being done of such drastic novelty that they seemed to breach all the inherited rules, not merely of practicality but of morality itself. Hence, if one wishes to look for utopianism in the 1930's, for an exalted faith in the intangibles of morals and character, and for moral indignation of the kind that had once been chiefly the prerogative of the reformers, one will find it far more readily in the editorials of the great conservative newspapers than in the literature of the New Deal. If one seeks for the latter-day equivalent of the first George Kennan, warning the people of San Francisco that it would do them no good to have a prosperous town if in gaining it they lost their souls, one will find it most readily in the 1930's among those who opposed federal relief for the unemployed because it would destroy their characters or who were shocked by the devaluation of the dollar, not because they always had a clear conception of its consequences, but above all because it smacked to them of dirtiness and dishonesty. In the past it had been the conservatives who controlled the settlement of the country, set up its great industrial and communications plant, and founded the fabulous system of production and distribution upon which the country prided itself, while the reformers pointed to the human costs, the sacrifice of principles, and drew blueprints to show how the job could be better done. Now, however, it was the reformers who fed the jobless or found them jobs, saved the banks, humanized industry, built houses and schools and public buildings, rescued farmers from bankruptcy, and restored hope—while the conservatives, expropriated at once from their customary control of affairs and from their practical role, invoked sound principles, worried about the Constitution, boggled over details, pleaded for better morals, and warned against tyranny.

Lamentably, most of the conservative thinking of the New Deal era was hollow and cliché-ridden. What seems most striking about the New Deal itself, however, was that all its ferment of practical change produced a very slight literature of political criticism. While the changes of the Progressive era had produced many significant books of pamphleteering or thoughtful analyses of society—the writings of such men as Croly, Lippmann, Weyl, Brooks Adams, Brandeis, the muckrakers, Socialist critics like W. J. Ghent and William English Walling—the New Deal produced no comparable body of political writing that would survive the day's headlines. In part this was simply a matter of time: the Progressive era lasted over a dozen years, and most of the significant writing it engendered came during its later phases, particularly after 1910; whereas the dynamic phase of the New Deal was concentrated in the six hectic years from 1933 to 1938. Perhaps still more important is the fact that the New Deal brought with it such a rapid bureaucratic expansion and such a complex multitude of problems that it created an immense market for the skills of reform-minded Americans from law, journalism, politics, and the professoriat. The men who might otherwise have been busy analyzing the meaning of events were caught up in the huge expanding bureaucracy and put to work drafting laws that would pass the courts, lobbying with refractory Congressmen, or relocating sharecroppers.

To this generalization there is one noteworthy exception: In his two books, *The Symbols of Government* and *The Folklore of Capitalism,* Thurman Arnold wrote works of great brilliance and wit and considerable permanent significance—better books, I believe, than any of the political criticism of the Progressive era.* But what do we find in these works, the most advanced of the New Deal camp? We find a sharp and sustained attack upon ideologies, rational principles, and moralism in politics. We find, in short, the theoretical equivalent of F. D. R.'s opportunistic virtuosity in practical politics—a theory that attacks theories. For Arnold's books which were of course directed largely against the ritualistic thinking of the conservatives of the 1930's, might stand equally well as an attack upon that moralism which we found so insistent in the thinking of Progressivism.

Arnold's chief concern was with the disparities between the way society actually works and the mythology through which the sound lawyers, economists, and moralists attempt to understand it. His books are an explanation of the ritualistic and functionally irrational character of most of the superficially rational principles by which society lives. At the time his books were written, the necessity of coping with a breakdown in the actual workings of the economy had suddenly confronted men with the operational uselessness of a great many accepted words and ideas. The language of politics, economics, and law

* Thurman W. Arnold: *The Symbols of Government* (New Haven, 1935), *The Folklore of Capitalism* (New Haven, 1937). By 1941 the first of these works had gone through five printings; the second, fourteen.

had itself become so uncertain that there was a new vogue of books on semantics and of works attempting to break "the tyranny of words," a literature of which Arnold's books were by far the most important. The greater part of Arnold's task was to examine, and to satirize, the orthodox conservative thinking of the moment. This is not our main concern, but what is of primary interest here is the extent to which Arnold's thinking departs from, and indeed on occasion attacks, earlier Progressivism. The deviation of Arnold's system of values from the classic values of American Progressivism was clear from his very terminology. I noted, in discussing the Progressive climate of opinoin, the existence of a prevailing vocabulary of civic morals that reflected the disinterested thinking and the selfless action that was expected of the good citizen. The key words of Progressivism were terms like *patriotism, citizen, democracy, law, character, conscience, soul, morals, service, duty, shame, disgrace, sin,* and *selfishness*—terms redolent of the sturdy Protestant Anglo-Saxon moral and intellectual roots of the Progressive uprising. A search for the key words of Arnold's book yields: *needs, organization, humanitarian, results, technique, institution, realistic, discipline, morale, skill, expert, habits, practical, leadership*—a vocabulary revealing a very different constellation of values arising from economic emergency and the imperatives of a bureaucracy.

Although primarily concerned with the conservatives of the present, Arnold paid his respects to the reformers of the past often enough to render a New Dealer's portrait of earlier Progressivism. He saw the reformers of the past as having occupied themselves with verbal and moral battles that left the great working organizations of society largely untouched. "Wherever the reformers are successful—whenever they see their direct primaries, their antitrust laws, or whatever else they base their hopes on, in actual operation—the great temporal institutions adapt themselves, leaving the older reformers disillusioned, like Lincoln Steffens, and a newer set carrying on the banner." * Respectable people with humanitarian values, Arnold thought, had characteristically made the mistake of ignoring the fact that "it is not logic but organizations which rule an organized society"; therefore they selected logical principles, rather than organizations, as the objects of their loyal-

* *The Symbols of Government,* p. 124.

ties. Most liberal reform movements attempt to make institutions practice what they preach, in situations where, if this injunction were followed, the functions of the institutions could not be performed.* Where the Progressives had been troubled about the development of institutions and organizations, Arnold's argument often appeared to be an apotheosis of them.

At one point or another, Arnold had critical observations to make on most of the staple ideas of Progressive thinking. *The Folklore of Capitalism* opened with a satire on "the thinking man," to whom most of the discourse of rational politics was directed; and the thinking man was hardly more than a caricatured version of the good citizen who was taken as the central figure in most Progressive thinking. While Progressive publicists had devoted much of their time to preachments against what they called "lawlessness," one of the central themes of Arnold's books was an analysis of law and legal thinking showing that law and respectability were so defined that a good many of the real and necessary functions of society had to go on outside the legal framework.† Similarly anti-Progressive was his attack on the anti-trust laws—a source of some amusement when he was later put in charge of the enforcement of these laws. But Arnold did not deny that the laws, as they had been interpreted by reformers, had had some use. Their chief use, as he saw it, had been that they permitted the organization of industry to go on while offering comfort to those who were made unhappy by the process. They had, then, a practical significance, but a far different one from that which the reformers had tried to give them. The reformers, however, had had no real strategy with which to oppose the great trusts: "The reason why these attacks [against industrial organizations] always ended with a ceremony of atonement, but few practical results, lay in the fact that there were no new organizations growing up to take over the functions of those under attack. The opposition was never able to build up its own com-

* *The Folklore of Capitalism,* pp. 375, 384.

† Cf. *The Symbols of Government,* p. 34: "It is part of the function of 'Law' to give recognition to ideals representing the exact opposite of established conduct . . . the function of law is not so much to guide society as to comfort it. Belief in fundamental principles of law does not necessarily lead to an orderly society. Such a belief is as often at the back of revolt or disorder."

missary and its service of supply. It was well supplied with orators and economists, but it lacked practical organizers. A great cooperative movement in America might have changed the power of the industrial empire. Preaching against it, however, simply resulted in counterpreaching. And the reason for this was that the reformers themselves were caught in the same creeds which supported the institutions they were trying to reform. Obsessed with a moral attitude toward society, they thought in Utopias. They were interested in systems of government. Philosophy was for them more important than opportunism and so they achieved in the end philosophy rather than opportunity." *

Arnold professed more admiration for the tycoons who had organized American industry and against whom the Progressives had grown indignant than he did for the reformers themselves. He spoke with much indulgence of Rockefeller, Carnegie, and Ford, and compared John L. Lewis with such men as examples of skillful organizers who had had to sidestep recognized scruples. "Actual observation of human society . . . indicates that great constructive achievements in human organization have been accomplished by unscrupulous men who violated most of the principles which we cherish." † The leaders of industrial organization ignored legal, humanitarian, and economic principles. "They built on their mistakes, their action was opportunistic, they experimented with human material and with little regard for social justice. Yet they raised the level of productive capacity beyond the dreams of their fathers." ‡

Not surprisingly Arnold also had a good word for the politicians, who, for all their lack of social values and for all the imperfections in their aims and vision, are "the only persons who understand the techniques of government." One would prefer a government in the hands of disinterested men, to be sure, but such men are so devoted to and satisfied with the development of good principles that they fail to develop skills, and hence fail to constitute "a competent governing class." Hence society is too often left with a choice between demagogues and psychopaths on one side, or, on the other, "kindly

* *The Folklore of Capitalism,* p. 220.
† *The Symbols of Government,* p. 5.
‡ Ibid., p. 125.

but uneducated Irishmen whose human sympathies give them an instinctive understanding of what people like." * Several pages of *The Folklore of Capitalism* were given to a defense of the political machines for the common sense with which they attack the task of government and for the humanitarian spirit in which their work is conducted.†

Taken by itself, Arnold's work, with its skepticism about the right-thinking citizen, its rejection of fixed moral principles and disinterested rationality in politics, its pragmatic temper, its worship of accomplishment, its apotheosis of organization and institutional discipline, and its defense of the political machines, may exaggerate the extent of the difference between the New Deal and pre-war Progressivism, but it does point sharply to the character of that difference. ‡

* Ibid., pp. 21–2.

† *The Folklore of Capitalism*, pp. 367–72; cf. pp. 43, 114–15; cf. *The Symbols of Government*, pp. 239–40.

‡ There are many points at which Arnold yields to the need to seem hard-boiled and at which (rather like F. D. R. himself) he becomes flippant over serious questions. While such lapses have a good deal of symptomatic importance, I do not wish to appear to portray his writing as an attack upon political morality as such: it was not an effort to destroy political morality, but to satirize a particular code of morality that he considered obsolescent and obstructive, and to substitute for it a new one, the precise outlines of which were obviously vague. In my judgment, Arnold did not even successfully pose, must less answer, the very real and important questions that were suggested by his books concerning the relations between morals and politics, or between reason and politics. For a searching criticism see the essay by Sidney Hook in his *Reason, Social Myths, and Democracy* (New York, 1950), pp. 41–51 and the ensuing exchange between Hook and Arnold, pp. 51–61, which to my mind succeeds only in underscoring Arnold's philosophical difficulties. The great value of Arnold's books lies not in the little they have to say about political ethics, but in their descriptive, satirical, and analytical approach to the political thinking of his time, and in their statement of the working mood of a great many New Dealers.

I should perhaps add that my own comments in this area are not intended to be more than descriptive, for there are large questions of political ethics that I too have not attempted to answer. In contrasting the pragmatic and opportunistic tone of the New Deal with the insistent moralism of the Progressives, it has not been my purpose to suggest an invidious comparison that would, at every point, favor the New Deal. Neither is it my purpose to imply that the political morals of the New Dealers were inferior to those of their opponents. My essential interest is in the fact that the emergency that gave rise to the New Deal also gave rise to a transvaluation of values, and that the kind of moralism that I have identified with the dominant patterns of thought among the Progressives was inherited not so much by their successors among the New Dealers, who tended to repudiate them, as by the foes of the New Deal.

To emphasize, as I have done, the pragmatic and "hard" side of the New Deal is not to forget that it had its "soft" side. Not all its spokesmen shared Arnold's need to pose as hard-boiled.* No movement of such scope and power could exist without having its ideals and its ideologies, even its sentimentalities. The New Deal had its literature of inspiration and indignation, its idealistic fervor, its heroes and villains. The difference I hope to establish is that its indignation was directed far more against callousness and waste, far less against corruption or monopoly, than the indignation of the Progressives, and that its inspiration was much more informed by engineering, administration, and economics, considerably less by morals and uplift. For the New Deal not only brought with it a heartening rediscovery of the humane instincts of the country; it also revived the old American interest in practical achievement, in doing things with the physical world, in the ideal that had inspired the great tycoons and industry-builders of the Gilded Age but that afterwards had commonly been dismissed by sensitive men as the sphere only of philistines and money-grubbers.

At the core of the New Deal, then, was not a philosophy (F. D. R. could identify himself philosophically only as a Christian and a democrat), but an attitude, suitable for practical politicians, administrators, and technicians, but uncongenial to the moralism that the Progressives had for the most

* I have been referred to David Lilienthal's *TVA: Democracy on the March* (New York, 1944) as an illustration of the idealism and inspirational force of the New Deal, and as a work more representative of its spirit than the writings of Thurman Arnold. Lilienthal's book is indeed more unabashedly humanitarian, more inspirational, more concerned with maintaining democracy in the face of technical and administrative change, more given to idealization of the people. It also shows, however, a dedication to certain values, readily discernible in Arnold, that would have been of marginal importance to all but a few of the Progressives. Like Arnold, Lilienthal is pleading the cause of organization, engineering, management, and the attitudes that go with them, as opposed to what he calls the "fog" of conventional ideologies. He appeals to administrative experience, technology, science, and *expertise*, finds that efficient devices of management "give a lift to the human spirit," and asserts that "there is almost nothing, however fantastic that (given competent organization) a team of engineers, scientists, and administrators cannot do today." (Pocket Book ed., New York, 1945, pp. ix, x, 3, 4, 8, 9, 79, 115). In the light of this philosophy it is easier to see that Lilienthal's more recent defense of big business does not represent a conversion to a new philosophy but simply an ability to find in private organization many of the same virtues that as TVA administrator he found in public enterprise.

part shared with their opponents. At some distance from the center of the New Deal, but vital to its public support, were other types of feeling. In some quarters there was a revival of populistic sentiment and the old popular demonology, which F. D. R. and men like Harold Ickes occasionally played up to, chiefly in campaign years, and which Harry Truman later reflected in his baiting of Wall Street. Along with this came another New Deal phenomenon, a kind of pervasive tenderness for the underdog, for the Okies, the sharecroppers, the characters in John Steinbeck's novels, the subjects who posed for the FSA photographers, for what were called, until a revulsion set in, "the little people." With this there came, too, a kind of folkish nationalism, quickened no doubt by federal patronage of letters and the arts, but inspired at bottom by a real rediscovery of hope in America and its people and institutions. For after the concentration camps, the Nuremberg Laws, Guernica, and (though not everyone saw this so readily) the Moscow trials, everything in America seemed fresh and hopeful, Main Street seemed innocent beyond all expectation, and in time Babbitt became almost lovable. Where Progressivism had capitalized on a growing sense of the ugliness under the successful surface of American life, the New Deal flourished on a sense of the human warmth and the technological potentialities that could be found under the surface of its inequities and its post-depression poverty. On the far fringe there was also a small number of real ideologues, aroused not only by the battle over domestic reform but by the rise of world fascism. Although many of them were fellow travelers and Communists, we stand in serious danger of misunderstanding the character of the New Deal if we overemphasize the influence of this fringe either upon the New Deal core or upon the American people at large. It has now become both fashionable and, for some, convenient to exaggerate the impact of the extreme left upon the thinking of the country in the 1930's. No doubt it will always be possible to do so, for Marxism had a strong if ephemeral impact upon many intellectuals; but the amateur Marxism of the period had only a marginal effect upon the thought and action of either the administrative core of the New Deal or the great masses of Amercians.* For the people at large—that is,

* Granville Hicks, in his *Where We Came Out* (New York, 1954), chapter iv, makes a sober effort to show how limited was the Communist

for those who needed it most—the strength of the New Deal was based above all upon its ability to get results.

The New Deal developed from the beginning under the shadow of totalitarianism, left and right. F. D. R. and Hitler took office within a few months of each other, and from that time down to the last phases of the New Deal reforms not a year went by without some premonition of the ultimate horror to come. In the earliest days of the Roosevelt administration a great many of its critics, influenced by such models of catastrophe as they could find abroad, saw in it the beginnings of fascism or Communism. Critics from the left thought, for instance, that the NRA was a clear imitation of Mussolini's corporate state. And—though this is now all but forgotten—critics from the right at first thought they saw fascist tendencies in the "violations" of fundamental liberties with which they regularly charged the architects of the New Deal. Only later did they find it more congenial to accuse the New Deal of fostering Communism.

To a sober mind all of this rings false today, for it is easier to see now that Roosevelt and his supporters were attempting to deal with the problems of the American economy within the distinctive framework of American political methods—that in a certain sense they were trying to continue to repudiate the European world of ideology. Between the London Economic Conference and Roosevelt's "quarantine" speech of 1937, the New Deal, for all its tariff-reduction agreements, was essentially isolationist. What it could not escape was the reality of what even some of the Republican leaders later began to characterize as "one world." After 1939 that reality was the dominant force in American life. The beginning of the war meant

influence even in those circles which were its special province. A complementary error to the now fashionable exaggeration of the Communist influence is to exaggerate its ties to the New Deal. Of course Communists played an active part in the spurt of labor organization until the experienced labor leaders expelled them, and in time Communists also succeeded in infiltrating the bureaucracy, with what shocking results we now know. But it was the depression that began to put American Communism on its feet and the New Deal that helped to kill it. The Communists, as consistent ideologues, were always contemptuous of the New Deal. At first they saw fascism in it, and when they gave up this line of criticism during the Popular Front period, they remained contemptuous of its frank experimentalism, its lack of direction, its unsystematic character, and of course its compromises.

that Americans, with terrible finality, had been at last torn from that habitual security in which their domestic life was merely interrupted by crises in the foreign world, and thrust into a situation in which their domestic life is largely determined by the demands of foreign policy and national defense. With this change came the final involvement of the nation in all the realities it had sought to avoid, for now it was not only mechanized and urbanized and bureaucratized but internationalized as well. Much of America still longs for—indeed, expects again to see—a return of the older individualism and the older isolation, and grows frantic when it finds that even our conservative leaders are unable to restore such conditions. In truth we may well sympathize with the Populists and with those who have shared their need to believe that somewhere in the American past there was a golden age whose life was far better than our own. But actually to live in that world, actually to enjoy its cherished promise and its imagined innocence, is no longer within our power.

Richard S. Kirkendall

THE CONTINUITY OF CHANGE

RICHARD S. KIRKENDALL, Professor of History at the University of Missouri, disagrees strongly with Richard Hofstadter and Carl Degler on the nature of the New Deal. This selection, a portion of a long and valuable essay in which the author methodically discusses the degree of change that the New Deal brought to American life, is based upon a wide acquaintance with the literature of twentieth-century American history and upon Kirkendall's own writing about agricultural policy and the role of the intellectual in the 1930's.

Kirkendall argues that the New Deal was simply an important episode in the development of American "collectivistic capitalism," an economic system characterized by large units and a high degree of organization. There is little doubt in the author's mind that the development of collectivistic capitalism was underway well before the 1930's. *Laissez-faire* had long been abandoned, and progressive intellectuals had formulated the basic ideas of the New Deal a generation in advance. The central concerns of the New Dealers, moreover, were substantially the same as those of the progressives.

From "The Great Depression: Another Watershed in American History?" by Richard S. Kirkendall in *Change and Continuity in Twentieth-Century America*, edited by John Braeman, Robert H. Bremner, and Everett Walters, pp. 145–154, 188–189. Copyright © 1964 by the Ohio State University Press. All rights reserved. Reprinted by permission of the Ohio State University Press.

The New Deal was not a "watershed" in either American life generally or the history of American reform in particular.

Critics of Kirkendall's thesis doubtless would question his handling of the significance of Keynesian economics. Probably, in addition, they would assert that he places too much emphasis on the continuity of ideas and plays down the actual changes effected by the New Deal. His conclusion, after all, admits that, whatever the progressives thought or attempted to accomplish, it was the New Deal which established big government as a permanently powerful force in American life, promoted the rise of big labor, and imposed a high degree of organization upon agriculture. Is not this admission a large concession to the watershed thesis?

The decade of the 1890's, acording to Henry Steele Commager, is "the watershed of American history," but a few historians point to the 1930's, with its Great Depression and New Deal, as a major watershed. When applied to history, the term is used in its British sense as synonomous with "divide" and amounts to an attempt to suggest that points or periods in history resemble geographical features such as continental divides, the lines separating drainage basins. Although not many historians employ this concept in their interpretations of the depression decade, several of them use similar terms and at times identify them with "watershed." In a major essay interpreting the New Deal as a revolution, Carl N. Degler writes: "as the Civil War constituted a watershed in American thought, so the depression and its New Deal marked the crossing of a divide from which, it would seem, there could be no turning back."

The idea of a watershed renders a distorted view of the flow of history in the 1930's for it exaggerates the role of change in the period and neglects the importance of continuity. While significant changes took place during those years, the decade also had important ties with the past. The concept of continuity as well as of change needs to be employed in an analysis of the Great Depression and the New Deal. The chief significance of the latter lay in its major contribution to a development that had been under way since the third quarter of the nineteenth century: the rise of a collectivistic or organizational type of capitalism.

Those interpreters of the 1930's who use concepts that stress breaks with the past usually begin with emphasis on the great expansion of government that took place during the period. "Buffeted and bewildered by the economic debacle, the American people in the course of the 1930's abandoned, once and for all, the doctrine of laissez faire." "The state had previously been a passive or impartial force. . . . Now it became the interventionist state." In these words, two leading historians, Louis M. Hacker and Carl N. Degler, describe what they call "the Third American Revolution."

In pinning the laissez faire label on the pre-New Deal period, these historians accept a myth, for long before the 1930's Americans had come to expect the government to deal with economic affairs in many important ways. General aspects of the New Deal can, in fact, be traced to late nineteenth- and early twentieth-century critics of laissez faire theories. The New Deal's pragmatic approach to the use of state power, its rejection of both socialism and the negative state, its efforts to strengthen the free-enterprise system by introducing essential reforms and by equalizing opportunity, its belief that liberal democratic values could be attained in a complex industrial society only by practical state action—all of these ideas had been developed by theorists of an earlier day, men such as Lester Ward, Henry George, Richard T. Ely, John R. Commons, Herbert Croly, and Louis Brandeis. Richard Hofstadter, in a famous essay emphasizing discontinuity in the New Deal, notes that it failed to produce a significant body of political writing comparable to that produced in the Progressive period. A perceptive critic, Andrew M. Scott, maintains that the New Deal did not need to do this:

> the task of criticizing the old ideas and shaping the new had largely been completed *during the Progressive Era.* It was because the basic thinking had already been done that the general approach to the crisis . . . could be agreed upon so quickly and with so little need for agonizing reappraisal.

Specific programs of the New Deal as well as its theoretical approach to problems had been worked out in the past.

Franklin Roosevelt's administration employed both types of programs that the Progressives had developed to deal with big business. The emphasis upon acceptance and regulation of it that Theodore Roosevelt had called for in the New Nationalism reappeared in the National Industrial Recovery Act, while the anti-bigness point of view of the Sherman Anti-Trust Act of 1890 and Woodrow Wilson's New Freedom of 1912 came to the fore again in such features of the New Deal as the Public Utilities Holding Company Act and the Temporary National Economic Committee. In other words, both of the leading Progressive philosophies figured in the New Deal's enlargement of government.

To support his thesis that the New Deal marked a "drastic new departure . . . in the history of American reformism," Hofstadter calls attention to the "many men" who had endorsed the Progressive movement but "found in the New Deal an outrageous departure from everything they had known and valued. . . ." It is true that Newton Baker, for example, lashed out at the increase in power of the national government occurring under the New Deal. Baker's reputation as a progressive, however, rested chiefly on his activities on the municipal level, in Cleveland, from 1901 to 1916. Another survivor of the Wilson administration, on the other hand, Josephus Daniels, applauded the New Deal enthusiastically. Idaho's Senator Borah, another carry-over from the Progressive era, criticized the New Deal on the grounds that it did not do enough to restore the old competitive economic system of small units, a system that he assumed would require only a small government. Borah, however, represented but one type of Progressive, the type labeled "traditionalist" by John Braeman and opposed to the "moderns" who looked to Theodore Roosevelt for political leadership. Three former followers of T.R., William Allen White, Peter Norbeck, and Gifford Pinchot, looked upon the New Deal as a revival of the Progressive movement. In short, since that movement contained conflicting groups and the New Deal contained more than one part, old Progressives surviving in the 1930's responded in varied ways to the programs of that decade: as Progressives, all of them rejected laissez faire; they disagreed, however, about the types of government action they desired.

The Hacker-Degler interpretation is somewhat confusing in

regard to early rejections of laissez faire in theory and practice. Hacker, although aware of government intervention before the 1930's, seems to suggest that prior to the New Deal Americans had a "laissez faire, or passive, state." Degler, while admitting that "the rejection of laissez faire had a long history" and that the Progressives "limited business" and "assisted agriculture," implies that earlier departures had been temporary while "with the depression the nation at large accepted the government as a permanent influence in the economy"; thus, the New Deal was not "repudiated by the Eisenhower administration, the first Republican government since the reforms were instituted."

Of crucial significance here are distinctions that these historians make between types of state action. For example, they argue that prior to the New Deal the state "had refused to interfere significantly in the interests of the security and the welfare of its laboring peoples," that the "progressive impulse . . . continued to conceive of the state as policeman or judge and nothing more," and that the New Deal's "primary and general innovation was the guaranteeing of a minimum standard of welfare for the people of the nation." Hacker refers to New Deal government as "the social-welfare state" while Degler calls it "the guarantor state."

Related to this is one of Hofstadter's important distinctions between the Progressive movement and the New Deal. The latter, he suggests, had "a social-democratic tinge that had never before been present in American reform movements." Earlier movements had been "concerned very largely with reforms of an essentially entrepreneurial sort and only marginally with social legislation," while from the 1930's on "American political reformism" took "responsibility on a large scale for social security, unemployment insurance, wages and hours, and housing."

In the depression crisis, the federal government did take on vast new responsibilities in the social-welfare field and make new efforts to reduce economic inequalities. Note the relief programs, labor provisions of the National Recovery Administration codes, and legislation dealing with social security, housing, labor standards, and taxation. These responsibilities and efforts, however, grew out of the past; and they included certain features of the Progressive movement, especially the ideas and activities of the social workers, a group that played an important, not a marginal, role in that movement. "Without minimizing the importance of the social-reform measures inaugurated during the 1930's," Robert H. Bremner writes, "it may be said that the measures then adopted were largely implementations, amplifications, and—in some instances—but partial fulfillments of the preventive social work formulated before World War I." "By standing firm in the old progressive faith, by exploring new lines of theory and practice," Clarke A. Chambers points out, "the partnership of social reformer and social worker anticipated [during the 1920's] in broad concept and often in intimate detail the welfare consensus which marked the New Deal." In this connection, attention should be paid to pre-New Deal reform movements in Wisconsin, New York, and Massachusetts; Theodore Roosevelt's proposals; the Progressive party platform of 1912; Woodrow Wilson's suggestions in the same year, his programs a few years later; and the work of such groups as the National Child Labor Committee, the National Consumers' League, and the American Association for Labor Legislation. Furthermore, individuals who contributed in major ways to the development of New Deal social-welfare programs, including Frances Perkins, Robert F. Wagner, David I. Walsh, Edwin E. Witte, and Arthur J. Altmeyer, had developed their basic ideas in this field back in the Progressive era. In short, Arthur Link's conclusion that "the Second New Deal" represented "the full flowering of social-justice progressivism" provides a more adequate view than Hofstadter's of the relations between this aspect of the New Deal and the past.

Hofstadter's emphasis upon the depression in his interpretation of the relations between the New Deal and the Progressive movement should also be questioned. He argues that the former was different "because its central problem was unlike the problems of Progressivism" and maintains that the central problem was the depression. Of course, the Progressives of the early twentieth century had operated in a period of prosperity, and Herbert Hoover was the first President to insist that the central government was obliged to combat dips in the business cycle. On the other hand, the anti-depression efforts of the New Deal represented its major failure: millions remained unemployed when war provided the stimulus the economy needed. Most of the ideas that New Dealers hoped to put into action had been formed to deal with other problems. This suggests that New Dealers did not believe that the problem of depression should monopolize the center of the stage. They were vitally interested in the more general problems of an urban industrial civilization. Like the Progressives before them, they sought ways to realize liberal democratic values in an America that had been changed radically by the rise of industry and the city, and they found opportunities in the depression situation to enact laws embodying ideas that had been developing for more than half a century.

Furthermore, the major anti-depression formula that emerged from the new experiences, the "Keynesian" emphasis upon deficit financing, had ties with the Progressives' fundamental assumptions concerning the role of government. While the formula enlarged somewhat the economic responsibilities and significance of government, making it "the indispensable partner of business," Keynesianism employed well-established powers of government, the taxing and spending powers; attempted to make capitalism work rather than to substitute another system for it; and reflected confidence in the ability of an active government to deal with economic problems.

This stressing of the New Deal's links with the past does not deny that significant changes took place in American political practices during the 1930's. Washington, D.C. became a much more important place; the number of federal employees increased more than in any earlier decade, with the executive branch growing from slightly less than six hundred thousand persons in 1933 to well over nine hundred thousand by 1939. One historian of American cities, however, notes that Washington had been emerging "as the political center of national affairs" for a number of years; that as early as World War I state authority "had dwindled to a shadow of its former importance. Boston's and Albany's, Denver's and Sacramento's loss was Washington's gain." And a student employing a statistical approach to the trend of government activity in the United States, while recognizing that the depression and the New Deal played important parts in producing the great increase during the twentieth century in the size of government, rejects the hypothesis that this increase is to be explained by "a changed concept of government's functions brought into being under the New Deal." Instead, he suggests, the development was "part of a trend already established before the great depression."

When looking, then, at the enlargement of government that took place during the 1930's, there seems no good reason to reject the conclusion that Henry Steele Commager reached nearly twenty years ago. Writing in 1945, he insisted that "the Roosevelt revolution was no revolution, but rather the culmination of half a century of historical development. . . ." The depression provided the climate in which ideas that had been taking shape for a number of years could become more widely accepted by the public and more firmly fixed in government practices. As a consequence, Americans came out of the decade with many new and permanent national programs and with what could justifiably be labeled a "big government." This matched the earlier rise of "bigness" in the business world.

The watershed concept, as well as others that emphasize breaks with the past, should be avoided in interpretations of the 1930's. The Great Depression and the New Deal created major changes in American life but also maintained important connections with an earlier America. The leading developments of the depression decade which are associated with the New Deal should not be viewed as radical new beginnings in American history but chiefly as significant parts of a large-scale transformation of American capitalism that had been under way for at least half a century before the 1930's. During those pre-New Deal years, American business lost its individualistic character and, although some unsuccessful attempts were made to restore that, somewhat more successful efforts sought to bring government and various economic groups into harmony with the collectivistic trends. Then in the years of the depression and the New Deal, big government became firmly established, promoted the rise of big labor, and conducted similar, fairly successful efforts designed to get the farmer to conform to the new type of capitalism. Big business lost some of its power but little of its size, and so Americans emerged from the decade with an economy dominated by the interplay among large public and private organizations and with lower-income groups hoping and expecting to improve their status within the system, not to destroy the system—which, in later years, became even more firmly established.

Leslie H. Fishel, Jr.

A CASE STUDY: THE NEGRO AND THE NEW DEAL

FEW EARLY twentieth-century progressives had much interest in the problems of the Negro; in fact, many were frankly racist in their attitudes. By the late 1960's, however, the aspirations of the Negro had become the central concern of American liberalism. This growing attachment to the cause of racial equality unquestionably has been the most important change in the twentieth-century American reform tradition. As Leslie H. Fishel, Jr., Director of the State Historical Society of Wisconsin, demonstrates in this selection, the New Deal played an important transitional role in this development.

Negroes found President Roosevelt personally inspiring, and many of FDR's lieutenants were strongly committed to the cause of civil rights. Many New Deal programs, moreover, provided much-needed economic benefits to a black population which had suffered terribly from the depression. Yet, as Fishel observes, "Roosevelt's actual commitments to the American Negro were slim." There was no significant New Deal program to meet the special problems of the Negro; FDR was preoccupied with the depression and the need to obtain Southern votes in Congress for New Deal economic reforms. Many of the New Deal agencies ac-

From "The Negro in the New Deal Era" by Leslie H. Fishel, Jr., *Wisconsin Magazine of History,* XLVIII (Winter, 1964–1965), 111–117, 120–123; reprinted in abridged form in *The Negro American: A Documentary History* by Leslie H. Fishel, Jr., and Benjamin Quarles. Copyright © 1967 by Scott, Foresman and Company.

tually practiced racial discrimination of one type or another. Even in 1941, when Roosevelt under great Negro pressure established a Fair Employment Practices Commission, he refused to integrate the armed forces.

For the Negro then the New Deal was a period of progress, but its mixed record was acceptable only because of the barrenness of the past. It moved well beyond the reformism of the progressive era, yet did little more than lay the groundwork for the increasingly frank and thoroughgoing approach to civil rights which has characterized the liberalism of the post-World War II era. Several factors have contributed to this new liberal concern: the growing sophistication and militance of the Negro leadership, the national commitment against fascism during the World War II years, and, after the war, a prosperity which made it possible for white liberals to turn their attention to civil rights. But who can say that the new liberalism would have developed as it did had the New Deal not haltingly shown the way?

His voice exuded warmth and a personal inflection which brought him close to his listeners. His own physical affliction and the way he bore it earned him deserved admiration and gave encouragement to those who had afflictions of their own, even a darker skin. John Gunther testified to Roosevelt's attraction for people as "concrete and intimate. . . . He set up goals in human terms that the average man could grasp for." The general public responded to his magnetism; one of his secretaries selected a list of salutations which were used on letters addressed to him, and they ran the gamut from "Dear humanitarian friend of the people" to "My Pal!" and "Dear Buddy." Almost all of his callers remarked on his personal charm and persuasiveness.

These characteristics of FDR the man, taken with his consummate ability to personalize his understanding of human exploitation and underprivilege, made him the most attractive President, for Negro citizens, since the Civil War. Robert Vann, publisher of the Negro weekly Pittsburgh *Courier,* who was brought into the 1932 campaign by some of Roosevelt's lieutenants, advised his race to "go home and turn Lincoln's picture to the wall. The debt has been paid in full." Yet, like Lincoln, Roosevelt's actual commitments to the American Negro were slim. He was more a symbol than an activist in his own right. His compassion, though real, was tempered by his own background, by the enormity of the decisions which came up to him, and by political considerations. An enthusiastic politician, he used political weights and measures on a political scale to judge the evidence, and the Negro was often found wanting. When Walter White, the executive secretary of the NAACP, obtained an audience through the good graces of Mrs. Eleanor Roosevelt to plead for the President's public support of the antilynching bill, FDR demurred because he needed Southern votes in Congress on other matters.

Nevertheless, the FDR image eventually became a favorable one; his picture hung in living rooms and infant sons carried his name. At first, though, Negroes waited to be shown. Their publications granted him the benefit of doubt when he spoke about justice and equality, in the hope that he was talking, too, to Negroes. He called lynching murder, remarked W. E. B. DuBois, and "these things give us hope." His acknowledgment, through his Secretary of Labor, of the National Urban League's survey of economic conditions among Negroes was, in the words of an *Opportunity* editorial, "an evidence of his deep interest in the Negroes' welfare." By midway through his first term, FDR had captured the admiration and affection of the Negro people and, with that, their votes. During the campaign of 1936, Negroes were outspoken in their support of the Democratic national ticket. Sixteen thousand Harlem residents traveled to Madison Square Garden in September of that year to attend a political rally, and sixty other cities held similar and simultaneous rallies. The New Yorkers mixed a rich fare of music and entertainment with leading New Dealers talking politics, but it was an African Methodist Episcopal Bishop, the Reverend C. Ransome, who symbolized the affair and its meaning by reading a "New Emancipation Proclamation." The vote in November was anticlimactic; the second Roosevelt had weaned the Negro away from the Republican party.

Roosevelt did not publicly associate himself with Negro projects or Negro leaders before 1935, but his programs and some of his associates were more aggressive. Early in 1933, he approved of a suggestion that someone in his administration assume the responsibility for fair treatment of the Negroes, and he asked Harold Ickes to make the appointment. A young white Georgian, Clark Foreman, came to Washington at Ickes' request to handle the task, and brought in as his assistant an even younger Negro of great promise, Robert C. Weaver. Foreman successfully made his way through the burgeoning maze of new agencies which were springing up and did a respectable job of calling to the attention of agency heads and their assistants an awareness of the special problems of Negroes. Along with Ickes, Daniel Roper, the Secretary of Commerce; Harry Hopkins, FDR's relief administrator; and Aubrey Williams, a Hopkins deputy, were sympathetic to committing the New Deal to work more generously with and for Negroes.

From the first, the various New Deal agencies carried the major burden of this emphasis, since they translated words into bread and butter, shelter and schooling. For the Negro, the most significant were the Federal Employment Relief Administration (FERA), the National Recovery Administration (NRA), the Works Progress Administration, later called the Work Projects Administration (WPA), the Agricultural Adjustment Administration (AAA), the Tennessee Valley Authority (TVA), the National Youth Administration (NYA), the Civilian Conservation Corps (CCC), and the public housing efforts of several agencies. There were others in the alphabetical jungle which assisted Negroes, as whites, in more specialized ways, such as the Federal Writers' Project and the Office of Education studies. The very number of agencies added credence to the emergent fact that, for the first time, the federal government had engaged and was grappling with some of the fundamental barriers to race progress.

It was one thing to engage and grapple with a problem at the federal level, and another thing to implement it at lower levels. Most of the New Deal agency programs ran afoul of local laws and customs and most of them capitulated on very practical grounds. As a consequence, Negroes vigorously attacked the inequities, even while they appreciated the limited benefits. FERA, the first New Deal agency to work directly to alleviate the plight of the destitute, tried by locally administered dole and work-projects to pump more money into circulation. Until the end of 1935, when it was abolished, it administered most of the direct relief and work relief programs which the New Dealers initiated, distributing about four billion dollars. Its progress was dogged by racial discrimination, since the design of projects and allocation of funds remained in local hands. Jacksonville, Florida, Negro families on relief outnumbered white families three to one, but the money was divided according to proportions of the total city population. Thus 15,000 Negro families reçeived 45 percent of the funds and 5,000 white families got 55 percent. Along the Mississippi River, from Natchez to New Orleans, Negroes were passed over for skilled jobs and frequently received less than the stipulated minimum wage. When the state of Georgia squeezed out of the FERA administrator the right to fix hourly wages for Negroes below thirty cents an hour, *Opportunity* mournfully questioned, "Does this presage the end of that heralded concern for the Forgotten Man?"

If the relief program raised questions of discrimination, the NRA brought howls of indignation. In the words of a Negro labor specialist, the NRA administrator, General Hugh A. Johnson, was "a complete failure" for not properly recognizing the Negro. The industrial codes established under NRA deferred to geographic wage and employment consideration so that the Negro worker generally earned less money for equal time and was frozen out of skilled jobs. A young Negro lawyer, John P. Davis, organized the Joint Committee on National Recovery in the fall of 1933 to persuade federal authorities to rectify these policies. "It has filed briefs, made appearances at public hearings," he wrote, and "buttonholed administrative officers relative to the elimination of unfair clauses in the codes," but to little avail. In self-defense, NRA officials explained the difficulty in bucking local customs, pointing out also that the NRA was responsible only for industrial workers. Agricultural laborers, domestic servants, and the service trades were not included, and most of the unskilled workers were exempted by statute from wage and hour minimums. "It is not fair," wrote an NRA administrator in a Negro journal, "to blame the NRA for not curing all these ills, if such they be, within a year." Until the Supreme Court decreed its demise in the spring of 1935, the NRA was a favored whipping boy for Negroes, as well as for others. "The Blue Eagle," a Virginia newspaper observed, "may be [for Negroes] a predatory bird instead of a feathered messenger of happiness."

The TVA and the AAA came under fire in the early years of the New Deal for similar reasons. Negro critics raged at the all-white model towns, such as Norris, Tennessee, which were established in conjunction with TVA. Homes for white workers on the project were substantial, while Negro workers lived in substandard temporary barracks. Skilled jobs went first to whites and most labor crews were segregated. TVA, it appeared to two observers in 1934, "aims to maintain the *status quo*." A year later, the situation seemed little better. In one sample two-week period, Negroes were 11 per cent of the working force, receiving only 9.5 per cent of the payroll. Under AAA, Negro tenant farmers and sharecroppers, as the most dispensable laborers, suffered first from the crop-reduction policy and found themselves without employment. Concerned about the evolving discriminatory pattern, the NAACP in 1934 devoted a major share of its energy to trying to prevent white landlords from illegally depriving their Negro tenants of crop-reduction bonuses.

Two New Deal programs for young people operated with a minimum of discrimination: the CCC and the NYA. The CCC established segregated camps in the South and in some parts of the North; the great bulk of the integrated camps were in New England. By 1935, its peak year, CCC had over a half million boys in camp. In general, Negroes stayed in CCC camps longer than whites, were not moved up to administrative posts in camps as readily as whites, and were restricted to less than 10 per cent of the total enrollment. Since the proportion of young Negro men in need was substantively higher than this, the quota system was actually inequitable. The NYA, which Mary McLeod Bethune served as administrator of Negro affairs, was shaped to help young men and women in school and with schooling. It grew out of the university and college student relief program established under FERA, and by the end of its first six months, in late 1935, had distributed more than forty million dollars. Conforming to existing state and regional patterns, the NYA still managed to help a critical age group among Negroes.

The debit side of the New Deal's efforts to assist Negroes fell far short of its material and psychological credits. Never before had Negro leaders participated in government affairs as freely and as frequently. The Department of Commerce had E. K. Jones, on leave from the National Urban League; the NYA had Mrs. Bethune; Interior had William H. Hastie and Weaver; the Social Security Board had Ira DeA. Reid; Labor had Lawrence W. Oxley; the Office of Education had Ambrose Caliver, to mention a few. Never before had there been so great a stress on improving the education of Negroes. Many relief programs included elementary education and training classes as part of the regimen. Negro colleges and universities received funds for buildings. The Office of Education, along with other agencies, began an important study of the status of Negro education.

Professional opportunities opened up in government, although not at the rate at which Negroes were graduating from college. For the first time, Negroes were employed as architects, lawyers, engineers, economists, statisticians, interviewers, office managers, case aids, and librarians. Nonprofessional white-collar jobs, which had rarely been within reach of the race, now became available to trained stenographers, clerks, and secretaries. While many of these jobs centered around programs for Negroes within the government, such as Negro slum clearance projects, Negro NYA offices, and the like, they broke the dam which had hitherto kept Negroes out of these kinds of positions.

Harold Ickes, a former president of the Chicago chapter of the NAACP, was the first New Dealer to be recognized as a tried friend. He quickly ended discrimination in his department and set the example by placing professionally-trained Negroes in responsible positions. He first drew FDR's attention to Hastie as a candidate for the federal judge vacancy in the Virgin Islands, and Roosevelt made the appointment in 1937. Ickes appeared at predominantly Negro functions and in 1936, on the occasion of an address at Howard University, even went so far as to wear a University of Alabama hood with his cap and gown because "it seemed to have the best color effect. . . ." While Ickes could not breach established segregation patterns in housing, one-eighth of the federal housing projects planned before the end of 1935 were in mixed neighborhoods. Approximately one-half of them were in Negro slum areas and, thanks to the negotiating skill of Ickes' assistant, Robert C. Weaver, the contracts for a substantial portion of these called for the employment of both skilled and unskilled Negro workers.

Eleanor Roosevelt, the New Deal's conscience, made it her business to reaffirm by word and deed her faith in the equality of opportunity for all. She included Negro and mixed organizations on her itineraries, welcomed mixed groups of adults and children to the White House, and spoke up for the race at critical times. In 1936, as part of a long memo on political strategy in the presidential campaign, she urged party leaders to ask respected Negroes like Mrs. Bethune to participate among Negro groups. The penalty for her unflagging advocacy of the Negro's cause was abuse or occasionally embarrassing questions. As the European war spread after 1939, she confronted questions about the Negro's loyalty. "Rarely," she told a group of New Jersey college women in 1940, "do you come across a case where a Negro has failed to measure up to the standard of loyalty and devotion to his country."

Eleanor Roosevelt was more than a symbol of the New Deal's conscience; she was a vehicle for approaching and influencing the President. She performed this service for Walter White when the antilynching bill was before Congress. When the DAR refused to allow Marian Anderson to sing in Constitution Hall, Mrs. Roosevelt was the intermediary who secured permission to use the Lincoln Memorial for the concert. It was useful for the President to have his wife serve in these varying capacities, absorbing some of the criticism, supplying him with information he could get from no other source, and sparking his conscience, when that was needed. This relieved the President from having to punctuate his speeches and press conferences with references to the Negro. Before 1935, these were almost nonexistent; after 1935, they increased in frequence and directness, but Roosevelt did not directly commit himself, as his wife did, until his famous Executive Order 8802 of June, 1941, established a Fair Employment Practice Committee to supervise all defense-contract industries.

In many ways, 1935 seemed to be a pivotal year for the President's public statements to and about the Negro. His annual message to Congress in January asserted that "in spite of our efforts and in spite of our talk, we have not weeded out the overprivileged and we have not effectively lifted up the underprivileged." Uplift and underprivilege were two words which Negroes understood, two words which footnoted their history; yet Roosevelt did not mention the Negro specifically. Shortly after that, he told WPA state administrators that "we cannot discriminate in any of the work we are conducting either because of race or religion or politics," and although he went on to speak of political pressures, the word "race" was there for Negroes to see. In two other public statements later in the year, FDR paid lip service to the accomplishments of the race and by 1936, an election year, he proclaimed his policy that "among American citizens there should be no forgotten men and no forgotten races." The transformation was more one of degree than of conviction; Roosevelt was beginning to speak to the Negro, however rarely, rather than to lump him without identification into massive generalizations. But his eye was ever on the balance of political forces and he never voluntarily came out foursquare for the Negro.

In perspective, Roosevelt's circumspection on some domestic issues was less significant than his New Deal legislative program. Labor unions received substantial encouragement from Section 7a of NRA and from the Wagner Act, although the White House maintained an equivocal position toward both labor and management. The jump in union memberships and the rise of the Committee on Industrial Organization, first within the AF of L and later as the independent Congress of Industrial Organizations (CIO), gained impetus from the newly established right to strike and the newly created federal board to mediate labor disputes. A strengthened labor movement confronted, as one of its problems, the question of Negro members. Older unions such as the United Mine Workers and the International Ladies Garment Workers Union welcomed Negroes without distinction. When the CIO broke from the AF of L, its nucleus of unions including the new and somewhat fragile organizations in the automobile, rubber, and steel industries accepted Negroes on an equal basis, except in those localities where race friction was high. The United Textile Workers attempted to do the same, but the existence of textile plants in southern states made this task more onerous. It was not enough for a union to resolve, as the CIO did, to accept members without regard to race, creed, or color, or even, as the UAW and the organizing committies of the steelworkers did, to offer Negro workers a chance to join up. Negroes still hung back, alternately tempted and frightened by management's offers and threats. The wave of the future was with the industrial unions, and *Opportunity's* declaration to Negro steelworkers that it would be "the apotheosis of stupidity" for them to stay out of the union battling for recognizance in 1937, was prophetic. The success of the Brotherhood of Sleeping Car Porters, under the leadership of A. Philip Randolph, in gaining recognition as the bargaining agent with the Pullman Company after a twelve-year struggle, marked the beginning of the race's influence in national labor circles and on national labor policy. After his union was recognized, Randolph prodded the AF of L to grant it an international charter, making it an equal with other member unions, and he never eased up his fight to liberalize the AF of L's racial policies. Even though he was not persuasive enough to break down these craft and railway-union prejudices, Randolph emerged before World War II as a dominant voice in Negro circles and a power to be reckoned with in American unionism.

When Harlem rioted in 1935, *The Crisis* explained that only the patience of the Negro had delayed it that long. Patience was not enough to counter the "sneers, impertinence, and personal opinions of smart-aleck investigators, supervisors and personnel directors." Unemployment, rent gouging, and the belief that Harlem had not received its share of relief money snapped the uneasy calm; the riot erupted with a frenzied attack on whites and the purposeful looting of food and clothing stores. The prompt on-the-scene appearance of New York City's popular mayor, Fiorello H. La Guardia, helped restore rationality. When the United States entered World War II, Harlem still seethed from overcrowding, white insolence and price gouging, and again rioting broke out, followed by riots in other cities, most notably Detroit. The hands of the clock had swung half circle and the Negro had learned from the white how to use violence and lawlessness when order and the law were not sufficient.

Toward the end of the 1930's the federal government turned more and more of its attention to the European conflict, the economy flourished as the industrial bastion of the embattled Allies, and the Negro had committed himself to the New Deal and to President Roosevelt. Polls in 1940 showed that Negro voters overwhelmingly supported Roosevelt for a third term, and the polls were right. The reason for this support was not difficult to surmise. Outside of what the Democratic Administration had tried to do directly and indirectly, the decade itself was marked with identifiable milestones of progress. In athletics, Jesse Owen was an Olympic champion, and Negro football players starred on many of the major college teams. Professional baseball still resisted, but its time was not far off. In interracial activities, conferences on a variety of subjects began to meet with overbearing regularity and, though self-consciously interracial, the pattern developed almost irrevocably. College students and adults met to talk about education, religion, economic matters, and, of course, civil rights. Even in the South, the indomitable Mrs. Bethune organized an interracial conference at the college she founded, and the white University of Florida tentatively sent delegates. In the deep South, interracial conferences were held on a segregated basis; Eleanor Roosevelt told of attending one in Birmingham and inadvertently sitting in the colored section. "At once the police appeared to remind us of the rules and regulations on segregation. . . . Rather than give in I asked that chairs be placed for us with the speakers facing the whole group." White Southerners began to speak up for the Negro. They were still a small minority, but the mere fact that a white state supervisor of schools in Georgia would admit to the inequalities of segregated schools, or a white North Carolina legislator would question a decreased appropriation for a Negro college, was a sign of change. The rise of Huey Long in Louisiana brought a different attitude, one of ignoring race differences without changing race relationships. The all-white Mississippi Education Association established a committee in 1938 to recommend ways in which students might study Negro life, and several Northern newspapers in 1940 editorially acknowledged the importance of Negro History Week. The tide had turned, and Negroes credited the turning to the New Deal.

The sudden shock of the surprise attack which drew the United States into World War II served more to expose sore spots than to blanket them in loyalty. In the First World War, the protests against unequal treatment were slow to develop and not widely heard, but the Second World War was different. Even before Pearl Harbor, clamors arose from the South warning that the Negro was not going to "come out of this war on top of the heap as he did in the last one." However distorted the comparison, the attitude was clear, and it influenced the government's decision to extend pre-Pearl Harbor patterns into the war period.

The Negro soldier remained separate in the armed services, and not always welcome. Judge William L. Hastie resigned as civilian aide to the Secretary of War in protest against the dissembling tactics of the Army Air Corps to keep the Negro on the ground. *The Crisis,* returning to a World War I cry, criticized the appointment of Southern white officers for Negro troops and the explanation that they could handle them better. When FDR queried Walter White about the carelessness of the Negro press and the consistency of its attack on the war effort, White replied that better treatment for Negroes in the armed services and the invitation of Negro editors to presidential press conferences and top briefings would clear up the problem.

White became an important man in the war effort and was finally sent overseas as a war correspondent in early 1944. He toured every major front in Europe and the Pacific and his reports did not make soothing reading. Wherever he went, he later wrote, "there was a minority of bigots who were more determined to force their bigotry on others than they were to win the war." This was particularly true of officers, both Northern and Southern. Separation, he found, bred this spirit, especially when key officers were "prejudiced or weak, or both." When Negroes and whites actually fought together, as they did during the Battle of the Bulge in December of 1944, attitudes changed, according to polls among white officers and men. "After the first day," a white South Carolinian admitted, "when we saw how they fought, I changed my mind." The top combat brass, such as General Dwight Eisenhower and Admiral Chester Nimitz, were willing to co-operate, but they were hemmed in by Washington orders and junior officer reluctance.

At home, the intense feelings bared by war boiled up with wearying constancy. In the spring of 1941, A. Philip Randolph organized the March on Washington movement which threatened to march if the White House did not declare for fair employment practices in defense industries. President Roosevelt issued his famous Executive Order 8802 in June, establishing the FEPC and the principle of government concern with employment discrimination. Randolph continued the movement during the war, but it lapsed as the older organizations themselves became more militant.

The prosperity of war industry and the proscriptive Southern mores once again attracted thousands of Negroes to Northern cities. The consequent overcrowding and war tension heated racism to the boiling point, as the riots in New York, Detroit, and Los Angeles demonstrated. For the Negro, racism was the same wherever it appeared. In Roy Wilkins' words, "it sounds pretty foolish to be *against* park benches marked 'Jude' in Berlin, but to be *for* park benches marked 'Colored' in Tallahassee, Florida." Negroes could not understand why whites drew distinctions between the Nazi ideology of Aryan supremacy and the American ideology of white supremacy. Even back in 1933, the *Crisis* expressed its "unholy glee" at Hitler's attack on the Jews: "Now that the damned include the owner of the [New York] *Times*, moral indignation is perking up." The paradox which Wilkins illustrated could only be resolved by a change of face on the part of white America.

The war itself, by drawing thousands of men and women into a collaborative effort with whites, made such a change possible. Negroes served in the armed services in all ratings and at all ranks, though segregated. War industries hired skilled Negro men and women at supervisory and managerial levels. Government used colored workers in great numbers and in more sensitive positions than ever before. The Negro's political power was organized in an unprecedented manner during the wartime presidential election. The younger generation of Negro men and women who had grown up in prosperity and matured in depression were awakened to the infinite possibilities of an assimilated society, and from them came the trained leadership to plan the campaign.

The death of Roosevelt and the end of the war in 1945 terminated an era. The office of the Presidency now symbolized a concern for justice and equality for all Americans, including Negroes. The White House had taken a stand in favor of the principle of equal rights, although the practice had lagged. The new President, Harry S. Truman, a man of lesser parts, was to take the next practical step and declare in specifics his belief in the equality of men of whatever race under the law. Where Roosevelt concealed the particular in the general principle, Truman spoke out without check. Where Roosevelt used the excuse of war to delay integration, Truman used the excuse of peace to accelerate it. Where Roosevelt used the federal government to increase economic opportunities for all, Truman used the federal government to increase economic opportunities for Negroes. While the Truman Fair Deal never approximated the energy and the excitement of the Roosevelt New Deal, it was the former which capitalized on the Negro's readiness to take an equal place in American democracy.

Howard Zinn

THE NEW LEFT VIEWS THE NEW DEAL

HOWARD ZINN, Professor of Government at Boston University, author of a significant historical study, *La Guardia in Congress*, and editor of a widely-used collection of primary sources, *New Deal Thought*, has established himself as an important historian and interpreter of twentieth-century American reform. An activist in the peace and civil rights movements and a social thinker convinced of the need for a radical reconstruction of American society, Professor Zinn has become known as a spokesman of the contemporary New Left. His analysis of the New Deal is the work of a thoughtful historian, but it provides in addition insights into the outlook of an important social-intellectual movement.

Zinn agrees with Richard Kirkendall that the New Deal was not a period of revolutionary change. Kirkendall, however, writes from within the dominant liberal tradition and appears inclined to accept the New Deal on its own terms. Writing from a radical perspective, Zinn seems more involved with his subject's relevance to present-day social problems; his treatment of the New Deal at times borders on indignation.

The author is convinced that Roosevelt and his associates were extremely cautious and their accomplishments, if undeniably im-

From "The Grateful Society" by Howard Zinn, *Columbia University Forum*, X (Spring, 1967), 28–32. Copyright © 1967 by Howard Zinn. Reprinted by permission of the author.

portant, very limited. The New Deal may have left "a mountain of accomplishment behind," but it as well as succeeding reform movements failed to scale other important peaks. It in fact ignored a bold and searching dialogue among important social thinkers and radical politicians. Its often-praised "pragmatism" was actually a method for avoiding a careful inquiry into the nation's social problems and a systematic and far-ranging formulation of liberal objectives. In the main, its benefits were directed toward either the middle class or certain groups which were well enough organized to demand government assistance; those who were most needy, and least organized, received much less. The effect was to restore an old and inequitable social structure, not create a new one. Actually, World War II brought forth more important social and economic experimentation and even "saved the reputation of the New Deal."

Much of Professor Zinn's critique is not new; the foundations of his interpretation were laid by a more conventional liberal, James MacGregor Burns, in the mid-1950's, well before the advent of the New Left. Those who disagree with this critical analysis would argue that it ignores the limitations of the political context within which the New Dealers worked. They probably would also assert that Zinn's intense concern with the problems of the present has led him to undervalue the real achievements of the New Deal. Nevertheless, the viewpoint expressed in this valuable and thought-provoking article seems to be winning some acceptance among younger historians; the New Left interpretation of the New Deal probably will be increasingly influential.

We have been extravagantly, almost obsequiously, grateful for the New Deal and its successors. Yet our gratitude is rooted in a failure of sense. We do not see to what extent war and preparations for war have kept our economy flowing. We are pleasantly aware of the carbohydrate prosperity of the class, the upper-middle, that verbalizes contentment best, but our ears are not attuned to the drugged mutterings of the TV-watching, beer-drinking, politically cynical poor. We refuse to see the world as one and can toast our economy while two thirds of the world's people starve beneath the drone of tourist charter flights, and some die in the explosions of our surfeit.

It is instructive to compare the New Deal and the Great Society because the two rubbed together bring a small flash of understanding while separately they just shine dully, pleasingly. True, these are the prosperous 1960s and those were the depressed 1930s. But somehow, now as then, some among us live high, and some live low, and there is a chronic malaise—of lost opportunities and wasted wealth—in the economic air. Now as then, we leave unsolved the major domestic problem of our time. That is, how to bring the blessings of immense natural wealth and staggering productive potential to every person in the land. Also unsolved is the political corollary of that problem: how to organize ordinary people to convey to national leadership something more subtle than the wail of crisis: the day-to-day ache felt in garbage-strewn ghettos and crowded schools, the environment of tens of millions of Americans clawing for subsistence in the richest country in the world.

The New Dealers were articulate, humane, and on occasion profound. Their ideas fathered an unprecedented body of welfare legislation, and pulled the nation from the edge of economic disaster. Without clearly defined goals beyond getting over the depression, they found themselves creating new laws and institutions: the Tennessee Valley Authority, the social security system, farm subsidies, minimum wage standards, labor relations boards, public housing. The Roosevelt programs refurbished middle-class America, restored jobs to the jobless, and gave just enough to the lowest classes to create an aura of good will.

When the reform energies of the New Deal began to wane, around 1939, the nation was back to normal, with a permanent army of unemployed and a poverty-ridden 20 million effectively blocked from public view by a huge, prosperous, consuming middle class. Once again, we had a tremendously efficient and wasteful productive apparatus—efficient because it could produce limitless amounts of those goods selected for production, wasteful because the selection was determined not by usefulness to society but by profitability to business. That, we recognize with some reluctance, is a description of our nation in

1967—the Fair Deal, New Frontier, and the Great Society notwithstanding.

The word "pragmatic" has been used, perhaps more often than any other, to describe the experimentalism of the Roosevelt Administration—the improvisation, the absence of long-range programs or theoretical commitments. Richard Hofstadter, indeed, has said that the only important works of political philosophy to come out of the Roosevelt circle were Thurman Arnold's books, *The Symbols of Government* and *The Folklore of Capitalism.* Hofstadter described Arnold's work as "the theoretical equivalent of FDR's opportunistic virtuosity in practical politics—a theory that attacks theories." In both books Arnold cut away at "myths and symbols" and apotheosized pragmatism.

Pragmatism, however, is a method, and experimentation can be guided by a variety of social goals. Understanding is better served by an inquiry into ends: in what direction is government willing to experiment? What goals, what ideals, what expectations direct its course? How far will it go?

New Deal measures were directed toward preventing depression, helping the poor, curbing ruthless business practices. And Roosevelt's speeches often had the flavor of a moral crusade. In a campaign speech in San Francisco in 1932 he said: "Our government . . . owes to everyone an avenue to possess himself of a portion of that plenty sufficient for his needs, through his own work." In his 1936 speech accepting the nomination, he spoke of the power of the "economic royalists" and said: "Our allegiance to American institutions requires the overthrow of this kind of power."

But FDR's aims were not sharply enough defined to prevent his shifting from one policy to another: from constant promises to balance the budget to large-scale spending in emergencies; from an attempt to reconcile business and labor interests in the National Recovery Act to belated support for the pro-labor Wagner Act; from special concern for the tenant farmer in the Resettlement Administration to generous price supports for the large commercial farmer in the Agricultural Adjustment Act of 1938.

His political leadership showed the same indecisiveness as did his ideas on economic reform. Roosevelt was cautious about supporting the kinds of candidates in 1934—Socialist Upton Sinclair in California, for example, or Progressive Gifford Pinchot in Pennsylvania—who represented bold approaches to economic and social change. When he did decide to take vigorous action against conservative Congressional candidates in 1938, he did so too late and too timorously. His political acumen did not extend to building a new base among the poor, the unemployed, the tenant farmers, and other disadvantaged groups with whose support he might have given the country a bolder economic program.

The experimentalism of the New Deal, in short, had its limits: up to those limits, Roosevelt's social concern was genuine, his political courage huge, his generous spirit unfailing; beyond them, his driving force weakened. In 1938, with the nation out of the worst of the depression, with the skeletal structure of social reform on the statute books, and with that year's Congressional elections showing a sudden waning of political approbation, the Roosevelt program slid to a close. It left a mountain of accomplishment behind, and ahead, mountains still unclimbed. Many millions—businessmen and professionals, unionized workingmen, commercial farmers—had been given substantial help. Many millions more—sharecroppers, slum-dwellers, Negroes, North and South, the unemployed—still awaited a genuine "new deal."

What accounts for the sputtering out of the New Deal? For one thing, the urgency of 1933–1935 was gone. There were still 9,000,000 unemployed in 1939, but the sense of panic was over. After all, unemployment was normal in America. Harry Hopkins had said in 1937 that even with prosperity it was "reasonable to expect a probable minimum of 4,000,000 to 5,000,000 unemployed." The goals of the New Deal did not much exceed the restoration of the traditional structure of the American economy.

But why were the expectations of the New Deal so limited? Why didn't the New Dealers simply declare that the government would *continue* spending, experimenting, and expanding public enterprise, until no one was unemployed, until slums were gone, until no family received below-subsistence income, until adequate medical care was available to all, until anyone who wanted it could get a college education? There were—and are—political obstacles to such a program; but is not the first step toward overcoming the obstacles an open avowal of the objectives? Bolder aims might have enabled FDR to do what political historian James MacGregor Burns asserts was not done: to build "a solid, organized mass base" among underprivileged groups.

Part of the answer, I think, is that humanitarianism can go only so far in the redistribution of privilege; self-interest must carry it further. In 1933 Paul Douglas, then an economics professor at the University of Chicago, wrote prophetically:

> Along with the Rooseveltian program must go . . . the organization of those who are at present weak and who need to acquire that which the world respects, namely, power. . . . Unless these things are done, we are likely to find the permanent benefits of Rooseveltian liberalism to be as illusory as were those of the Wilsonian era.

The groups that did organize—the larger farm operators, the several million industrial workers who joined the CIO—improved their position significantly. The aged, with a push from the Townsend Movement, got a bit of help. But many others—tenant farmers, the unemployed, the service and domestic workers (that is, mostly Negroes)—were left behind.

Madison's argument that political stability would be assured in a federal republic because an uprising in one state would die for lack of support in another is applicable also to economics: no single economic interest, fierce as it may be in its own domain, is wide enough to embrace society at large. Since the Civil War, crises have been met with enough conciliation to keep general resentment below the combustible level; isolated disadvantaged groups have fought their way up the social ladder—often only to the point of complacency. Reform from the top is humane but disinterested, and thus limited.

If it is only the underprivileged who can supply the driving force for a sharp change in their condition, then perhaps it is up to intellectuals to define expectations and work out programs. The New Deal experience indicates that the boldest programs, the largest expectations, come most often from intellectuals not closely associated with the White House, from those whose ideological reach is not impaired by their clinking glasses with the mighty.

John Dewey was one of these. An early American pragmatist, he believed, like Roosevelt, in moving step by step, but he proposed longer ones, taken two or three at a time. FDR wanted to preserve the profit system. Dewey was willing to see it reshaped. Roosevelt wrote to newspaper publisher Roy Howard in 1935 that the basic New Deal program had "now reached substantial completion." Dewey, lecturing at the University of Virginia that same year, urged "organized social planning" in which "the new forces of productivity are cooperatively controlled." Liberalism, Dewey said, "must now become radical. . . . For the gulf between what the actual situation makes possible and the actual state itself is so great that it cannot be bridged by piecemeal policies undertaken *ad hoc.*"

Roosevelt explored only one sector of the vast ground between Marxism and Hooverism. Edmund Wilson, for instance, also rejected Marxian dialectic yet found in it a kernel of truth: "if society is to survive at all, it must be reorganized on new principles of equality." Reinhold Niebuhr urged that "private ownership of productive processes" be abandoned. Economist Stuart Chase, shrewdly looking beyond the question of ownership, suggested that old alternatives had been swept aside by the onrush of technology. There was a need, Chase said, for some uncategorizable collectivist society whose "general objective will be the distribution of the surplus, rather than a wrangling over the ownership of a productive plant which has lost its scarcity position." William Ernest Hocking, the Harvard philosopher, asked for "collectivism of a sort" where "the totality of persons in a community . . . determine what is produced." Upton Sinclair talked of a cooperative society in which "every man, woman, and child would have the equivalent of $5000 a year income from labor of the able-bodied young men for three or four hours per day." It was, all in all, a bolder dialogue than any we have heard since.

Although Roosevelt told students at the Oglethorpe University during his 1932 campaign that he was in favor of "a larger measure of social planning," he was never willing to go as far as his own advisor, Rexford Guy Tugwell, to whom planning meant "something not unlike an integrated group of enterprises run for its consumers rather than for its owners." "Planning," Tugwell said, "implies guidance of capital uses, . . . and there is no way of accomplishing this except through a control of prices and of profit margins."

Roosevelt would plan on behalf of the lower classes; the Tennessee Valley Authority was a good example of this. But planning would not be national in scale; nor would it interfere with the fundamental character of an economy based on corporate profit; nor would it attempt any fundamental redistribution of wealth in the nation. The TVA was acceptable because it represented *piecemeal* planning.

In 1938, Roosevelt asked for a sweeping investigation of monopoly by the Temporary National Economic Committee, saying: "The power of the few to manage the economic life of the Nation must be diffused among the many or be transferred to the public and its democratically responsible government." But the TNEC, after producing enough testimony to fill 31 volumes and 43 monographs, was unwilling, as William Leuchtenburg writes, "to tackle the more difficult problems or to make recommendations which might disturb vested interests."

Roosevelt was cautious in his espousal of public enterprise and the federal spending it required. Even when he went all out for spending, it was only a fraction of what British economist John Maynard Keynes was urging as a way of bringing recovery. An American Keynesian, Alvin Hansen, argued to deaf ears that the economy was "mature" and therefore required much more frequent and powerful injections of governmental spending than were being given.

Roosevelt had introduced the idea of a "yardstick," represented by the Tennessee Valley Authority—a public enterprise that would, by competition, bend private enterprise more toward the needs of the consumer. But the vast implications of the concept were left unexplored. With TVA, with a brief golden period of federal theater and federally subsidized arts (the demise of which FDR mourned but did not fight), with a thin spread of public housing, and a public-works program called on only at times of desperation, the New Deal had reached its ideological and emotional limits.

It was World War II that saved the reputation of the New Deal. Economic and social experimentation blossomed in 1940–45 as it had not before; there was a certain measure of national planning, a job for everyone, a vast system of postwar educational benefits. Now there was little inhibition, for the objective was not economic democracy, but something more traditional and acceptable—winning at war. The war against fascism was regarded as profoundly moral in itself (a righteousness easily assimilated later in anticommunism) and there was no need to search for its Jamesian moral equivalent.

SELECTED BIBLIOGRAPHY

The most important and monumental study of the New Deal is Arthur M. Schlesinger, Jr., *The Age of Roosevelt,* three volumes of which are now in print: *The Crisis of the Old Order* (1957), *The Coming of the New Deal* (1959), and *The Politics of Upheaval* (1960). The best one-volume work is William E. Leuchtenburg, *Franklin D. Roosevelt and the New Deal* (1963). Basil Rauch, *A History of the New Deal* (1944), was an important pioneering effort. Dixon Wecter, *The Age of the Great Depression* (1948), remains a significant social history. Broadus Mitchell, *Depression Decade* (1947), is a standard economic history. Paul Conkin, *The New Deal* [also published as *F.D.R. and the Origins of the Welfare State*] (1967), is an influential New Left critique; also representative of the New Left is Barton J. Bernstein's interpretive essay in Bernstein, ed., *Towards a New Past* (1968).

Significant collections of documentary material are Frank Freidel, ed., *The New Deal and the American People* (1964), William E. Leuchtenburg, ed., *The New Deal: A Documentary History* (1968), and Howard Zinn, ed., *New Deal Thought* (1966). Among the most important published primary sources are Samuel I. Rosenman, ed., *The Public Papers and Addresses of Franklin D. Roosevelt* (13 vols., 1938–1950), Elliott Roosevelt, *F.D.R.: His Personal Letters* (4 vols., 1947–1950), Max Freedman, ed., *Roosevelt and Frankfurter: Their Correspondence, 1928–1945* (1967), John M. Blum, ed., *From the Morgenthau Diaries* (3 vols., 1959–1967), and Harold L. Ickes, *The Secret Diary of Harold L. Ickes* (3 vols., 1953–1954).

Frank Freidel has published three volumes of his *Franklin D. Roosevelt* biography: *The Apprenticeship* (1952), *The Ordeal* (1954), and *The Triumph* (1956); they give a penetrating and extremely important interpretation of Roosevelt's life until his ascension to the presidency. See also Freidel, *F.D.R. and the South* (1965). James MacGregor Burns, *Roosevelt: The Lion and the Fox* (1956), is the most important and persuasive critique of its subject. Other significant studies are Bernard Bellush, *Franklin D. Roosevelt as Governor of New York* (1952), Daniel R. Fusfeld, *The Economic Thought of Franklin D. Roosevelt and the Origins of the New Deal* (1954), and Alfred Rollins, Jr., *Roosevelt and Howe* (1962).

Among the most important books written by New Deal figures are Raymond Moley, *The First New Deal* (1967), Frances Perkins, *The Roosevelt I Knew* (1946), Samuel I. Rosenman, *Working with Roosevelt* (1952), and Rexford G. Tugwell, *The Democratic Roosevelt* (1957).

New Deal agricultural policy has attracted much attention. In addition to Christiana MacFadyen Campbell, *The Farm Bureau and the New Deal* (1962), see especially Richard S. Kirkendall, *Social Scientists and Farm Politics in the Age of Roosevelt* (1966), an important study which ranges farther than its title indicates. Other significant works are Dean Albertson, *Roosevelt's Farmer: Claude R. Wickard in the New Deal* (1961), David E. Conrad, *The Forgotten Farmers: The Story of Sharecroppers in the New Deal* (1965), John L. Shover, *Cornbelt Rebellion: The Farmers' Holiday Association* (1965), and Sidney Baldwin, *Poverty and Politics: The Rise and Decline of the Farm Security Administration* (1967).

Important studies of the New Deal and labor are Jerold S. Auerbach, *Labor and Liberty: The La Follette Committee and the New Deal* (1966), Irving Bernstein, *The New Deal Collective Bargaining Policy* (1950), Milton Derber and Edwin Young, eds., *Labor and the New Deal* (1957), Walter Galenson, *The CIO Challenge to the AFL* (1960), and James O. Morris, *Conflict within the AFL* (1958).

New Deal policy toward business receives attention in Wallace E. Davies and William Goetzmann, eds., *The New Deal and Business Recovery* (1960), Ralph F. De Bedts, *The New Deal's SEC: The Formative Years* (1964), and Sidney Fine, *The Automobile under the Blue Eagle* (1963). Ellis W. Hawley, *The New Deal and the Problem of Monopoly* (1966), remains the most important and comprehensive study.

New Deal work relief programs are studied in Searle F. Charles, *Minister of Relief: Harry Hopkins and the Depression* (1963), and John A. Salmond, *The Civilian Conservation Corps* (1967). Robert E. Sherwood, *Roosevelt and Hopkins* (1948), is valuable but devoted mostly to the war years.

James T. Patterson, *Congressional Conservatism and the New Deal* (1967), is the most important work yet published on New Deal politics. Bernard Donahoe, *Private Plans and Public Dangers: The Story of FDR's Third Nomination* (1965), and George Flynn, *American Catholics and the Roosevelt Presidency, 1932–1936* (1967), cover significant topics.

Otis L. Graham, *An Encore for Reform: The Old Progressives and the New Deal* (1967), is a thoughtful and valuable, although not entirely convincing, treatment of the relationship between the progressive movement and the New Deal. Bernard Sternsher, *Rexford Tugwell and the New Deal* (1964), discusses an important thinker of the 1930's. Frank Warren, III, *Liberals and Communism: The "Red Decade" Revisited* (1966), is an important study of the intellectual climate of the 1930's, but see also Daniel Aaron, *Writers on the Left* (1961), and Leo Gurko, *The Angry Decade* (1947). Donald McCoy, *Angry Voices: Left-of-Center Politics in the New Deal Era* (1958), is a standard survey of its subject.

Other important topics are covered in Arthur J. Altmeyer, *The Formative Years of Social Security* (1966), Edwin E. Witte, *Development of the Social Security Act* (1962), Paul J. Conkin, *Tomorrow a New World: The New Deal Community Program* (1959), Wilmon H. Droze, *High Dams and Slack Waters: TVA Rebuilds a River* (1965), Barry Dean Karl, *Executive Reorganization and Reform in the New Deal: The Genesis of Administrative Management* (1963), Jane De Hart Matthews, *The Federal Theater, 1935–1939: Plays, Relief, and Politics* (1967), and Timothy McDonnell, *The Wagner Housing Act* (1957). Two very significant essays are Richard S. Kirkendall, "Franklin D. Roosevelt and the Service Intellectual," *Mississippi Valley Historical Review*, XLIX (Dec., 1962), 456–471, and William E. Leuchtenburg, "The New Deal and the Analogue of War," in John Braeman, *et al.*, eds., *Change and Continuity in Twentieth-Century America* (1964), pp. 81–143.

Various types of opposition to the New Deal receive coverage in Edward C. Blackorby, *Prairie Rebel: The Public Life of William Lemke* (1963), Abraham Holtzman, *The Townsend Movement: A Political Study* (1963), Donald McCoy, *Landon of Kansas* (1967), Charles J. Tull, *Father Coughlin and the New Deal* (1965), and George Wolfskill, *The Revolt of the Conservatives: A History of the American Liberty League* (1962).

Historians have just begun to examine the impact of World War II upon the New Deal. Eric F. Goldman, *Rendezvous with Destiny* (1952), contains a pioneering chapter which Alonzo L. Hamby attempts to amplify in "Sixty Million Jobs and the People's Revolution: The Liberals, the New Deal, and World War II," *The Historian*, XXX (August, 1968), 578–598. Important studies of the Negro in wartime are Richard M. Dalfiume, "The 'Forgotten Years' of the Negro Revolution," *Journal of American History,* LV (June, 1968), 90–106, and Louis Ruchames, *Race, Jobs, and Politics: The Story of the FEPC* (1953). Significant and relevant are Eliot Janeway, *The Struggle for Survival* (2d ed., 1968), Bruce Catton, *The War Lords of Washington* (1948), Kenneth Davis, *The Experience of War* (1965), Joel Seidman, *American Labor from Defense to Reconversion* (1953), Walter W. Wilcox, *The Farmer in the Second World War* (1947), and Roland Young, *Congressional Politics in the Second World War* (1956).

An extremely useful bibliographical guide is William J. Stewart, compiler, *The Era of Franklin D. Roosevelt: A Selected Bibliography of Periodical and Dissertation Literature, 1945–1966* (1967). Richard S. Kirkendall, "The New Deal as Watershed: The Recent Literature," *Journal of American History,* LIV (March, 1968), 839–852, thoroughly surveys the contributions of the mid-1960's.